Always Another Adventure

By Robert F. Marx

Always Another Adventure

Pirate Port: *The Story of the Sunken City of Port Royal*

They Dared the Deep: *A History of Diving*

The Battle of Lepanto 1571

The Battle of the Spanish Armada 1588

Following Columbus: *The Voyage of the* Niña II

The Voyage of the *Niña II*

Always

·

Another

·

Adventure

·

by Robert F. Marx

The World Publishing Company
Cleveland and New York

Published by The World Publishing Company
2231 West 110th Street, Cleveland, Ohio 44102
Published simultaneously in Canada by
Nelson, Foster & Scott Ltd.
Copyright © 1967 by Robert F. Marx
Library of Congress Catalog Card Number: 67–24468
Printed in the United States of America

◆

In
Memory
of
John M. Goggin

◆

CONTENTS

Contents

PREFACE

Given the sort of life I lead, it would be logical to assume that I have written this book now because I expect to meet a sudden and violent end long before I reach the advanced age usually associated with the writing of an autobiography. Logical but incorrect. Contrary to what is commonly believed, most men whose lives involve more than the ordinary share of risks—whether they are test pilots, race drivers, deep-sea divers, or what—are not fatalists. They are convinced that they lead a charmed life, that the next guy may fail to come out of a spin or run out of air at 250 feet below the surface, but not they themselves. No, the death they fear is a slow one, from sheer boredom with their own exploits. And it is to ward off death by boredom that I have written this book.

Almost everyone enjoys talking about himself, but along about the five-hundredth time he is asked to recount a particular episode he either loses his temper or starts to invent variations on the original anecdote for his own entertainment. I have done both. So, to preserve my pleasant disposition, and before the stories become embellished beyond recognition even by me, I decided to write them down—cold sober, without an audience, and with my old log books for the sake of accuracy. Now, whenever anyone asks me about that shark attack off Belize, or whether the cat on the *Niña II* voyage *really* fell overboard, I can refer him—or her—to the appropriate chapter and continue talking about present activities and future projects, which interests me more than rehashing the past.

Another reason for the book is to explain a recent turn in my life, the apparent transformation from freewheeling adventurer (or pirate, or just plain nut, depending on one's point of view) to serious archaeologist, which has come as quite a surprise to many people I know. At the end of 1965, I began a large-scale archaeological program for the Jamaican government on the sunken city of Port Royal, considered by many the most important underwater site in the Western Hemisphere. A few people doubted my capacity for the painstaking work of excavation, methodical recording of data, and historical research required to interpret the data correctly. Most, knowing the way I have tackled other projects that interested me, conceded I could do it but puzzled over my reasons. Why should a restless pirate like me tie himself down to a job that requires such patient, often tedious work without even the prospect of striking it rich? Opinions ranged from "Marx must have an angle" to "Marx must have gone off his nut on that last voyage."

After reading this book they will be reassured that what seems an abrupt transformation from pirate to scholar has merely been a shift of emphasis. I began to study history and archaeology almost solely to help in locating and identifying shipwrecks I was looking for and became so fascinated by the subjects themselves that I eventually ended up by searching for shipwrecks, Maya temples, artifacts, and everything else that was relevant in order to learn more about history and archaeology. However, the transformation is not, nor ever will be, complete. That is, I have no more intention of settling exclusively for exploring archives and libraries in the future than I had of embarking on a venture strictly for thrills in the past. There are still too many buried ruins, sunken galleons, and routes of pre-Columbian voyages to America waiting to be discovered.

My third and final reason was to introduce some of the outstanding people I have come across. A few, like Taole, the pint-sized Maya Indian who struggled through the Quintana Roo jungle with me, could not tell their own stories because they can barely read or write. Then there are the good friends who probably do not realize how much they have helped me and would not say so if they did. There are three in particular who appear in the book and deserve mention: Capt. Robert Legge, USN (Ret.), who first aroused my interest in marine archaeology, as opposed to treasure hunting, by persuading me to search for the historically valuable though intrinsically worthless USS *Monitor* and encouraged me to keep trying until I found it; Clay Blair, who emphasized the importance of filling a tremendous gap in maritime history—the story of the Spanish treasure fleets—and persuaded me that the only way of doing so was through original research in European archives; and John Goggin, to whose memory this book is dedicated and who not only taught me much of what I know about archaeology but also, though a university professor himself, convinced me that the professions of archaeologist and historian need not be secret societies for which an academic degree is the only passport.

Unfortunately, many other friends had to be omitted in favor of some thieves and cutthroats whose contributions to the story were essential. One particular omission I regret was made for the sake of prudence rather than lack of space: a group of Cuban exiles from Miami about whom I was writing an article for a widely respected national magazine. The article was never run, and since official policy is still opposed to U.S.-based raids on Cuba, I decided against including this chapter in the book. Regardless of what one may think of their actions—right or wrong—it was impossible not to be impressed by the courage, dedication, and resourcefulness of this small group, and some day I hope to give a full account of the adventures, and misadventures, I shared with them.

R. F. M.

Kingston, Jamaica
May 1967

Always Another Adventure

Chapter
One

·

The
Making
of an
Adventurer

◆

I decided to become a deep-sea diver at the age of ten. Three years later I started on my first professional salvage job, and since then I've logged so many hours underwater that I check every once in awhile to see if gills are growing on my neck. Sometimes I settle for sailing on the sea instead of diving underneath it, and occasionally I've been beached for months at a time to follow some crazy adventure on land, but I'm really out of my element there and always make tracks for the nearest stretch of open water at the first opportunity.

Almost everyone I know, from casual acquaintances to my closest friends, has said to me at one time or another, "You must have been born and raised next to the sea, you love the water so much." I hate to disillusion them, but I never even laid eyes on the sea until a month before I went down in a helmet rig for the first time. All I knew as a child were sooty brick houses, hilly streets, and steel furnaces belching black smoke—Pittsburgh, Pennsylvania, where I was born December 8, 1935. Nothing could be further removed from ships and the sea, and maybe that's why I love them so much.

From as far back as I can remember I considered Pittsburgh the end of the world (They say it's changed since then. I wouldn't know; I haven't been back in seventeen years), and as soon as I learned to read, my one ambition was to leave. I spent all of my spare time in the school and public libraries poring over books on explorers and the faraway places they visited. All the money I made on my paper route was spent on maps, guide books, and magazines like the *National Geographic*, which I would read from cover to cover and then start all over again. I had little use for family, or school either, especially after I was thrown out of geography class (my favorite subject) in the fourth grade for correcting the teacher once too often. Nor did they have much use for me. I must have been a real headache to everyone who was responsible for me—my mother, the nuns at school, the Juvenile Courts—and why they went to so much trouble to keep me in Pittsburgh I'll never understand.

I must have been about eight when I made my first getaway attempt. It all started when one of my uncles, who was in the numbers racket, gave me a job as messenger boy because I refused to go to summer camp like the other boys my age. At first my job was just to keep him and his associates provided with cold beer while they were busy answering the phones in the back room of a pool hall from which they operated, but after awhile I was promoted to bookie status and sent around with pad and pencil to list the numbers the clients wanted to play and to collect the bets. Whenever someone won, he (or she) would always give me a good tip, and I found the job very profitable. But one day I happened to ask the wrong man if he wanted to play the numbers. He turned out to be a plain-clothes policeman, and I found myself in the hands of the Juvenile Court, probably the youngest person ever arrested as a numbers bookie. I was smart enough not to squeal on my uncle and his partners, and this act of loyalty resulted in their buying me a brand-new bicycle—my first—after I was released into the custody of my mother, who had not known about my rather shady job.

With wheels, the world was mine to see. A few days later I sneaked out of bed during the middle of the night, loaded a bag with food, plus maps on which I had marked the best route to San Francisco, and took off on my bicycle. By noon I was crossing the Ohio state line, and six days later I had reached Chicago, very hungry, since both my food and money had run out. I had two alternatives: give up or resort to crime. I chose the latter, but it amounted to the same thing, since I was caught stealing a handful of change from a newsstand, taken to the Juvenile Court, and sent back home to Pittsburgh, along with my bicycle.

Within two weeks I was on the move again, but I got only as far as Cleveland before I was caught, thanks to a national alert that was put out. This time my mother and the juvenile authorities decided that I was really a tiresome nuisance, and my bicycle was sold. I was left without wheels, but this wasn't going to stop me for long.

My next escape was more carefully planned. Having read so many stories in which adventurous boys ran away to sea and signed up as cabin boys, I decided to do the same. It occurred to me that they might no longer hire nine-year-old cabin boys, but I was tall for my age and often passed for twelve. After consulting all my maps I decided that the best way, mainly to avoid detection from the police, would be to head down the Ohio River and then the Mississippi all the way to New Orleans, where I could be sure of finding many outward-bound vessels. Two of my school companions, who looked upon me as a leader because of my past exploits, were of the same mind, and together we started to collect wooden boxes and crates to build a raft (I had just finished rereading *Huckleberry Finn* to get all the scoop). We discovered the remains of a burned houseboat tied up to the river bank, however, and decided to use that instead.

After spending nearly a week amassing our stores—we couldn't steal too much food from home at once or suspicion would be aroused—we set out one night, leaving behind notes for our parents saying that we were running away to Canada, which we figured would throw them all off track. By sunup we were well away from dirty, smoggy Pittsburgh and heading down river at a good clip, since the current was even stronger than usual because of recent flood rains. Our plan was to stay in midstream so that anyone ashore who spotted the raft would think it was just a derelict and not report us to the police.

Around noon we suddenly heard roaring water and saw that the river dropped off ahead. We hadn't noticed any falls on my maps and had never thought of meeting one on our river voyage. All three of us began to paddle frantically for the nearest shore, but before we could reach it, our raft was flung over the falls and into the foaming, sucking waters below. None of us could swim, and one of my companions drowned before the men from the nearby boat locks could jump in and pull us to safety. That really shook me up, since the raft had been my idea and in a way I felt responsible. Not that I gave up all ideas of escaping; I simply decided I would go it alone the next time.

As soon as summer vacation came around again, my mother packed me off to stay with my aunt and uncle in Detroit, figuring that I would just run away from home anyway, as I had done during the last two summers. After only three days, they found me completely unbearable also. (They should have been glad that I sneaked out of their house every morning to spend the day touring the city on my own, but I guess this worried them.) But rather than ship me back to Pittsburgh and admit total defeat, they sent me to stay with their married daughter, Shirley, and her husband, who were spending the summer in a cottage on Lake St. Clair in Canada.

My cousin and her husband, Philip, were glad to have me: Shirley, because she loved to cook, and I have a voracious appetite; and Philip, because he had just returned home from the Pacific, where he had fought for three years in the Marine Corps, and liked to play platoon sergeant with me. He was appalled when he discovered that I never played sports and preferred to spend most of my time reading instead. To him this was very unhealthy and unnatural, and after hiding all my books, he set about trying to make what he called a "normal kid" out of me.

In baseball I was a strike-out artist, in football I would trip over my own feet running with the ball, and in basketball I probably established some kind of record by missing more than two hundred baskets in a row. I was even worse at swimming, if that's possible. After three weeks of lessons, I was just as hopeless as on the first day, when he threw me in, ordering me to swim or sink, and I promptly sank, right to the bottom of the lake. The only thing I can say for myself is that I had guts: I was scared to death of the water, but I was willing to try it again after Philip jumped in and pulled me out. But the only way I seemed to be able to stay afloat was by lying on top of an inner tube. My lack of athletic ability soon resulted in family squabbles, since Philip would say after every unsuccessful lesson, "Thank God that uncoordinated misfit isn't from my side of the family!" Shirley would argue that I was a "brain," which was more important than being a star athlete. Philip would retort that any ten-year-old who knew what the capital of Baluchistan was, but not the name of one player on the Pittsburgh Pirates, was definitely abnormal. And so it went on.

One day Shirley returned from town with a present for me, a pair of swimming goggles. Philip was away playing golf, and I was planning to use the respite from his rugged training schedule to catch up on my reading, but it was very hot and I went in for a dip in the lake—that is, for a splash around on the inner tube. Since I hated to get water in my eyes, I decided to try out the goggles. I was surprised to find that I could stick my face in the water and see not only the lake bottom but also fish and eels swimming around through the grass and weeds that grew there. Philip was even more surprised when he returned home later to find me actually swimming, even making shallow dives to get a closer look at the fish. In my excitement over the new world the goggles opened for me, I had completely forgotten my fear of the water.

Within a week I had developed into quite an underwater swimmer. Philip made a spear for me out of part of a broom handle and one of Shirley's kitchen knives, which I used to chase after the carp and other fish. I never caught one the whole summer—most of them were too fast for me, and the slower ones I found too pretty to spear—but I was the happiest child alive. Even my precious books were forgotten, except for some new ones on fish life and underwater stories Shirley bought for me, which I would stay up half the night reading, hiding under my covers with a flashlight to avoid detection by Philip. The one I liked best was *Twenty Thousand Leagues under the Sea,* especially the part where they left the *Nautilus* to bury one of the crew members in their cemetery at the bottom of the sea. Even though I had never heard of an aqualung or any other type of SCUBA gear (nor had many other people in the United States at that time), and suspected that such a feat would be impossible in real life, that didn't stop me from imagining myself at the bottom of the ocean, moving freely among the fish.

Finally the summer was over, and it was time to return to Pittsburgh, which I hated, and school, for which I had no further use, since I had decided to become a deep-sea diver and figured that nothing I learned in school would be helpful in that occupation. Realizing that I would have to be a little older before I could fulfill this ambition, I put up with school and Pittsburgh for almost two years. I managed to keep out of trouble, too, mainly because I spent every weekend and school vacation, except for the coldest winter months, diving in any available body of water around Pittsburgh—lakes, rivers, reservoirs, streams, everything larger than a mud puddle. The only equipment I had was my own homemade hand spears and swimming goggles, which are not really designed for anything but the most shallow dives, since the pressure of the water pushes them, sometimes very painfully, against the diver's eyes. Face masks, in which the pressure can be equalized by blowing air through one's nose, snorkels, fins, and even the aqualung had already been invented and used by the military, but skin diving and SCUBA diving as sports were barely known in the United States. Unknown to me at the time, a number of men out in California were pioneering the sport, making and sometimes inventing their own equipment, but my activities were confined to the murky waters around Pittsburgh.

At that time deep-sea helmet rigs were the only kind of diving equipment I knew existed. There were several books out, supposedly true accounts of the underwater exploits of a handful of brave "hard-hat" divers who led adventurous and dangerous lives salvaging "sunken treasure-laden shipwrecks" in the tropical waters of the Caribbean Sea and the South Pacific. It is ironical that I should have accepted these books as hard fact, believing every word about fights with the eighty-foot octopi that invariably guarded the sunken treasure chests, about Spanish galleons lying still intact on the sea floor, and other products of the authors' imagination, only to find out years later that they were pure fiction; while at the same time I looked upon the exploits of Jules Verne's Captain Nemo as fantasy, only to find *myself* years later swimming around underwater with a tank of air on my back and no hose to the surface.

Of all the tales of sunken treasure I read, the one that fascinated me most was that of Port Royal, the old pirate headquarters in Jamaica which sank beneath the sea in 1692 during an earthquake, supposedly with a vast amount of treasure. The author-diver told of finding the city still standing at the bottom of the sea, of walking past houses with skeletons hanging out of windows, and entering the coral-encrusted nave of the cathedral whose bell could be heard ringing when the sea was rough. I spent many a sleepless night lying in bed and thinking how exciting it would be to dive on that sunken city and search for all the treasure there myself—completely unaware that the city, far from standing intact, is a huge pile of rubble buried under many feet of mud and silt at the bottom of a murky harbor and that the chances of finding the treasure, if it exists at all, are somewhere in the order of a million to one.

My mother thought that I must have been cured of my itchy feet, since I hadn't bolted once in almost two years, and for my twelfth birthday she gave me another bicycle. She was wrong. I was off again, heading over the snow-covered roads down to Miami, with the idea of working my way on board some ship to Jamaica, and Port Royal. I was so obsessed with this idea that I traveled over thirty hours straight before taking my first rest, and was back on the road after only a few hours' sleep in a barn. I was on the outskirts of Richmond, Virginia, several days later, with aching legs and numb from the cold but determined to keep on, when my trip came to an abrupt end: I was sideswiped by a truck and ended up in the hospital with a broken leg. As soon as I could walk I was taken back to Pittsburgh by a juvenile officer.

This time they decided to cure me of my itchy feet by committing me to an indefinite term in Thorn Hill, a juvenile detention farm. It wasn't so bad; at least it was in the country outside of foul-smelling Pittsburgh, although not nearly far enough to suit me. I was released on probation a year later and returned to my mother's custody, more determined than ever to make a successful break, knowing that if they caught up with me before I could reach Jamaica, they would put me back in Thorn Hill until I was eighteen.

I got an evening job as a bus boy in a restaurant and began to salt away all my money, not even buying any more maps or books, since I figured that I would need at least $100 to reach

Miami by train (bicycles were getting too risky). Then something else came up. Two older boys, about seventeen or eighteen, who lived in the neighborhood, stole a car and invited me to go with them to Florida. I jumped at the chance, stopping only to dig up the sixty-odd dollars I had saved by then. A few hours later we were tooling along Route 40 approaching the city limits of Washington, Pennsylvania, when we ran into a roadblock, which the police had set up to catch a carload of bank robbers who were reported heading that way after knocking off a bank in Pittsburgh. We assumed, however, that the roadblock was for our benefit. I was cursing my luck at being nabbed again, when, instead of stopping, the boy who was driving floorboarded the accelerator and tried to smash through. The police naturally thought this was the getaway car and opened up with a hail of bullets as we zoomed past. By some miracle none of us was hit but one of the rear tires was, and the car went careening over a seventy-foot embankment. All three of us were thrown clear before it exploded, and we were taken to the hospital unconscious.

My two companions weren't expected to live, but they recovered, only to receive stiff prison sentences. I was luckier: I had only a broken collar bone, fifty stitches in my face, and twice that number in the rest of me; and, although I found myself in the hands of the juvenile authorities once again, my father, whom I hadn't seen since my parents were divorced six years before, read about my latest fiasco in the newspaper and appeared on the scene to help. Luckily for me he had some influential friends who convinced the judge that I ought to be given another chance.

My new probation officer was a real mean cat, who assured me that he wanted nothing better than to have me sent back to the detention farm and out of his hair. I toed the line and everything went well for a few months, until a substantial amount of money was reported missing from the cafeteria at the school for "problem children" to which I had been transferred.

When my probation officer learned of it he decided that I was the culprit and informed the school principal that he was going to have me sent back to Thorn Hill. The principal, who was sure that I wasn't the thief, called me into his office to warn me. I didn't lose a moment. Borrowing a few dollars from a classmate, I left school, and Pittsburgh, that same afternoon, heading due east for Atlantic City, the nearest place I figured I could reach the ocean, which I longed to see and to dive in.

By hitchhiking I managed to reach Atlantic City in only two days, arriving to find a spring gale lashing the coast, with huge waves breaking over the famous boardwalk. I was spellbound: I loved the sea even more than I had expected when I witnessed its great power and fierceness. But I was also hungry, cold, and penniless. I had no luck finding any kind of a job, with the hotels almost completely shut down at that time of year, but I was dead set against resorting to crime, as I had done years before in Chicago: not that I wasn't desperate enough to steal; I just knew that I would make a lousy thief and get caught. So with my stomach growling almost as loud as the pounding waves, I located a vacant cabana and went to sleep.

I was so hungry the next morning that I decided to beg for a handout. I didn't seem to be getting anywhere. The few people I came across in the almost deserted resort looked so mean, I chickened out at the last minute and asked them directions to some phony street. Then I spotted a wiry little fellow with a kind face and summoned up my courage. My guardian angel must have been working overtime that day. The man, whose name was Joe Novak, not only took me home to his wife who stuffed me with good food, but also turned out to be a deep-sea diver with a small, local salvage business.

Joe had no children of his own, and he and his wife "adopted" me. Delighted to learn that my own ambition was to be a diver, Joe began to teach me the rudiments of the profession, more or less by example, since I had a hard time understanding his peculiar mixture of Polish and English. At first I worked only as his line and hose handler, but after a few weeks he let me take my first dive in a helmet rig. It is a fearful experience to go down in that heavy, cumbersome equipment for the first time, wondering how you will ever get to the surface if something goes wrong,' not even sure where the surface is, because the water is so murky that everything is pitch black only twenty feet down. Finally you do surface to find yourself soaking wet from perspiration, even though the water temperature below was near freezing. I wasn't half as frightened on the second dive, even less on the third, and after a few months I thought of going down a hundred feet as a routine chore, much less dangerous than arguing politics with a drunk.

The work with Joe, I must admit, was not what I had dreamed about at all—no walking in crystal-clear tropical waters, surrounded by brightly colored fish while I picked up tons of gold bars. But it was diving and that was enough to satisfy me. Joe didn't have much technical training (if he is alive today, I'm willing to bet he's still diving without the U.S. Navy diving tables for decompression), and his equipment was antiquated, with no diver-to-surface communications other than tugs on the air hose or guide line, but he knew what he was doing and was a very hard worker, diving six days a week no matter what the weather was like. For ten wonderful months, some days as hot as a furnace and others as cold as a deep freeze, we did all sorts of jobs. We installed underwater sewage pipes, blasted old pier pilings with primacord and erected new ones, raised small yachts that had foundered in rough weather, and patched damaged hulls and rudders on larger vessels. When regular business was slow we did wreck salvage, raising valuable brass propellers, brass and copper pipes and fittings, and tons of other scrap metal. We even salvaged a cargo of bootleg whiskey from an old rumrunner that had sunk during the days of Prohibition.

Then abruptly it all came to an end. One afternoon Joe's wife appeared at the wharf where we tied up our salvage barge with the news that a policewoman and a Juvenile Court officer were waiting at the house to take me back to Pittsburgh, and, no doubt, the detention farm. They had been searching for me for the past ten months (why I don't know; they should have been glad to get rid of me), and probably would never have found me if I hadn't sent a money order to my school chum to pay back the few dollars I had borrowed. I'm sure he didn't squeal on purpose, but he always was a blabbermouth. Joe sent his wife back home to keep the gendarmes busy, while he withdrew $500 in wages he had been saving for me from the bank, and put me on board a bus for Bridgeport, Connecticut. There he had a good friend, also in the diving business, who could look after me until the heat died down in Atlantic City.

Joe's friend was also a very kind-hearted man, but unlike Joe, a heavy drinker, and although he was offered many diving jobs, he was generally too drunk to perform them. I had to spend all the money Joe had given me on food, since what little we earned went for my employer's booze, and when that money ran out things were rough. Finally I lost all my patience and decided to leave. I was in his shabby office, which doubled as my living quarters, packing my few belongings when a telephone call came through from the vice-president of a local helicopter corporation: an experimental model of a new helicopter had been lost a few miles out in Long Island Sound and he wanted us to locate and raise it. My boss was lying at that moment in a drunken stupor on top of his desk, and I was about to say we couldn't accept the job, when I suddenly decided to do it on my own. I told the man that my "partner" was sick but that I would undertake the job if they could provide a tender with lifting gear and someone to help me. He agreed, and after only a few hours' work, mostly on board the tender dragging for the helicopter so that I could attach a cable to raise it, I was $2,000 richer. I gave $500 to my astonished boss, converted the rest into travelers' cheques, and headed for California, where, according to an article I had read shortly before in a magazine, a new sport called "skin diving" was becoming the rage.

I took my time getting there, swinging south first to give Pittsburgh a wide berth and making a disastrous stop at Las Vegas. Naturally I got cleaned out and arrived in Los Angeles flat broke again. However, I located an aunt of mine who agreed to take me in provided that I went back to school again. I had been at the end of the eighth grade when I left school over a year before, but I had no intention of spending the rest of my life in school. While I was living in Bridgeport I had thought it would be a good idea to have some kind of protection in case anyone started questioning my age, and passing myself off as eighteen, I had registered with the local Selective Service Board. With a draft card showing that age (even though I had just turned fifteen), I convinced the school authorities that I was a junior in high school. After some heavy cramming to start off, I soon caught up and by the end of the semester was receiving very good grades (granted that I had to be somewhat above cretin-level in intelligence to get away with this bluff, it still makes you wonder what they could have been teaching the other kids in the three years I skipped).

It wasn't long before I made contact with some divers in the Los Angeles area and sampled the sport of skin diving, California style. What a contrast! With fins I could reach the bottom twice as fast with half the effort; face masks in those days were primitive things made of hard rubber that had to be sand-papered down to fit the contours of one's face, and snorkels were usually nothing more than a length of garden hose, but primitive or not, both these pieces of equipment made a tremendous difference: one could dive deeper, see better, and never really have to surface completely. Soon I was initiated into the use of the Cousteau-Gagnan self-contained underwater breathing apparatus, or aqualung, which made the complicated helmet rig Joe Novak had taught me to use seem prehistoric in comparison, even though the streamlined SCUBA gear in use today, in turn, makes those early aqualungs, with their bulky, one-stage regulators, look like museum pieces.

I feel almost antiquated myself when I think how far skin diving has come since then. The skin-diving club I joined, the Los Angeles Neptunes, was one of the few in the world and the second one to be formed in the United States. Most of the other members were older men in their forties who had pioneered the sport in the late 1930s and 1940s, inventing or developing much of the equipment in use today. Skin divers were still such a rare breed when I joined the club that people would gather on the shore as we came out of the water in our weird equipment, half expecting one of us to say, "Take me to your leader."

People were beginning to find that this offbeat sport could have very practical uses, too. We spent a lot of our time just snorkeling around and challenging each other to spearfishing contests, but many weekends were devoted to collecting specimens of marine life for universities and government agencies, and also to commercial salvage jobs which, like my helicopter recovery work in Bridgeport, I discovered could be highly profitable. When we decided just to make "beer money," as we called it, we could average between $50 and $100 a day merely by recovering lost outboards, anchors, fishing tackle, even golf balls. Another lucrative line was diving for abalone, lobsters, and other seafood that we sold to restaurants up and down the coast. Just on weekend diving during the semester I was able to support myself (except for the small apartment my aunt gave me in the building she owned), and during the first summer vacation, when I could dive full time, I lived it up royally, buying everything from a hi-fi set to a new convertible, and flying to Hawaii for a three-week holiday—diving, of course.

My aunt was very much against my diving, an activity she, and many other people, put on a par with Russian roulette—with all the chambers loaded—and she always seemed surprised to see me return from a diving weekend in one piece. But if a person knows what he's doing and his equipment is in good shape, there is nothing particularly hazardous about diving in itself. Not that one can relax entirely; there are always some dangers, like sharks or killer whales. I had spent nearly four years diving in ocean waters without encountering any of the fierce and deadly "denizens of the deep" that, according to the sunken-treasure stories I had been so addicted to at the age of twelve, attacked divers every time they stuck a foot in the water. I had never even seen an octopus with tentacles longer than two feet; the few sharks I had come across seemed very docile, and, except for an occasional plague of jellyfish, or the sting ray I accidentally stepped on one day, which retaliated by sticking its barb through my leg, I had no reason to think that the creatures of the sea were not perfectly harmless. That, however, was before I met my first killer whales.

Bored with spearing fish except for food or money, I had gotten on a new kick of underwater photography and went diving off a rocky stretch of coast near the Palos Verdes cliffs to try out a special plexiglass case I had built to house a regular land camera. After taking a few photographs of the bright red Garibaldi fish, I saw a group of sea lions playing around some rocks nearby and swam toward them, hoping to get some good underwater shots of them. As I was approaching, they suddenly started to screech and swim around frantically, some trying to scramble onto the offshore rocks and others trying to reach shore. At first I thought they were afraid of me, but then I saw the real cause of their panic (a sight I'll never forget if I live to be a hundred): four killer whales, each about twenty feet long, among the most deadly animals in the sea, as vicious and powerful as sharks, but much more intelligent, since they are mammals. I was, if anything, more panic-stricken than the sea lions. I didn't even try to swim to safety, not that I could have outdistanced those monsters anyway. I just froze, sinking like a stone to the sea floor about thirty feet down, and this was probably my salvation (luckily I had plenty of air left in my tank), for, as I looked up, the killer whales closed in, expertly cutting off their victims' line of retreat to the shore. Seconds later the surface was a churning cauldron of blood. Smaller sea lions were cut in half with one crunch from those massive jaws; the larger ones, some weighing up to five hundred pounds, were finished off almost as quickly in three or four bites. In two minutes there was nothing left of the twenty-odd sea lions but gory bits and pieces that filtered down on top of me. Fearing that the killer whales might notice these little tidbits they had missed, and me in the bargain, I quickly set out for shore, hugging the bottom like a snake. I was so rattled by the horrifying scene I had just witnessed that I left my camera and camera case, which had taken me a month to build, on the bottom and never was able to locate it again.

The killer-whale episode showed me that not all marine life was completely harmless, but it certainly didn't put me off diving. In fact, I counted any time spent out of the water as so much time wasted. I had put up with school to finish my senior year; then, after spending a great summer knocking around Baja California, sleeping on the beaches and trading fish I speared for food and beer, I went on to Los Angeles City College to work for a degree in geography and geology. I even enrolled in night courses at UCLA to speed up the process, but this heavy schedule restricted my diving so much that I could hardly wait for summer vacation. When June finally came, I had already decided that I wasn't going to rot away in a classroom any longer (three years seems like a lifetime when you are seventeen). I got a summer diving job on an abalone boat that operated around the islands off southern California. As for future plans, it was a toss-up: either go into commercial salvage work straight away or sign up to fight in Korea first—hopefully as a Navy frogman. Time to worry about the decision when the fall came.

As it turned out the choice was made for me. One day, around the end of July 1953, I returned to the houseboat in Long Beach which I shared with some friends to find two FBI agents waiting to arrest me on charges of draft-dodging. I had completely forgotten about having registered with the draft board in Bridgeport, Connecticut, three years before with the phony age of eighteen. I had not bothered to notify them of a change of address nor had I registered in California yet, since I still wasn't eighteen. As luck would have it I was called up for induction into the Army, and when I couldn't be located in Bridgeport I was reported to the FBI, which eventually located me in California—how I never learned. I explained the whole story to them, and their office in Pittsburgh quickly verified the fact that I was really seventeen and not twenty-one. But I still found myself in trouble, since it is a federal offense to obtain a Selective Service card by fraud. So when they suggested that my enlisting in some branch of the service was a means by which my case could be closed without any problems for me, I took the hint and the same day headed for the armed services recruiting office in Long Beach.

Chapter
Two
•
The
Halls
of
Montezuma
•

I walked into the recruiting office with the idea of joining the Navy and volunteering for Underwater Demolition Team work in Korea and walked out with a bus ticket to the U.S. Marine Corps boot camp on Parris Island, South Carolina, instead. The recruiting officer had turned out to be a very persuasive Marine major who told me that Marines did underwater reconnaissance also and convinced me that if I wanted to see real action in Korea, the Marine Corps was the outfit for me. That was in August 1953, and only two weeks later the Korean armistice was signed. I just couldn't believe my luck. A three-year hitch in peacetime! Even before I reached boot camp I was already a typical Marine, hopefully scanning the newspapers for signs of another war someplace.

Graduating from boot camp at the head of my class, I was

given the chance to go to Officers Training School or Pilot Cadet School, or a choice of jobs in the enlisted ranks. When I explained to the major who interviewed me that I wanted to go to the Marine Corps Diving School, he just leaned back in his chair and guffawed: "Marx, you've been had. The Marine Corps has no diving school. That recruiting officer conned you royally." He searched around for something close to diving and came up with head lifeguard at Camp Lejeune, North Carolina.

That didn't last long. Perhaps I couldn't make any of those daring commando raids on enemy beaches that I had dreamed about before enlisting, but at least I could find something more interesting to do then tend the kiddies at a stateside swimming pool. I soon discovered that there was a great amount of diving work at Camp Lejeune and other Marine bases, but all of it was done by Navy divers, and this gave me an idea. Though quite unusual, and I wouldn't recommend it to other Marine Corps PFC's, I applied for a "General's Mast," which is a personal interview with one's commanding general. Mine turned out to be Major General Lewis ("Chesty") Puller, base commander and one of the most highly decorated Marines in the service at the time.

I was escorted to the headquarters building by my commanding officer, a colonel who was as frightened of "Chesty" as I was. Chesty had been known to throw other time-wasters out of his office on their ears, and all the while we were waiting outside, my CO kept shaking his head and saying, "Marx, you stupid idiot, we're both going to walk out of there privates. For you that's only one step down the ladder; for me it's a lifetime of sweat."

Finally, Chesty stuck his head out of the door and roared: "Get your tails in here on the double and quit wasting my time." As soon as we walked in, Chesty asked my CO what this was all about and why the CO couldn't handle it himself. Then, without waiting for him to answer, he turned to me and roared again, this time only inches from my face: "Boy, when I was a lowly PFC, I thought my commanding general was next to God himself. Now you misfits think we're your nursemaids and psychiatrists. You have exactly thirty seconds to tell me what you want, and it'd better be damned good or I'll have you shipped off to the Arctic."

I wasted a good ten of those seconds trying to overcome a sudden case of lockjaw but finally blurted out: "Sir, I think that the Navy is doing the Marine Corps a serious injustice, and I wanted to offer a suggestion to correct the matter."

Both Chesty and my CO looked as if I had denounced the President of the United States for un-American activities. Then Chesty smiled and said, "Son, as long as we Marines are just part of the Navy, that will always be the case, but let's hear your whole story."

I explained that I had learned that the Marine Corps underwater reconnaissance units had been disbanded after the Second World War, but I believed that the honor of the Marine Corps demanded that we do our own diving instead of having the Navy frogmen do it for us.

Much to my CO's surprise, Chesty agreed with me whole-heartedly. "Son, you have the makings of a good Marine and I hope you stick with it. But you have presented me with a little problem. I can't authorize a diving school here without approval from the Commandant of the Marine Corps, and he can't approve it without an OK from the Secretary of the Navy, and he won't give it. So, I think we'll have to act like Marines in this matter. You will be our unofficial base diver and we'll just have those Navy divers transferred. Say we don't need them anymore."

Chesty was as good as his word. The following day I was relieved of my lifeguard duties and ordered to take over all the duties of the Navy divers, who were soon transferred elsewhere. I was even promoted to corporal, and this naturally brought many jeers of "brown-noser" from my fellow PFC's, but that was the least of my worries. I found myself in a serious predicament: the Navy divers had not only been engaged in salvaging articles and equipment and recovering the bodies of drowned personnel, as I had thought, but were also experts in underwater demolition, welding, mine disposal, and several other specialties about which I hadn't the faintest idea. When I announced this to the colonel, who was still technically my commanding officer and who had only a few more months until retirement, he almost had a heart attack. But he soon solved the problem by sending me through a course at the base demolition school and another at the base maintenance school, where I learned the basic techniques of welding, metal cutting, and pipe-fitting, among others, so that I could adapt them to underwater work.

I soon had the situation well in hand, as the Marines say, and was able to take over all the diving at Camp Lejeune, as well as several other Marine bases to which I was loaned out for special jobs from time to time. One of my main duties was to locate bombs, rockets, and other high explosives that had been dropped in the water without detonating, and every time I had to grope for one of those babies in some muddy riverbed, or in the only slightly less murky waters offshore, I cursed myself for my bright ideas and wished that those Navy boys hadn't been transferred after all.

It was soon obvious that one person couldn't handle all the diving jobs, and although we had no official school at Camp Lejeune, I began to train other Marine volunteers in lung diving, underwater demolition, and salvage work. There was always some job to be done—recovering a plane's instrument panel so that the investigators could determine why it had crashed, repairing underwater installations, blasting underwater obstacles to navigation, and that tricky business of locating and disarming undetonated bombs. The big, twice-yearly maneuvers were our busiest time, since we had to raise all the equipment that was lost, including a great number of amphibious landing vehicles that had somehow turned out not to be completely amphibious.

The one job everyone, including myself, really disliked was

recovering drowned bodies. There was plenty of that work, for aside from the inevitable swimming accidents that occur on any seashore, both civilian and military, we were also called out whenever a plane crashed with its crew on board anywhere in the vicinity. Sometimes we took foolish risks ourselves, even when we knew there was little hope of rescuing these men alive and that we might find no more than mangled pieces of bodies, if that. But I suppose we realized how much it meant to the men's families.

A typical emergency call was one I received sometime in November 1954 from the base commander's aide, ordering me to rush with my diving gear to the parade ground where a helicopter would be waiting to take me to a swamp near Wilmington, North Carolina. A Navy bomber had crashed only half an hour before with its three-man crew still aboard. I was able to muster two of the best divers in the skin-diving club I had organized: Captain Robert Legge, a Navy orthopedic surgeon assigned to the base hospital, who was able to turn a routine operation over to an assistant; and Lt. Jerry Wright, USMC, who was glad to take a break from the boring work of drilling his platoon.

Arriving at the disaster area, which covered about two square miles of swamp with a river cutting through the middle, we found several helicopters already there and anxious men probing through the thousands of pieces of twisted wreckage for the bodies of the crew. Witnesses reported having seen the plane explode in a huge ball of orange flame, but there was still a large amount of high octane gas floating in water-filled craters, and this gave us the idea that perhaps the explosion had only been in one section and that there might be some intact sections underwater. Jerry, Captain Legge, and I first dove in the icy river and, despite poor visibility, recovered hundreds of pieces of the plane, including the instrument panel which was rushed to the investigators. But no bodies. Then I decided to try one of the largest craters (about twenty feet across and six feet deep) much against Captain Legge's advice, since the hole contained more high-octane fuel than water, and jagged pieces of the plane's fuselage were visible above the surface. I should have listened to him. The gasoline was so powerful that it soon ate holes right through my rubber diving suit, though it also warmed my body so that I didn't feel the cold. It also ate away the rubber on the edges of my face mask and burned my eyes, but I had found a helmet and a shoe on first jumping in and was convinced that at least one of the bodies was in the hole. I was right, for I soon recovered two legs and a torso. But by then my eyes were burning so badly I was completely blinded and had to give up the search.

Once out in the open air and practically naked, since there was nothing left of my diving suit but shreds, my body and face seemed on fire from the evaporating gasoline. As soon as I started hopping around from the pain, making it even worse, Captain Legge realized what was happening. He quickly threw me to the ground, covered me with mud and began to wash my eyes out with some medicine from a first-aid kit he had brought along. Jerry ran to have a helicopter readied, so that, after being wrapped in a blanket and placed on the floor next to a mail sack containing the parts of the man's body I had found, I was flown directly to the base hospital at Camp Lejeune for treatment. Several weeks later my body was still covered with blisters, but my eyesight was saved, which had been my main worry, and there was one compensation: I had a long vacation from shaving, since my beard did not start to grow again for months afterward.

The small group of volunteers I had started to train—along with Captain Legge, who had been one of the pioneer lung divers in California, and a few other experienced divers—started a real diving craze in Camp Lejeune that soon spread to other Marine bases in the U.S. Everyone wanted to take up this new sport, and by the time I left the Marine Corps, I had taught the techniques of lung diving to over one thousand Marines, including eight generals. It must have been the first time in the history of the Marine Corps that a corporal gave orders to a four-star general, even if they were only underwater hand signals.

The useful work my team and I did must also have set some wheels turning high up in the Marine Corps and Navy commands. That official Marine diving school which had been so out of the question was in fact established. During my last year in the Corps, I was suddenly given sergeant's stripes and ordered to set up a regular course of instruction for Marine reconnaissance companies on the small island of Vieques, between Puerto Rico and St. Thomas in the Virgin Islands. This new diving school was a sort of orphan outfit, and there was a short circuit somewhere in the supply route to Vieques, but we managed somehow. We obtained our diving gear in proper Marine fashion: that is, we stole it from the Navy, which had bases in nearby Puerto Rico and St. Thomas. Or sometimes we improvised, such as converting old fire extinguishers into compressed-air tanks, but this is a trick I wouldn't recommend generally—the improvised tanks have a nasty habit of exploding. We obtained the rest of our supplies by a thriving barter system: officers' clubs in all the services from St. Thomas to Florida were supplied with fresh lobster and fish in exchange for planeloads of beer and other essentials.

What we lacked in equipment we made up for in spirit, helped by the traditional rivalry between the Marine Corps and the Navy. Every new planeload of what I termed my "misfits," who sauntered off looking as if they thought they had volunteered for a Caribbean holiday, got a grueling training course which started out with an eleven-mile swim to the neighboring island of Culebra, egged on by shouts of: "Anyone of you idiots who doesn't make it is shark meat. Anyone out of breath at the end gets transferred to the Navy UDT." Then came the rudiments of lung diving and from there to specialized work in underwater demolition and air-sea rescue. Some of my men proved such good divers that we started experimenting with helicopter drops—sometimes from as high as fifty feet—equipped with a double tank weighing seventy-five pounds and other gear. I believe that these were the first experiments with this technique of air-sea rescue in any of the services, certainly in the Marine Corps. The school was short-lived, since it was closed down after my discharge, but by that time Marines had established themselves as qualified divers and continued to be trained at Navy diving schools. So Chesty Puller and I had contributed something to the Corps.

The average twenty to twenty-five hours a week I spent under water in my official duties for the Marine Corps left me only half waterlogged, and I spent every available hour of my free time trying to complete the process. My main interest was wrecks. Since I first started diving I had been fascinated by tales of locating and salvaging old shipwrecks. Although I eventually realized that 99 per cent of them were completely fake, describing wooden hulls still lying intact on the sea floor with a skeleton draped over the wheel and a giant octopus guarding the treasure chest on the deck, I never lost this fascination nor my interest in finding old shipwrecks myself. Part of it is the mystery attached to something lost long ago—like an ancient Egyptian tomb buried in the sand—and part is the excitement of searching for a sunken treasure.

I was determined to be scientific in this underwater sleuthing, so that by the time I joined the Marine Corps I already had a large wreck file full of information gleaned from newspaper articles, hydrographic charts, history books, and naval records—and of course books on sunken treasure itself. It didn't take me long to discover that Camp Lejeune was only a twelve-hour drive from an area I had picked out as one of the most promising hunting grounds in the United States—Cape Hatteras, North Carolina, sometimes called the "Graveyard of the Atlantic" because of the more than two thousand ships that over the centuries have either foundered close by or been wrecked on its treacherous shoals.

There was nothing particularly romantic or mysterious

about the first sunken treasure I went after at Cape Hatteras: two German submarines that according to U.S.Navy records had been sunk there during World War II with over $200,000 worth of mercury as ballast. I figured that this would at least make a down payment on a special ocean-going salvage vessel I had been dreaming about to cruise around the world in search of more interesting wrecks. My first futile trip to Cape Hatteras proved that my scheme of locating the submarines by myself in a skiff was hopeless. The seas were so mountainous that not even an obsessed nut like myself would venture out in so small a boat. I knew that I would need help, mainly financial, since nothing smaller than a fifty-foot shrimp boat or fishing trawler would do as a diving tender in those waters, and such a vessel would charter for between $60 and $100 a day. I placed an ad in the base newspaper: *Anyone with diving experience interested in locating two sunken subs with a fortune in ballast contact Cpl. Robert F. Marx. Must be willing to share costs.* Much to my surprise, over fifty people, ranging from privates to colonels, contacted me, but perhaps not so surprising, since few of us can resist the lure of a get-rich-quick scheme.

By taking about ten or twenty "shareholders" with me to Hatteras each weekend, I was able to charter the best vessels available, and since the members belonged to different units on the base, we never lacked any necessary equipment. If we needed buoys to mark out a search area, a lieutenant from the motor pool supplied fifty ten-gallon drums, painted in red and white stripes (for easy visibility) by a sergeant from a construction unit; and a corporal from the supply depot provided the rope to connect them to the buoy anchors, which were empty shell cases supplied by a major from an artillery battalion. Another member happened to be the quartermaster, who saved us from the astronomical food bills that a pack of hungry divers would have run up: he arranged for a supply truck full of food to be conveniently stationed every Friday afternoon in the parking lot where we assembled, so that we could set off well stocked for a weekend's diving—compliments of the U.S. Marine Corps.

Cape Hatteras is no diver's paradise. The same nasty weather, strong currents, and shifting shoals that have earned it such a bad reputation with seamen help to guard those two thousand-odd wrecks from would-be salvagers. Our first two weekend expeditions were a total loss, since on both occasions such a gale was blowing that no one was willing to take us out. Even on the "good" weekends on which we were able to get in the water, the wind never fell below twenty knots, and in most places we had to work in a six- or seven-knot current with visibility no more than ten feet, at the most.

Our search method was to cover systematically an area of ten square miles that I had plotted according to the approximate locations of the sinkings given by the Navy and some of the survivors. On the first trip out we laid out all fifty peppermint-striped buoys in a grid pattern covering part of the area. Then the boat cruised slowly back and forth between them, running its fathometer to catch any irregularities on the sea floor, which usually were wrecks. Whenever a contact was made, two divers, connected by a line to each other and to the boat (because of the strong currents) went down to inspect the contact. This system was repeated in a different section each time we went out, so that we eventually located a whole sunken fleet of old sailing vessels, six fishing trawlers, three freighters, one super-tanker, and one U.S. Navy sub-chaser, which we later learned had been sunk by one of the German subs we were searching for.

Finally, after four full months of searching, on our sixteenth trip to Hatteras, the grid system paid off: we found both submarines within a mile of each other. The first one was lying upright on the sand in seventy-five feet of water with two gaping holes in her hull, one amidships and the second in her bow (two direct hits scored by U.S. Navy depth charges); the second was in one hundred feet of water and, although she was buckled in several places, there were no holes in her hull. In fact, by banging on the hull, we found that a few of the compartments were still water-tight. We first tried prying open the conning-tower hatches on both subs with crowbars, and when that failed, with the winches on the chartered shrimp boat. They still wouldn't budge, so we got good bearings, attached buoys to both wrecks, and left for the base with plans to return the next weekend equipped with acetylene torches.

A few days later I called a meeting of all the men who had participated in the weekend expeditions until then (forty-one in all) to discuss how we would tackle the problem of salvaging the mercury, now that we had located the wrecks. I had a long list of equipment we would need, such as air compressors, acetylene torches, and underwater lights, but before I could start asking who could contribute what, one of our members, a major who was the base legal officer, walked in and announced that he had some very bad news. A few weeks earlier I had asked him to see about getting permission from the U.S. government to salvage the two subs, just to be on the safe side, and only the day before he had received replies from the Navy and State Departments. We were ordered not to salvage or even enter either submarine, since it was expected that they were booby-trapped. Also, we might discover something in them embarrassing to the German or United States governments.

Well, there went sixteen weeks of effort and all our plans for a nice packet of money—my plans most of all, since I had a one-third interest in the venture, with the rest divided equally among the other forty-one men who had helped. We were willing to take the risk of a booby-trap and couldn't imagine what embarrassing items we might find, but there was no point arguing with the United States government. I felt especially bad, not only because of the money but also because I had led the other men into the venture in the first place. We were all sitting around looking glum or making unprintable remarks about the Navy brass and the State Department, when Captain Legge stood up and called the meeting to order. He told everyone that even though this was a bad piece of luck, none of us had lost any great amount of money, and we had all gained valuable experience. He proposed that we form a permanent club for general diving, and any of us still interested in salvage could continue our weekend expeditions and search for other wrecks that had no legal, or diplomatic, complications. So Captain Legge, who had been a member of the first diving club in the United States, the "San Diego Bottom Scratchers," helped form the first Marine Corps club, the "Camp Lejeune Sea Urchins," of which I was elected president and Captain Legge vice-president, and which soon grew to a membership of over three hundred.

Sometimes alone, but usually with some of my fellow Sea Urchins, I made many other trips to the Outer Banks, which includes several long sand spits and islands as well as Cape Hatteras, to continue our search for sunken treasure. We first looked for a fleet of Spanish treasure galleons reported sunk off Hatteras in 1715, which we never found nor ever could have found, since, as I later learned, this fleet had actually been wrecked off the Florida coast. Then we went after a ship of Blackbeard the Pirate, who operated in the area during the eighteenth century. We found the wreck, sunk off Ocracoke Island in a battle in which Blackbeard was killed, but none of the reported treasure was on board. Another promising item from my wreck file was the American clipper ship *Central American,* sunk in 1857 with a large amount of gold from the California gold fields. We thought we had located her, but were pretty embarrassed to learn it was the wrong wreck after the papers had reported our $2 million discovery.

One of the most interesting wrecks I found during my time in the Marine Corps I literally bumped into by accident, not off Hatteras but at Wrightsville Beach, about fifty miles south of Camp Lejeune. Two days after Hurricane Hazel had swept over the area in October 1954, leaving behind over $150 million damage and many dead, I received a phone call from the editor of the local North Carolina newspaper offering me $500 to search for the body of one of his staff photographers who had been swept away while trying to take close-range photos of the sea lashing the coast. Even though I was always broke and in need of money to buy more diving equipment or finance some expedition, my conscience made me tell him that he would be wasting his money. The currents would have carried the body miles away by then, and there wasn't one chance in a million of finding it. But he urged me to try anyway, and I agreed to start out immediately for Wrightsville Beach, where a police launch would be waiting to take me out.

Even though the hurricane had already passed, the sea was still so rough that the police launch capsized soon after we left the dock, and after salvaging my gear (fortunately well secured below deck), I had to transfer to a more seaworthy fishing boat. A strong current was running parallel to the coast from north to south at a velocity of six to eight knots, so that ordinary search methods were out of the question. I decided to take advantage of the current; I would jump off the fishing boat about two hundred yards north of the Wrightsville Beach fishing pier and let the current sweep me along the bottom; an inflated life jacket floating on the surface, and secured to my waist with a long line, enabled the skipper of the fishing boat to follow me closely, and when I had been carried two hundred yards to the south of the pier, he would grab the line and haul me back to return and repeat the process at a different distance from the shore.

After checking the area from about a thousand feet seaward to the end of the pier, which jutted out at right angles to the shore, the really difficult work began, since I then had to search underneath the pier, where the body might have been caught by the pilings. On my first run, which was to be right under the seaward end of the pier, I was being swept along the bottom at the usual fast clip, barely able to see two feet in front of me, when I smashed right into the side of some large structure. Still slightly stunned, I was able to hold on and take a quick look before I was swept past by the current. It looked to be an old side-wheeled paddle steamer, buried halfway up her main deck in the sand, but almost upright with a slight list to port.

After making several other runs I was able to estimate her size at about one hundred and fifty feet in length and from thirty to forty across the beam. She lay at right angles to the shore partly under the north end of the pier, and one of the pilings had been driven through her bow. The deck house and the rest of the hull seemed intact, although I was not sure since she was like a huge porcupine, bristling with thousands of old fish hooks that had caught in her hull and deckhouse, which were also covered with razor-sharp barnacles, and I couldn't hold on against the current for more than a few seconds each time.

By the time it started to grow dark, I still hadn't found the man's body, even after searching the entire area under and to several hundred yards south of the pier up to the shore line. On the way back to the dock I told the skipper of the fishing boat that I had seen an old paddle-wheeler under the pier and asked if he knew anything about her.

"That's the *Fanny and Jenny,*" he said. "People around here say she's got a gold sword on her that belonged to General Robert E. Lee. I think it's a lot of hogwash myself."

I promptly forgot about the *Fanny and Jenny,* believing along with the fishing boat's skipper that the gold sword was just another wild treasure story. Then a few days later I happened to be reading a book about North Carolina called *The Devil's Tramping Ground* and came across an entire chapter devoted to the *Fanny and Jenny* that quickly set me off on another treasure hunt.

According to this book (and other sources I checked on later) the *Fanny and Jenny* was a Confederate blockade runner launched on the River Clyde in Scotland in November 1863. Many people in England sympathized with the Confederate side during the American Civil War, and before the newly built *Fanny and Jenny* set out on her maiden voyage, her captain had been entrusted with a gold sword, its hilt studded with jewels, which was a gift to Robert E. Lee from a group of wealthy admirers. Lee probably would have found a couple of artillery pieces more useful, but that is beside the point. Legend has it that the *Fanny and Jenny*, in addition to her cargo of weapons, munitions, and other materials badly needed by the Confederacy, was also carrying half a million gold sovereigns, but no documentary evidence has ever been found to support this story.

Setting out across the Atlantic, the *Fanny and Jenny* made a brief stop at Bermuda to obtain more fuel for the hungry steam engines that moved her two large paddle wheels and then headed for North Carolina, intending to discharge her cargo at Wilmington. At sunrise on the morning of February 19, 1864, she was surprised by several Union gunboats off Wrightsville Beach and, receiving a hit below the water line, began to take on tons of water a minute. Everyone quickly abandoned ship and was able to reach the shore before the *Fanny and Jenny* sank, about a hundred yards out. Then the captain and purser remembered the sword and their special assignment to deliver it personally to General Lee and headed back to the ship, whose deckhouse was still clear of the water. Before reaching her, their boat overturned and they were drowned. A few days later the *Fanny and Jenny* was swept farther out to sea during a heavy norther, and that is the last recorded information about her.

The very next weekend after reading this, I drove down to Wrightsville Beach with about twenty other members of the diving club and rented the same fishing boat I had used as a tender during my search for the photographer's body. The same strong current was running along the coast, but the sea was fairly calm by then, so that we were able to anchor safely off the north side of the pier, fairly close to the wreck. But there was one diving hazard we had not reckoned with: the hundred or so line fishermen who were fishing off the pier. As soon as they saw us strapping on our diving gear they began to hurl bottles, sinkers, and everything else they could think of down on us, figuring, I suppose, that divers would scare away all the fish. At first we just tossed the things back at them, but we were clearly outnumbered, and when one of my team got a nasty gash above his eye from a broken bottle, we called it quits and made a run for it.

After taking our casualty to a doctor for stitches, I went to see if we could come to an agreement with the owner of the pier. Relations between skin divers and line fishermen have never been very cordial, but my chat with the pier owner must have set some kind of record. According to him, millions of sheepshead made their home around that wreck, and he didn't want me or anyone else disturbing them. Nothing could persuade him to relent, not even an offer of a share in the sword we planned to recover, and his parting words were a threat to have me arrested if he ever caught me near his pier again.

As usual, it was Captain Legge who came up with some good advice. Noticing on the jacket of the book I had read on the *Fanny and Jenny* that the author was a prominent businessman from Greensboro, North Carolina, Captain Legge suggested that I try to enlist his support. The man could not have been more helpful. He took me to Raleigh, the state capital, and introduced me to the director of conservation and development, who expressed great interest in my project, especially since I offered to sell the sword, if recovered, to the state of North Carolina. He, as well as Governor Luther Hodges, asked the mayors and chambers of commerce in Wilmington and Wrightsville Beach to give me every assistance, and I returned triumphantly to Camp Lejeune, convinced that I had outsmarted both the pier owner and his fine fishermen (whom skin divers hold in secret, and not so secret, contempt anyway).

Meanwhile, the Wrightsville Beach chief of police, after receiving a written complaint from the pier owner blaming *us* for starting the fracas, had contacted the military police at Camp Lejeune with the result that I was ordered not to take my diving club back to Wrightsville Beach for a period of six months. But after a little intensive reasoning. I decided that, since the order said nothing about me personally, and since Captain Legge, the senior Naval officer on the entire base, could not be expected to heed an order issued for Marines, the two of us could go alone.

We arrived at Wrightsville Beach late in October 1954, after notifying my contacts in Raleigh, and found quite a welcoming committee of local and state officials, and almost everyone else but the disgruntled pier owner, who was still opposed to the idea. He eventually decided to make the best of it by charging fifty cents admission to the pier to watch the salvage operation.

The mayor provided us with his own cabin cruiser, which we anchored close to the pier with lines fastened from the stern to some pilings to keep right over the wreck. The sea was rough, although nothing to compare with my first dive there shortly after Hurricane Hazel, and visibility was excellent for the area— over ten feet. Captain Legge and I jumped overboard, connected by a safety line because of the current, and, as luck would have it, landed right on top of the *Fanny and Jenny's* deckhouse, which we soon discovered was packed with a cement-hard mixture of sand and fine silt. She had taken quite a beating before sinking, since we counted over forty cannon-ball holes in the deckhouse alone. Working our way forward we found two large anchors fastened on the deck, as well as a large windlass and a metal box which we pried open later and found full of cannon balls. We completed our preliminary survey, finding four six-foot cannons and another smaller windlass aft of the deckhouse, and then surfaced to find our own diving tender in danger of sinking. It was jammed with about thirty or forty reporters and photographers, one of whom nearly smashed my face mask while leaning over the side to take a close-up as we climbed aboard. I threatened to dump them all overboard if they didn't clear off and get back to shore fast, then relented and said they could stay alongside in the launches that had brought them, on the condition that they stayed at anchor while we were in the water (most divers would rather work in a school of sharks than have motorboats with their slicing props cruising around overhead).

After Captain Legge and I had rested and talked over our next move, while he extracted two fish hooks caught in my leg from the wreck, we jumped back in with fresh tanks and armed with crowbars and axes. Figuring that the sword and any other interesting items would be in the deckhouse, we smashed a large hole in the after end and began to dig out the hard-packed silt and sand with our hands. After several hours, with a brief trip to the surface for new tanks, we had dug away enough debris to squeeze halfway through the opening. Then we began to feel solid objects in the sand, which we pulled out excitedly, only to find that they were all pots, pans, and other cooking utensils— we must have been in the galley and not the captain's cabin as we had hoped.

While we were below, a free-for-all had started on the surface unknown to us. The pieces of wood we had smashed from the deckhouse had floated to the surface, and all the history-minded Sons of the Confederacy standing on the pier wanted one of these relics from the Old South. Several boys did a thriving business climbing down the pilings to fish out the wood and sell the pieces to the highest bidder, sometimes getting as much as five dollars for a sliver no larger than a pencil. But two of the boys fell into the icy water and had to be fished out by a Coast Guard cutter that had come alongside with a television crew.

By that time Captain Legge and I were completely out of air, and our teeth were chattering so hard that we couldn't have held the mouthpieces anyway. We surfaced, and after answering millions of questions from the flock of press people, we had a dockside conference with the local officials on our plan of action. Both Captain Legge and I agreed that the only sensible way to find the sword and any other goodies was to rig a boom right on the end of the pier. After using the boom to lift the heavy objects like cannons and anchors, and then to rip off the deckhouse roof and some of the deck planking, we could use a large suction pump to remove all the sand and silt from the hull and deckhouse. The officials agreed and promised to have a heavy lifting boom rigged up by the following Saturday, when we planned to return.

We had to postpone it for a day because of a bad gale in the area, and when we arrived we not only found the sea still very rough but also no boom on the pier. The owner had been advised by his insurance company that the pier would be damaged by the lifting operations, and he also believed that the piling that went through the forward deck of the *Fanny and Jenny* would collapse if we started to rip the wreck apart. But with NBC and ABC television crews ready on nationwide hookups, as well as over fifty members of the press, the show had to go on. The mayor had a large fishing trawler waiting for us with a winch they said would be strong enough for the job.

We decided to lift one of the large cannons, which must have weighed at least three-quarters of a ton. After Captain Legge and I had secured a heavy cable firmly around the cannon and climbed back aboard, the winch was started. But instead of lifting the cannon, the trawler pulled itself right against a piling, crashing into it with a jolt that shook the whole pier. We pulled off quickly but not before the pier owner, almost in a state of apoplexy (and this time I had to admit that he had a legitimate gripe), leaned over to shout that he'd have us all jailed for life, including the mayor. The trawler captain agreed to give it one more try, but this time asked us to secure one of the anchors, which he judged from our description to be only half the weight of the cannon. Apparently it wasn't light enough; the same scene was repeated, with the hundreds of spectators stampeding to the shore for safety, since it felt to them as if the whole pier were collapsing. By that time the trawler captain had also had enough and insisted on returning to the boat dock.

But Captain Legge and I weren't prepared to give up yet, and we persuaded the mayors of both Wilmington and Wrightsville Beach to find another fishing trawler, which we would use only to rip off the deckhouse roof, leaving the cannon and anchors in place. This operation was much easier, and we had removed nearly all of the roof, when a swarm of state troopers, summoned by the frantic pier owner, appeared above and ordered us to come ashore immediately. Fortunately the lieutenant governor and the two mayors were among the crowd of spectators, and they intervened on our behalf. After much discussion, it was decided to suspend operations while the question of whether or not our salvage work would damage the pier was looked into. The lieutenant governor assured us that it would be settled to everyone's satisfaction by the following weekend, and he even offered to have one of the North Carolina State Fisheries vessels ready for our use as a diving tender.

Captain Legge and I drove back to the base laughing over the day's events, but, as it turned out, the pier owner was to have the last laugh. He sued everyone involved in the salvage scheme, from the mayor of Wrightsville Beach to the State of North Carolina, for damaging his pier and ruining his business. (We had supposedly scared away all the fish as well.) He did not win his case, but it dragged on for over a year, and the court issued an injunction against any further salvage work until the suit was settled.

In addition, an enterprising local newspaper editor published several editorials condemning the idea of two "Yankees" (Captain Legge and me) raising this precious relic of the Confederacy, instead of some "loyal Southerners." Not everybody took the editorials seriously, but enough zealots did to keep us from getting permission to return to the wreck. As far as I know no one else has made any attempt to raise General Lee's sword since then, but then maybe the friendly pier owner doesn't discriminate between Yankee carpetbagging divers and "loyal Southern" divers.

I made many other treasure hunts during my two and a half years at Camp Lejeune, all with about the same success as the *Fanny and Jenny* venture. We never found most of the wrecks we looked for (mainly because they never existed in the first place) and those we did find yielded nothing more than a large collection of steering wheels, ships' bells, portholes, cannons, cannon balls, and assorted crockery.

Not that this discouraged me: half the thrill was in the

search itself, and, strangely enough, my most interesting diving venture during my Marine Corps days had nothing to do with a treasure at all. One evening, late in the summer of 1954, when I was having supper at Captain Legge's quarters, he said: "Bob, why don't you find the *Monitor?*" I told him that I had heard many tales about it on my various trips to the Outer Banks and was interested in its history as the first American ship specifically designed as an ironclad, but couldn't see wasting my time trying to locate a wreck that had no treasure, but only historical value.

Captain Legge argued that it wouldn't be a waste of time, since if I found and raised the *Monitor,* I could write my own ticket in the salvage business when I left the Marine Corps. I still wasn't convinced. Then he started talking about what a challenge it would be, how people had been intrigued by the mystery of the *Monitor*'s whereabouts almost since the day she went down, how I would be doing a service for my country, and by the end of the second after-dinner brandy, I was more enthusiastic than he was.

The *Monitor* (also known as the "Yankee Cheesebox on a Raft") was a Federal ironclad that had defeated the Confederate *Merrimac* at Hampton Roads, Virginia, on March 9, 1862, a battle that probably did little to affect the outcome of the Civil War but which marked a new era in the history of naval warfare, since it was the first in the world fought between two ironclad ships. On December 29, 1862, the *Monitor* was towed out of Fort Monroe, Virginia, by a paddle steamer, the *Rhode Island,* to help blockade the Confederate-held port of Charleston, South Carolina. The *Monitor,* built so low in the water that her decks were usually awash and only her circular gun turret amidships was visible, was well designed for a battle in calm, protected waters, but she was not very seaworthy. During a storm off Cape Hatteras on the night after leaving port, she developed a leak at about the same time that the towline parted. At the sign of a rocket flare from the *Monitor,* the towship *Rhode Island* lowered lifeboats, rescuing all but sixteen of the crew, but when they returned for the rest they were unable to locate the low-lying vessel in the darkness and high seas. It was assumed that the *Monitor* had sunk, and the *Rhode Island* continued on to Charleston alone.

After reading all the books on the *Monitor* I could lay my hands on and seeing that no two of them agreed on where she had sunk or even her position when the towline with the *Rhode Island* had parted, except that it was in the general vicinity of Hatteras anywhere between ten and thirty miles from shore, I decided to do some original research on the subject. As soon as I could get a week's leave, I went to Washington, D.C., and started to track down information, mostly in the Library of Congress and the National Archives. Searching through the original log of the *Rhode Island,* I found that the captain estimated his position at twenty-one miles from the Cape Hatteras lighthouse when the *Monitor* disappeared. However, that still left a huge area to be covered, since there was a very strong onshore current running at the time, which might have carried the foundering *Monitor* with it.

On my way back to Camp Lejeune I made brief stops at several of the fishing villages on Hatteras Island, and nearly all the old salts I spoke to claimed that they had heard from their fathers or grandfathers that the *Monitor* lay fairly close to the Hatteras Lighthouse. I didn't put much stock in these tales, since I was trying to be scientific in my search, but when I saw Captain Legge at the base and told him what a lost cause I thought it was, he urged me on and suggested that I return and pump the local fishermen for more clues. They can often be more helpful than all the documents put together, he said, and I have since learned this to be true.

The next weekend I was back in Hatteras again, and one of the old seamen, a retired captain named Gray, who heard me asking about the *Monitor,* said he might have something that would interest me. Inviting me to his house, he pulled out an old family ledger in which births, deaths, marriages, and other events were recorded. One of the items was about a family picnic held on the beach near Hatteras Lighthouse one Sunday in early January 1865—only two years after the *Monitor* had disappeared—and mentioned that they had seen the "Yankee Cheesebox on a Raft" in the breakers right off the lighthouse!

This was all I needed. After arranging to charter a fishing boat for the following weekend, I rushed back to share the news with Captain Legge and to call a special meeting of the diving club to ask for volunteers to help in the search. Over 150 raised their hands (and there would have been more, but I was about the only pampered Marine on the base who could get liberty every weekend), so that we had to pick forty names out of a hat.

That next weekend, like the ten or twelve that followed, brought no success: a total of two hundred divers spent over twenty-four hundred hours in those cold, rough waters covering every inch of the bottom from the shoreline to a distance of five hundred yards out and for two miles each side of the lighthouse, without finding one sign of the *Monitor*. The weather got colder and the sea rougher as winter set in, and I finally had to suspend operations. It was foolish to risk the club members' lives when it had become obvious that the *Monitor* just wasn't where I had been led to believe it was.

Once more Captain Legge urged me on, persuading me to give it one more try. I took another week's leave in January 1955 and returned alone to Hatteras in search of more clues. My first task was to make sure that the lighthouse was the same one mentioned in the Gray's family record book. It wasn't; but it was built only two hundred yards from the old site, and this made little difference since we had searched up and down the coast for two miles on either side of the new one.

I decided to make another search off the lighthouse, on the off-chance that we had missed an area before. In my first attempt to get a small rented skiff through the heavy surf, it overturned, ruining the outboard motor, and after paying $75 damages claimed by the owner, I was left with exactly $4.83 for the rest of the week. Room and board were no problem—I just slept on the beach and traded fish I speared for hot meals from some of the Hatteras villagers—but now I couldn't afford to rent even a skiff. Too stubborn to quit, I decided to work without one. This meant fighting my way through the breakers wearing a seventy-five pound double-tank aqualung and other heavy equipment, back in through the breakers when I ran out of air, and then out again with a new set of tanks, making about four or five excursions a day. Dozens of people gathered on the beach to watch, telling me what a nut I was every time I crawled out of the water to change tanks. But I had to be grateful for their presence: on two occasions when I was swept out to sea by strong currents, spectators rushed to the nearby Cape Hatteras Coast Guard station, and a lifeboat was sent out to rescue me.

By the end of the week I had nothing to show for my efforts but dozens of cuts and bruises from being battered around by the big breakers, and a case of pneumonia from sleeping on the cold beach, which put me in the base hospital for two weeks. That seemed the end of the *Monitor* business, but a piece of valuable information turned up that set me off on my search again. One of the club members came to visit me in the hospital one day to tell me that he had been reading through an old atlas, published in 1870, and had noticed that the location of the Cape Hatteras Lighthouse, about a mile back from the shore line at that time, did not tally with its present location, only twenty or thirty yards from the high-water mark. As soon as they let me out of the hospital I went up to Raleigh to check out this new lead. Other old maps and charts also placed the lighthouse about a mile inland, and several state geologists I consulted confirmed that the coastline of the Outer Banks in the Hatteras region had receded almost a mile in the last hundred years. In fact it would have receded even farther, they said, if dune grass had not been planted during the 1930s to cut down the erosion from the strong currents and surf. This meant if the *Monitor* had been in the breakers when seen by the picnickers in 1865, it would be a mile offshore today.

Returning to the base, I found still another valuable lead waiting for me in the mail. Reading in some history book that the Union 20th Indiana Regiment had been stationed on Hatteras at the time the *Monitor* was lost, I had written to the Indiana State Historical Society asking if there were any regimental records existing from that period, and the society sent back photostats of the regiment's record book for a month following the *Monitor's* disappearance. Pay dirt again. Two days after the *Monitor* had gone down, some soldiers had found five bodies of her crew washed ashore near the lighthouse, and the bodies had been buried near a large cedar tree on a high knoll a half mile behind the lighthouse.

Back again at Hatteras the following weekend, I easily located the knoll, as well as the stump of a long-dead cedar tree. Then searching through the bushes for signs of a grave, I stumbled upon a large hole with many stones lying about. Since Hatteras is pure sand, I figured that the stones must have been brought there—perhaps to cover over a grave—and began to scoop away the sand eagerly with my bare hands. A twig snapped behind me and I turned to find myself staring into a rifle barrel held by an elderly man who demanded, "What are you doing trespassing on my property?" As I explained to him what I was looking for, he lowered his rifle and said in a friendly tone, "That's very interesting. Come up to the house for a drink and tell me about it."

Entering his house, or cottage, I could scarcely believe my eyes: The walls of the small living room were covered with drawings and paintings of the *Monitor,* as well as a large chart of the Cape Hatteras area, showing the different positions where the *Monitor* had been reported lost. On it a spot about a mile off the lighthouse was marked with an "X" in heavy red ink and the words, "Here is where I found her."

My host, I soon discovered, was Mr. Ben Dixon MacNeill,

a retired journalist and an amateur historian who had devoted most of his life to studying the Civil War, mainly the history of the *Monitor*. Somewhat of an eccentric, he lived alone and was considered a crazy hermit by the local people, since he rarely went out, spoke to no one, and kept a fierce dog tied at his gate to discourage visitors, which is why, I suppose, no one had directed me there during all that time I had been asking about the *Monitor*.

After we had been talking for awhile, MacNeill took a small box from a drawer and, handing it to me, said, "Is that what you were looking for?" Inside were buttons and five belt buckles from Union naval uniforms from the Civil War period. "I dug that grave up several years ago," he continued, "and verified that the five *Monitor* crewmen had been buried there. I also knew all five bodies had been washed ashore at the same spot and I realized that the *Monitor* had to be close to the shore or the bodies would have scattered. With that idea, I started my air search. That was twelve years ago. During the first six years I made seventy-five flights without spotting her, but on the seventy-sixth, I finally did. Since then I've made about twenty more flights, but I've only seen her six times, because the water gets dirty sometimes and sometimes she gets covered over with sand."

I sat there absolutely flabbergasted, not knowing whether to believe him or not. It seemed impossible that this recluse could have found the *Monitor* without someone knowing about it, and no one in Hatteras had ever mentioned it to me. Yet his facts and the position he had marked certainly jibed with what I had learned. As if reading my mind, he said: "You don't believe me, do you?" I said that I did though it was difficult, and he invited me to visit him again, which I promised to do, providing it was all right with that huge dog at the gate.

Back in Hatteras village, I asked many of the people I knew about MacNeill's story. They all said that they had heard him make some noise about sighting the *Monitor* from the air, but that since three different diving expeditions financed by some Yankees had ended in failure, they assumed that MacNeill had invented the whole thing.

I made several other trips back to visit MacNeill, each time bringing him several bottles of whiskey and boxes of food—he looked half-starved and I certainly didn't want the old man to die, at least not before he helped me locate the *Monitor*. He refused to tell me her exact position and had prudently taken the chart from the wall after my first visit so that I couldn't get a good fix from land features. The press, he said, had criticized him so badly after the last major expedition (sponsored by some retired mailman from Michigan) that he didn't want to go through the same thing again if I failed to locate her. I finally persuaded him to help me by promising that we would work in complete secrecy: if we were successful, then he would have the last laugh at his newspaper critics, and if not, no one would know the difference.

We agreed to mount a small-scale expedition that would not attract much attention and decided upon June (1955) as the most likely month for (relatively) calm, clear water—although you can never count on Hatteras weather. MacNeill would provide a plane for spotting the *Monitor* from the air, or rather borrow it from his nephew who happened to own one, and I would furnish all the diving equipment. MacNeill let the sheriff of Hatteras village in on our secret too, because he had been helpful before (and also backed MacNeill's story, claiming to have seen the *Monitor* twice from the air himself), and he promised to loan his dory with an outboard motor as a diving tender.

In order to insure secrecy at my end, I told no one on the base about the expedition except the Legges and one of the members of the diving club, whom I asked along to help— Donald "Andy" Anderson, the best diver in the club and, most important, very close-mouthed. I also at the last minute told my girl friend, a woman Marine named Marcia, and this turned out to be a mistake.

Andy and I arrived at Hatteras on June 5 in a station wagon loaded with equipment and found that MacNeill had everything ready; he had even managed to get us a free room in a comfortable motel, although we had been expecting to camp out on the beach. The following day we began our search, even though— June or no June—the seas were enormous and the water very dirty. Andy rode in the plane to search for any signs from the air, while the sheriff and I cruised below in the dory. Whenever Andy saw any dark spots that might be the wreck, he dropped a weighted float from the plane and we maneuvered over to the spot so that I could dive down and investigate. Each time it turned out to be only a dark patch of seaweed on the bottom— except once, when it was a school of menhaden, so closely packed together that I was almost able to walk over them to get back to the dory.

We spent all that day and the five days that followed in the same tiring work. It was tiring not only for me but for everyone, including MacNeill, who directed the plane's searches from the beach with a walkie-talkie I had borrowed from the base. Our tempers grew shorter with each day of fruitless searching, especially MacNeill's, who faced the prospect of still another fiasco, and by the evening of the sixth day he was in a real state, calling all of us blind, incompetent nitwits. Then came the last straw. Toward sunset a light plane landed on the highway near the lighthouse (which we also had been using as an airstrip), and out stepped my friend Marcia and Larry Holland, a friend of mine who was assigned to the Camp Lejeune newspaper. Deciding to pay me a little visit, Marcia had persuaded Larry, who saw a chance for a good story, to fly her up to Hatteras. It was the end of our joint expedition. As soon as Marcia introduced Larry as a reporter from the base newspaper, MacNeill flew into a rage, accusing me of breaking my promise of secrecy and denouncing us all as "Marine Corps publicity hounds." He stalked off, and I followed, trying to explain what had happened, but I have to admit that the whole thing looked like a double cross, and all MacNeill would say was that he was withdrawing from the venture and that I was on my own.

I was so furious with Marcia and Larry that I could have strangled them on the spot, but I realized that I now had no plane, except Larry's, and I persuaded him to stay for the weekend and help out. The next day's search was no more successful than the previous ones, even though Larry and Andy were able to get very close looks—every time the single engine died out on the lower octane automobile gas, which was all we could get in Hatteras. But by evening the water was getting much calmer and clearer, and our hopes rose again.

I went to see MacNeill that night to try to patch things up but got no farther than his gate. He threatened to turn his dog loose if I didn't leave his property, so that was that. I was determined to find the *Monitor,* with or without MacNeill.

On Sunday morning, June 12, Andy went up on his thirty-eighth flight of the week. The sea was almost flat calm, and the water so clear that I could look over the side of the dory and see bottom thirty feet down—remarkable for Hatteras. Suddenly Larry banked the plane sharply and came toward us, making several low passes and wagging the wings. At first I thought that the plane was in trouble again, but then I saw Andy's arm sticking out and waving me toward shore. I was so impatient that when the sheriff couldn't start the outboard motor immediately, I dove in, swam to shore, and ran to the highway just as the plane was taxiing to a stop.

Andy jumped down, shouting above the engine, "Marx, Marx, we saw it, we saw it! Get in, you'll see it too!" I climbed in quickly, practically knocking Andy over with a passing thump on the back. Larry gunned the motor, and we careened down the highway, when suddenly we heard a sickening crunch from the right wing and jolted to a stop. Neither of us had noticed a high road sign or heard Andy's shouts of warning. It looked as if only the wing fabric was torn, so we jumped in again—after removing two more signs farther ahead—and took off.

Once airborne I saw that the water was clearer than I had ever imagined it could be around Hatteras. Larry flew out several miles to sea to gain altitude, and I saw wrecks lying all over the bottom like toy boats in a bathtub. Then he turned and headed for the site. I was so excited I could hardly breathe. At exactly 11:15 A.M. I saw the *Monitor* for the first time. There was no mistaking her: the dark oval outline of her hull, the circular gun turret amidships, and the smaller square pilothouse in her bow were all clearly visible. Larry made several passes over the spot until the engine started to cough and sputter badly, and I asked him to go over just once more so that I could throw out a buoy marker—a ten-gallon can attached to a concrete block. The block plummeted straight down, but the lighter can was carried against the paper-thin fuselage, tearing a hole large enough for a person to crawl through. By this time the engine had died out completely, and Larry said he would have to land on the beach.

Leaving Larry to replace the rear wheel that had been knocked off by a piece of driftwood as we landed, and patch up the fuselage and wing, I rushed to the motel to get more buoys— the first one had landed to one side, and also there was danger of its being torn loose in any heavy seas. Andy and I loaded the dory with more buoys, and although we couldn't see the *Monitor* from the surface, I had made a rough fix from landmarks I had noted from the plane and laid out a number of markers in the area. Returning to the beach for our gear so that we could rush back and dive on the *Monitor,* we found MacNeill waiting for us with that same old rifle.

"So you found her," he said. "Well, she's mine, and you aren't going to dive on her, even if I have to shoot you."

Luckily, several of the local people were standing around, and they grabbed the rifle from him. Then he burst into tears. I

really felt sorry for the old man—I had spent a year looking for
the *Monitor,* but he had spent most of his life—yet no amount
of arguing would get him to accept my offer to work together
again. Then, as I was standing there arguing with him, the
sheriff came up to tell me that he would be needing his dory and
motor for something else and couldn't take us out again.

The whole *Monitor* business was beginning to look like a
bad dream, and to make matters worse I soon had what I thought
was positive proof that I was cracking up as badly as MacNeill.
Returning to my motel room exhausted, I flopped on the bed and
must have dozed off after dropping a dime in the motel radio for
an hour's music. Suddenly I woke up to hear: "This is Monitor
calling. Beep-bup-beep-a-rup. Monitor calling." Then silence. I
was ashamed to say anything to Andy and the others and only
weeks later learned that NBC radio had started a new weekend
program that same day, called "Monitor."

I found Marcia, Larry, and Andy on the beach trying to get
the plane in shape to fly back to the base. After we helped patch
the torn fuselage and wing with parts of the Sunday newspaper
and refix the rear wheel with bits of wire, Larry declared her
ready to go. I was a little more skeptical and later learned that
they had barely made it back: the right wing spar had been
broken when we hit the road sign, although it fortunately waited
until they touched down at the base air strip to fall off altogether.

But Andy and I were too excited about the prospect of
diving on the *Monitor* to worry about anything else, and as soon
as they took off we raced back to the village to rent one of the
dozens of boats tied up at the Hatteras dock. No business; they
were all "needed for something else," too. By the time we had
scouted all the five other villages on Hatteras Island with the
same luck, we began to wonder what was going on. Finally,
someone told me MacNeill had been around threatening to
shoot the first person who loaned or rented us a boat. Maybe that
was it, or maybe they just naturally sided with one of their own

people against outsiders (and Yankee outsiders at that), but whatever the reason, we were at a dead loss. There we were with the *Monitor* located and all we could do was sit on a sand dune and stare out at our buoys, floating on the still incredibly calm sea, and make periodic trips to the dock to offer the local fishermen double, triple, or whatever they wanted to charge to take us out. At the end of the week we finally packed up and drove back to the base in disgust.

Marcia and Larry had already spread the word of our discovery, figuring, I guess, that the damage had already been done with MacNeill and that real publicity could not make it any worse. News items had appeared all over the United States and in some foreign countries as well (we had been completely unaware of all this, since we had seen no newspapers at Hatteras and no one there would talk to us), and I was summoned to see the base commander, Major General Reginald Ridgely, who had replaced my old friend Chesty Puller. He was very interested in the discovery and ordered me to go to Washington to tell my story personally to the Secretary of the Navy. He, too, was very interested, but I failed to convince him that the Navy should send a barge to salvage the *Monitor*. In fact, almost everyone in Washington took a keen interest in my discovery, except for a few skeptics in the press who labeled me as a fraud. Perhaps that is why the Navy and the Smithsonian Institution, which I also went to for help, were reluctant to give me any direct backing. Everyone suggested that I go back to the *Monitor* and either get a good photograph of her on the bottom or pull off something that would prove her identity. But no one was willing to supply either the money or the boat I needed for such a project—that is, until the editors of *Life* magazine saw the possibility of a good article.

Several days after I returned to Camp Lejeune, a *Life* reporter named Clay Blair appeared and announced that *Life* was prepared to finance an expedition back to Cape Hatteras to photograph the *Monitor* underwater. Clay, like any good reporter, was also skeptical of my claim, and we didn't hit it off very well at first, but eventually he became as enthusiastic about the *Monitor* as I was, and the *Monitor* became the first in a long series of projects we were to collaborate on closely.

The Marine Corps was generous enough to give me all the time off I needed from my regular diving duties, and because Andy Anderson had been transferred to Japan while I was in Washington, General Ridgely gave another member of my diving club, Lieutenant Keith Ingram, permission to be my new assistant.

The three of us—Clay, Keith, and I—arrived at Hatteras on July 8. At first we found the atmosphere as hostile as when Andy and I had left a few weeks before, but the unlimited amounts of money that *Life* was prepared to pour into the project soon overcame any fear of MacNeill's rifle. At Hatteras village we were able to charter a sixty-four-foot shrimp boat, the *Sterling,* for about three times the price our diving club had paid on previous expeditions, but the owner claimed that it was the hurricane season and he was taking a serious risk going out at all. I tried once again that same day to reach an understanding with MacNeill, but he would have none of it, and I decided to give up and ignore him from then on.

When we cruised out to the *Monitor* site the next morning, we found that all the buoys we had left were gone—probably torn loose during a recent gale that had lashed the area for over a week, although we were prepared to suspect that MacNeill had had a hand in their disappearance. We dropped out more buoys in a grid pattern covering a large area that I plotted from bearings I had taken before, and began to cruise back and forth with the fathometer running, as we had done to locate the two German submarines. The *Sterling's* fathometer was not very sensitive, but we figured that it was good enough to find the large hulk of the *Monitor,* especially since I was sure I had put us within five hundred yards of her either way.

All day long we kept obtaining a reading near the southeast

corner of the grid. It seemed too small to be the *Monitor,* but after spending all day without finding anything else, I decided to check it out in the late afternoon. We dropped anchor, but the seas were so heavy that by the time I had strapped on all my equipment the anchor had dragged considerably, and my fifteen-minute search on the bottom revealed nothing but sand and seaweed.

Clay telephoned the managing editor of *Life* that evening and told him that none of the fathometers on the local fishing boats was very sensitive, but we had heard that several Coast and Geodetic Survey vessels with very refined equipment were work-ing in the area. The editor exerted a little pressure that same evening, and by the following morning the *Stirni,* a 110-foot vessel with the latest electronic detection gear, was on its way to aid us.

We met the *Stirni* at the site where our grid pattern was laid out and were welcomed aboard by Commander C. R. Reed, who was very eager to help us, since their specialty happened to be locating wrecks to plot on navigational charts. They decided to use their fathometer first, and then, if that didn't produce results, the sonar, which is the best wreck-locating device but not always effective in shallow waters close to shore. The only reading produced during the fathometer runs that could possibly be a wreck was over the same spot on the southeast corner of the grid where we had picked up an outline the day before. We anchored, and moments after the sonar was turned on, the operator reported a positive metal contact. We plotted his bear-ings on a chart and again it was that same spot the fathometer had indicated.

Clay, Keith, and I figured that this was enough evidence that the *Monitor* or at least some wreck was down there and wanted to rush back to the *Sterling* so that we could check it out. But Commander Reed said that, since his boat and the other two Coast and Geodetic Survey vessels had to leave for Norfolk the following day, he wanted to make certain that there were no other wrecks in the general vicinity which we could check if this contact turned out to be something other than the *Monitor*. He radioed the other two vessels to join him, and later that afternoon they set up draglines to sweep the bottom for any other wrecks or obstructions. The only snag occurred in the same spot as the fathometer and sonar contacts, and by then we were all convinced that it was the *Monitor*. It was already dark by the time the last sweep was completed, so we decided to anchor the *Sterling* for the night and accepted the comfortable bunks Commander Reed offered us aboard the *Stirni*.

As soon as it was light, a boat was lowered to drop a buoy directly over the spot that had given the sonar contact, and after thanking Commander Reed and his crew, we rushed back to the *Sterling* to move her over the site. At 0812 I was over the side. I swam to the buoy line and pulled myself down hand over hand to keep from being swept away by the swift current.

Reaching the bottom forty-five feet down, I expected to see the whole outline of the *Monitor* as I had seen her from Larry's plane; instead, about ten feet in front of me I spotted a gutter-like depression running in a slight curve across the bottom—the kind of depression made when a strong current scours the sand away from the lee side of a buried object. Digging my hands deep into the sandy bottom to brace myself, I half swam, half pulled myself toward it. Soon I was able to make out a large metal bulkhead sticking three or four feet out of the sand, and by holding on to the rim and working my way around, I discovered that it was a circle about twenty feet in diameter. After all the hours I had spent during the previous year poring over blueprints and drawings of the *Monitor,* I knew that this could only be the *Monitor*'s round gun turret. I dug down farther in the sand and found the two gun ports right where they should be, but my hands were so numb from the cold that I couldn't tell whether they were closed or only filled with sand.

My air was running low, so after circling the gun turret once more, I headed up. Surfacing about fifty feet seaward of the

Sterling, I shouted that right below me was the *Monitor*'s turret, and Clay tossed over a buoy, while Keith swam over with a line, since I was losing way against the current.

Back aboard, as Keith strapped on his diving gear, I quickly changed tanks, putting on a brand new one that Clay had bought in a small town on the way up from the base. Holding on to the new buoy line Clay had placed, Keith and I landed squarely on top of the turret, where the buoy anchor rested— Clay had scored a bull's-eye. Our plan was to search out from the half-buried turret and determine if any other part of the *Monitor* was sticking out of the sand. We started to follow the gutter-like line toward the spot where I estimated the small pilot house would be in her bow, when I began to feel dizzy. I drew a deep breath from my mouthpiece to make sure that the air was flowing properly and noticed that the air had a foul taste. My head whirled more and more; then I felt a sharp pain in my chest. Spitting out the mouthpiece, I pulled the emergency cord on my life vest and felt myself flying to the surface, and the next thing I remember was waking up on the deck with blood pouring out of my ears, nose, and mouth.

Clay had seen me reach the surface and start to drift seaward face down in the water and had jumped in and pulled me back to the *Sterling*. When Keith came up a few minutes later, after he couldn't find me on the bottom, they opened the valve on the tank I had been wearing to see what was wrong and staggered back from a strong whiff of what smelled to them like exhaust fumes. We decided that someone must have used it after it left the factory and had refilled it with unfiltered air.

Meanwhile, a squall hit the area, lasting several hours. Not until it lifted did we see that the *Sterling* had swung around in the changing wind, snagged both buoy lines in her propeller, and dragged her anchor about three hundred yards away from the *Monitor* site. Clay, seeing that the three survey vessels were raising anchor and getting ready to steam off, rushed over in a skiff to tell Commander Reed about the calamity. Reed marked the *Monitor*'s location on a chart with her precise bearings, which he gave to Clay assuring him that we would have no trouble locating the wreck again. The bearings he gave were: 20 degrees 27 minutes—Loran Tower to Cape Hatteras Lighthouse; 95 degrees 51 minutes—Cape Hatteras Lighthouse to Kinnakeet Coast Guard Station (Askins Creek); 31 degrees 28 minutes—Cape Hatteras Lighthouse to Buxton Water Tower; and 23 degrees 8 minutes—Cape Hatteras Lighthouse to Cape Hatteras Auxiliary Lighthouse.

By the time Clay returned with the chart and bearings, I had stopped bleeding and wanted to make another dive (this time with one of my own tanks) to make sure that we buoyed the exact site again. Clay and Keith tried to talk me out of it, and I finally agreed to make only one dive to check the buoy anchor after Keith had located the wreck. Keith made several dives in the area Commander Reed had marked on the chart but failed to spot any signs of the *Monitor,* and so I decided to try my luck. Usually I can shoot right down to the bottom no matter how deep, but this time I had gotten less than ten feet down when my head seemed to explode. I felt as if I were reeling around in a drunken daze and had to surface immediately. Keith was in almost as bad shape as I was, numb from the cold in spite of the heavy track suits we wore, and we decided to head back for Hatteras. As we were pulling in the *Sterling*'s heavy iron anchor, it caught on something, finally surfacing with one of its huge flukes bent 90 degrees out of shape. Only later did it occur to us that the fluke must have caught the rim of the *Monitor*'s turret, since there were no other wrecks nor any large rocks in that area.

Keith insisted that I go to the doctor in Hatteras, who confirmed my suspicion that my left eardrum had ruptured, probably when I ascended so rapidly after inflating my life vest, and he advised me to stay out of the water for at least a month. (Later, at Camp Lejeune, Captain Legge had one of the ear specialists from the base hospital examine me also, and he warned that if I went diving again within three months, it might be the end of my diving career).

Clay telephoned his editors again that evening from Hatteras and learned that *Life's* underwater photographer, Peter Stackpole, was on his way down and would be able to help Keith relocate the *Monitor*, since I was temporarily out of commission. Peter arrived the next morning, and early the following day we were anchored again over the site marked by Commander Reed. I sat on deck burning with envy while Keith and Peter made dive after dive in a wide radius around the *Sterling*, each spending a total of three cold hours on the bottom before rising winds forced us to run to port.

The rising winds were the beginning of a gale that lasted for days and days. First Peter and then Clay had to return to New York, and finally Keith and I gave up also and left for Camp Lejeune. We were in very low spirits, which sank even lower when we heard that some of the newspapers were condemning this second finding of the *Monitor* as a fraud also. The idea of photographing the *Monitor*, or better yet raising her intact, was becoming more and more of an obsession with me, if only to silence those doubting Thomases.

Clay at least was able to convince the editors of *Life* that we had found the *Monitor*, and they agreed to back another expedition. This time we got the full support of the Navy, which lent us three top divers, and the Department of the Interior, which ordered the same three Coast and Geodetic Survey vessels to help us in the search again.

By August 4 everything and everyone—diving tender, survey vessels, photographers and divers—were assembled in Hatteras and ready to start. The water was calm and fairly clear, and this time I was certain we couldn't miss: the *Monitor* would be on the cover of *Life* within a few weeks.

Commander Reed and his superior, Commander Mathieson, who headed the team of survey vessels, assured us that they could put us directly over the *Monitor* in a matter of minutes, and the sonar units on all three vessels started pinging away. When no contact had been made after several hours of probing, the fathometers were brought into action, but no irregularities appeared on the almost flat bottom. Finally, draglines were set up, and the ships swept back and forth over an area of several square miles—still no results. We were completely baffled; Keith and I had seen and touched the *Monitor* and knew she was there. We were speculating over whether there could have been a mistake in the bearings, when Commander Mathieson called a conference aboard his command ship. The only explanation that occurred to them, he said, was that the *Monitor* had been covered over by shifting sand during the several severe gales that had been battering Cape Hatteras since we had been there the month before. They offered to stand by for several more days, but since there was really nothing more they could do, Clay and I decided not to keep them from their regular work any longer.

We still had not given up hope, and for the next three days Keith, Peter, and the three Navy divers searched the bottom, until on the third day I made an interesting discovery. We were anchored over the spot that Commander Reed had buoyed again before leaving, and bumping the *Sterling*'s fathometer switch accidentally, I noticed that the depth reading was only forty feet, whereas the *Monitor* had been lying at a depth of forty-five feet, sloping down to forty-eight feet, when we had found her on the previous expedition. We had the divers go down and check the fathometer reading with their depth gauges, while we did the same from the surface with weighted lines. There was no doubt about it. The sand was now more than five feet higher in the spot where we believed the *Monitor* to be—more than enough to cover over any trace of the gun turret, which had been only partially uncovered before.

So Commander Mathieson's theory was correct. And if we needed any further convincing we soon had it from the many local fishermen and the officers at the Hatteras Coast Guard Station whom we talked to. They all assured us that such rapid changes in depth were a common occurrence around Hatteras. Straight out from Cape Hatteras were the famous Diamond Shoals, shallow sand banks fifteen miles long and six to eight miles wide, which are constantly shifting in area and position. In a bad gale, they said, depending on the direction of the wind and currents, tons of sand are washed off the shoals toward shore, sometimes for miles up and down the coast, only to be scoured away again and redeposited on the shoals during the next gale. That was that. All we could do was pack up and wonder how long it would be before a favorable storm would uncover the *Monitor* again.

During the more than ten years that have passed since I dove on the *Monitor,* many people have asked me why I never went back to relocate her and at least try to take a photograph. The answer is simple. That would mean waiting on the beach for weeks, maybe months, for good weather. Then, more time, and great expense, would be needed to find her again—that is, if she weren't completely buried in the sand. And all this without much chance for a decent photograph: visibility is never more than ten feet where she lies (usually less) and at that distance only a small part of her turret could be shot in one photograph. But raising her is something else again. I would like to see her raised and preserved as one of the most interesting relics of our country's naval history, and if someone could find a spare $100,000, which is what it would cost to refloat her, provided her hull is still reasonably intact, then I'm more than willing to do it.

My hitch in the Marines kept me busy, but not too busy to yield to the Marx adventure lust now and then. The wildest escapade, and the funniest, occurred during a slack period in Camp Lejeune, when I was waiting for my transfer to the Caribbean to become official. Since I was virtually in limbo, neither part of the base nor formally separated from it, there was nothing much for me to do. I was bored out of my wits. Mail call was the big event of the day, and even that could be disappointing, if there wasn't a perfumed letter or two. On one particularly dull day I received two letters, and thorough sniffing made my heart sink. It rose again as soon as I opened them, but looking back, I'm convinced I would have been better off following my nose that time.

The first came from a man in Winston-Salem who wanted to hire me for some underwater work in his private lake. "Underwater" was the key word here, as it always is with me: I was interested. But another look at the letter revealed that the nature of the work was unspecified, and nowhere was there a mention of money, so I cooled off in a hurry. The second letter came from a place I had never heard of (I'll call it "Willisville" to protect the guilty), and the sender was a man who claimed to be a scientist, diviner, geologist, and treasure hunter, among other things. Well, I had my doubts, because the handwriting looked like the maiden effort of a backward six-year-old, but I read on anyway. This jack-of-all-trades informed me that he had followed the newspaper accounts of my discovery of the *Monitor* and decided I was just the man he needed to help him recover $200,000 in gold, which lay at the bottom of a river. The letter ended: "Come to Willisville pronto. Yore freind, F. R. Blackstone." Short, sweet, and mysterious.

I sat on my bunk for a good fifteen minutes, thinking it over. Common sense told me Blackstone was a crackpot and the story of the submerged gold a fairy tale. Paying attention to common sense isn't the Marx way, though. Not when it comes to treasure: I've made finds after listening to stories more fantastic than Blackstone's. It seemed to me that I had a choice between taking off on a wild-goose chase or lying on my bunk and staring at the ceiling indefinitely. I was just about ready to flip a coin when in walked my friend Lowell Murphy, otherwise known as "Horsefly." I handed him Blackstone's letter without a word, watching his face carefully. It was glum as he began reading (there wasn't a hint of perfume on any of the letters he tossed on his bunk), but by the time he finished his mouth was open and his eyes threatened to pop out of his head.

That settled it—we were going to Willisville. Since Horsefly was in the same boat I was in, waiting for a transfer, we had no trouble getting a few days' leave. We loaded my car with diving gear and set off, talking calmly about how we would spend the gold when we had it. (I don't think there was an "if" in either of our minds by then.) Horsefly wanted to build a mansion on top of a mountain and surround himself with enough beautiful women to keep him happy for the rest of his days. I sneered at the mansion—the indoor life has never appealed to me—and plumped for a yacht, but I had no quarrel with the harem. I didn't allow myself to get too carried away by daydreams, though. We had to pass through Winston-Salem en route to Willisville, which was way up in the North Carolina mountains, and I decided to stop off and accept the lake job in order to pay for the expedition. Horsefly protested, but he couldn't shake me from my decision to follow this practical scheme. It was my concession to common sense—or so I thought at the time.

The owner of the lake was overjoyed to see us, and agreed readily to pay us the $100 I asked. He was desperate. His man-made lake had a drainage system, used when the lake waters rose too high after a heavy rain and endangered the numerous summer cottages circling the lake. About a week before he had opened the drain and, after letting out a sufficient amount of water, had tried to close it. It wouldn't close, and his lake was draining dry. At one end of the lake, a platform was anchored to the bottom and on it was a hand winch connected to a door, which shut off the flow of water piped out through the side of the mountain to a valley below. It was this door that wouldn't close, and the water level of the lake had already dropped below ten feet.

Horsefly and I put on our rubber suits and aqualungs and went down. We found the problem immediately: a large tree trunk was caught in the pipe. When no amount of pushing or pulling could dislodge it, we surfaced to plan strategy. We decided that we would both take saws down; Horsefly would work at the lake end of the pipe, while I would enter the pipe from the mountain end and work there. The hope was that we could make the tree trunk small enough to be pulled out of the doorway and into the lake.

As soon as I looked over the side of the mountain and saw there was a drop of more than a hundred feet to the spot where the pipe was, I realized the plan was far more dangerous than I had supposed. But looking at the sad eyes of the owner of the lake, I foolishly made up my mind to go through with it. Wearing a double-tank aqualung and carrying a small saw, I was lowered down the side of the mountain on a line. I fought my way into the pipe and, though it was very narrow, I managed to work my way through against the pressure of the water, which did not fill the entire pipe because the drain door was partially closed.

The larger portion of the tree trunk was inside the pipe, so I had most of the work. Horsefly sawed vigorously and so did I, though I had to duck as pieces of wood came flying at me with the outrushing water. We made good progress, but the more we sawed the larger the opening at the end of the pipe became, and the more water gushed out. After nearly an hour and a half of work, I knew I would soon be out of air, so I decided to surface and fill the tanks.

I started out backward, because the pipe was too narrow to turn around in. When I was about halfway out, the top of my aqualung regulator got caught in a joint that connected two sections of the pipe. Reaching back over my head with both hands, I tried to get loose. Nothing doing. I jerked my body every which way, wriggled, and did just about everything I could think of. It was no use—I was stuck fast. I considered ditching the tank, but doubted that I could hold my breath long enough to swim all the way out to the opening. The water was gushing out full force now, and I realized that I had to go out of the pipe fairly slowly, or I might miss the end of the rope on which I had descended; if I did, I would be swept out into space by the water and end up in a mess on the valley floor. As though there weren't cause enough for panic, a piece of the tree trunk smashed my mask and cracked the glass. I wasn't hurt, except for a bloody nose, but I was forced to maneuver with my eyes closed.

I removed both of my rubber tennis shoes and let the lake water sweep them out, hoping that the people waiting for me to come up would see them and guess I was in trouble. Then, before I had a chance to think of other measures to take, I began to have difficulty breathing and knew that I was almost out of air. I could do nothing but wait for rescue—if there was going to be a rescue. I tried to conserve each breath of precious air as long as I could, which meant until my lungs felt like bursting. With only a few breaths left in the tank, I started saying what I figured were my last prayers. Very elaborate prayers they were too: having as many sins as I did, I wanted them to be winners.

Suddenly I heard a voice way off in the distance say, "What the hell are you doing in there?"

I opened my eyes, to discover that the pipe was completely free from water, and the drain door was closed. Well, nobody can say I hadn't been concentrating on those prayers. Spitting out my mouthpiece, I breathed deeply. The air in the pipe was fetid, but it was air. "I'm stuck," I shouted. "Send somebody with a can opener."

The next thing I knew, someone appeared at the drain door—with a can opener. I began cursing a mile a minute, and he withdrew in a hurry. Then Horsefly crawled through the door and helped me take off the aqualung. When I got out into the light, I vowed never to dive anywhere but in the open sea again. Horsefly laughed, so I invited him to take a breath from my tank. He did, and there wasn't a drop of air in it. He stopped laughing.

The owner of the lake was generous with his thanks and pats on the back. Saying he had a very important engagement, he told us we could swim in his lake anytime, handed each of us a ten dollar bill, and raced to his car. Looking at his retreating back, I was speechless. I flung the ten dollars to the ground and found my voice just as he was starting the car. From the way the car took off, I knew the motor wasn't drowning out my words. Then I stomped to my own car, still cursing. As I gunned the motor, I nerved myself for Horsefly's "I told you so."

But all he said was, "You shouldn't have been so hasty. Ten bucks pays for a lot of gas."

I had to laugh, and that cooled me off. By the time we reached Willisville a few hours later, we were in pretty good spirits again. For that town, we needed all the good spirits we could muster. At first glance, it looked like a place time forgot. The main street, rather the only street, consisted of a narrow dirt road with about ten buildings on each side. In front of some, weather-beaten signs announced the presence of an undertaker, a doctor, a sheriff, a post office, rooms to let, and a general store. What was in the others I have no idea to this day, and I prefer not to think about it. The store seemed the likeliest bet, both for finding out Blackstone's address and for the cold drink we wanted badly, so we pulled up in front of a gasoline pump that must have been one of the first in use. (Among my many regrets about the whole venture is my failure to cart off that pump—the Smithsonian would have been crazy about it.)

Stopping to lock the car, I entered the store a few paces behind Horsefly, and the first thing I noticed was the stupefied expression on his face. I looked where he was looking, and I'm sure I gawked as much as he did. It was a scene straight out of a hillbilly movie. There were about a dozen people, men with long beards and overalls, women with bonnets and calico dresses down to their ankles, all of them gathered around a red-hot, potbellied stove. The room was a jumble: saddles, farm tools, and coils of rope dangled from the ceiling; the walls were lined with shelves holding cloth, packages of food coated with dust, and bottles of medicine that cured everything and grew hair as well; on the counter, flies were having a picnic on jelly beans, peppermint sticks, and other goodies.

I closed my mouth, then opened it again to ask if some thirsty travelers could get a cold drink.

No answer. Just stares full of suspicion, the kind I might give to somebody who stepped out of a flying saucer on my lawn.

I tried again. A warm drink? Whiskey? Anything?

One of the men spat at the stove. There was a loud, sizzling noise.

Clearly we weren't going to get anything to drink there. I gave up and asked where I could find Blackstone.

Again, no response.

A dangerous glint came into Horsefly's eye. He asked if everybody in the place was deaf and dumb.

The man who had spat stood up, lifting the shotgun that leaned against his stool. "Mister," he said, "we folks don't like strangers around here, so 'spect no help from us-uns."

That seemed to be final or, if it wasn't, the way he was pointing the shotgun barrel was. We beat a hasty retreat. Once in the car, we felt a lot safer, and decided to cruise around and check mailboxes to find Blackstone, rather than seek any more help from "us-uns." The search didn't take long. I spotted a ramshackle house about two hundred yards from the street, and a hunch told me it was Blackstone's. I was right.

The house had been built years before the Civil War, and I'm willing to bet trash had been piling up all over the yard and the porch ever since. I don't know what color the house was originally, since the last vestiges of paint had flaked off long before. The windows were in a sorry state—broken, with most of the shutters gone and the rest barely hanging on. The inside of the building was as unprepossessing as the outside. We were ushered into a parlor crammed with junk; I was able to identify old butter churns, wool spinners, broken axe handles, and a few other objects, but most of the stuff was unrecognizable. A thick film of dust lay over everything, indicating that none of it had been moved for years. I've been in some holes in my time, but I can truthfully say that not one of them could hold a candle to Blackstone's parlor.

As for the man himself, he looked as though he belonged there. In his eighties, he had a long, white beard and hair covered with a tassled cap—an unwashed St. Nicholas. He was very friendly, sweeping some treasures off two chairs so we could sit down, telling us how happy he was to see us. His wife didn't seem so happy, but maybe a scowl was her natural expression. (We learned later that she was reputed to be a witch who could turn herself into an owl at night.) She brought us tea, in cups so unbelievably filthy that we lost all our thirst when we saw them, and left the room. Pretending the tea was too hot to drink, Horsefly and I set the cups down on the floor and settled ourselves comfortably in our chairs to hear Blackstone's story.

It was a lulu. The gold was the property of a Mr. Angus, the owner of a roadside inn during the years before the Civil War. No doubt he found the hotel business a little slow, because he had a sideline: he was the leader of a gang of cutthroats who preyed on travelers, stealing money, mounts, and all valuables that could be sold without suspicion, burying the rest with the bodies of the unfortunate victims. Booty too large to bury, such as carriages or coaches, was dumped in the river. Though his neighbors suspected Angus was up to no good, nothing was ever proved against him, and over a couple of decades he amassed more than $200,000 in gold. Before he could retire from his interesting occupation and enjoy his ill-gotten gains, he was taken ill. Convinced he was dying, he felt pangs of conscience and made a confession, begging God's forgiveness and telling the handful of neighbors at his bedside that he had placed his savings in a large apple-butter pot and dropped it in the river. Then he died and, according to eyewitnesses, instantly turned black.

(At this point in the narrative, Horsefly got so carried away that he picked up his cup of tea and took a sip. Recollecting himself, he spat it out and apologized for his bad manners. Blackstone didn't even notice: he was all wrapped up in his story.)

The neighbors present when Angus died fled the room the moment the corpse turned black. They wanted no part of the gold, believing it was cursed and would bring nothing but trouble. They refused to go back to the inn, even to give the body a decent burial. The only one ever to set foot in the inn again was a ten-year-old boy named Gum Shepard, who had worked for Angus as an errand boy. It was said that he knew where the gold was buried, having been shown the location by the old slave who had helped Angus bury it. If he knew, he did nothing about it during his lifetime.

Through the years, the legend spread that the inn was haunted. Nocturnal passersby told of hearing moans, groans, and screams, which were assumed to come from the spirits of Angus's victims, unable to rest in peace. A superstitious people, the mountaineers gave the inn a wide berth by day as well as by night. Only once was it inhabited again, by a young couple from Ohio, who purchased it from the county for back taxes. No one bothered to tell them about the ghosts, of course—they were strangers. They didn't stay long, leaving after a particularly grisly night during which they had seen visions of the long dead cutthroats murdering their victims. Or so they said. Soon afterward, the inn was burned down, and so great was the legend that people avoided going near the place where it had stood.

(By now Horsefly and I were exchanging skeptical glances. The account of the treasure's origin had been convincing enough; ghosts were something else again. Nevertheless, there was no doubt in our minds that Blackstone believed it all, so we heard him out to the end.)

For a long time, no one made any effort to recover the gold. Then, about thirty years after Angus's death, two boys who were swimming in the river were swept downstream by the current and found themselves near the site of the inn. Though their parents had told them the place was haunted, they apparently didn't take the curse seriously. They began to dive from the branches of an old tree on the shore, and suddenly one of them saw the apple-butter pot on the river bottom. He called to the other boy, and together they tried to roll it to the shore. They couldn't budge it. One of the boys ran home, sneaked into his father's barn, and returned with a coil of heavy rope and a horse. Tying one end of the rope to the horse, they dived into the water and tied the other around the handles of the pot. As the horse moved, the pot moved too, but the strain on the rope was too great: it snapped, sending the pot over a ledge on the river bottom and into water about twenty-five feet deep. Since neither boy had the wind to dive to such a depth, they gave up and went home. They didn't dare tell their parents what they had been up to, but the whole story came out with the discovery of the broken rope. Both boys were soundly thrashed. That was only the beginning of their troubles, though: a short time later, one of the boys cut his leg while chopping wood and bled to death; the other was struck by lightning. These disasters, naturally, intensified the belief that the gold was cursed by evil spirits.

Blackstone finished telling his story and started quaking in his boots, as though he feared the mere mention of the gold would bring the curse down on his head. Watching him, we were uncomfortable; we were sure now we had come on a fool's errand. All the blather about curses and ghosts made us doubt that the gold had ever existed. So I told Blackstone we would dive for the gold only if we were given its exact location, and I asked him if he could give it to us, figuring he would say no.

Instead, he nodded like somebody with St. Vitus's dance and said he "sure as hell could." Years before, he and Lemm Shepard, the grandson of Angus's errand boy, had made plans to recover the gold, but at the last minute they had both lost their nerve.

I looked at Horsefly, shrugged, and told Blackstone we

weren't afraid of the curse. We were willing to dive for the gold if he took us to the spot.

At that, he trembled even more. "No, no," he said. "I will never go to the site of the old inn." The poor guy could barely get the words out.

I waited for him to calm down a bit, then asked him, as gently as I could, how the hell he expected us to find the gold when he wouldn't show us where it was.

He stopped shaking at once, and said there was no problem. It seemed a friend of his named Cooke had a special immunity against ghosts (I think it had something to do with the way he came out of the womb, but Blackstone talked so fast I wasn't able to get it straight), and Cooke would lead us to the spot. Then hastily giving us directions for finding Cooke, he pushed us out the door and bolted it behind us.

We got in the car and talked it over. It struck us both that if there was a treasure, too damn many people knew exactly where it was. Maybe it was superstition that had kept the local yokels away from it all these years. Or maybe nobody in town knew how to dive, and Blackstone had cooked up the legend to entice some suckers—namely us—to bring it up from the bottom for him. Who knew? We thought seriously about cutting our losses and running, but not for long. After all, we had come a long way. Why not see the thing through? Famous last words.

We set out to find Cooke. It wasn't hard. Well, not very hard, anyway. He wasn't in the shack Blackstone had directed us to, but we heard peculiar noises in back of it, investigated, and found him in the bush behind the shack—seated on top of a broken-down hearse, believe it or not. It looked like a pretty uncomfortable perch, but it was obvious he felt no pain. The noise we had heard was his singing, produced whenever he removed his jug from his mouth. The moment he saw us, he climbed down from the hearse and flung his arms around our necks. A warm, effusive greeting. We didn't appreciate it, though: we were too busy holding our breaths so we wouldn't be overcome by the stench emanating from Cooke, his clothes, and the moonshine.

We told him why we had come, and he said he was willing to lead us to the gold, if we gave him half of it. I wondered where this would leave Blackstone, who undoubtedly expected a half-share too, but I figured we would settle things when we found the gold. Putting Cooke and his jug in the car between us (I took the precaution of emptying a bottle of after-shave lotion on the floor matting—opening the windows wasn't enough), we started out. The drive along Main Street was a bit nerve-wracking, because the friendly souls from the general store lined both sides of it and gave us the suspicious stare as we passed. Fortunately, it wasn't a very long street.

We followed the directions Cooke gave us between swigs of moonshine and bits of gossip about the citizens of Willisville; he was the kind of talker who doesn't care whether anybody listens or not. Suddenly he started on a new line of chatter, about ghosts, hauntings, curses, and what not. He himself wasn't afraid of twenty million ghosts, he said proudly, but how about us? Horsefly assured him we were both wearing very potent charms around our necks, and there was no need to worry about us. This appeased him, and he gave his full attention to his drinking.

It probably didn't take more than fifteen minutes to reach our destination, but it seemed like hours with Cooke in the car: his presence was, to say the least, overpowering. Horsefly and I got out of the car, then discovered that Cooke had passed out. No amount of shaking could bring him to, so we left him in the car and began investigating the river bank. We spotted a large tree, which might or might not have been the tree the boys had dived from. There was no way of knowing, but at least it was reassuring to find any tree at all. Cutting inland a bit, we found ourselves in a clearing that contained the foundation of a building. It might have been Angus's inn. Again, it might not. No way of knowing that either. We went in different directions to pursue this enlightening exploration. Horsefly was searching the bush near a well, when suddenly he shouted, "Catch!" I turned quickly and saw a human skull flying through the air toward me. I caught it, letting Horsefly know what I thought of his wit. He laughed. Poking around a bit longer, we found more skulls and human bones—relics to substantiate the story of Angus's activities. We returned to the car, where Cooke was still in his drunken stupor.

It was almost dusk by then, too late to dive, and we started back to town. On the way, we discussed the situation. It occurred to both of us that we had only Blackstone's and Cooke's word for the truth of any part of the story. The only thing resembling proof was the skulls, and objectively speaking, they proved only that the town's burial customs left something to be desired. Horsefly suggested that we look up Lemm Shepard, to find out if his story agreed with Blackstone's. This sounded like a good idea to me, so I stopped the car, and we tried everything from tickling Cooke's nose with the cork from his jug to slapping his face in an effort to bring him to. The last method worked, and he sobered up enough for me to tell him I wanted him to take us to see Lemm Shepard. He refused with vehemence, insisting that Shepard was mean, hated foreigners, and would shoot us just as soon as look at us. I told him we were wearing bulletproof vests, but he still refused. Then I threatened to take him back to the site of the haunted inn, tie him to a tree, and leave him there all night. He didn't care for the idea, immunity from ghosts or no immunity, and allowed as how maybe Lemm wasn't so ornery after all.

Off we sped, raising clouds of dust as we rode over mule trails that had never seen a modern car before, and arrived at a backwoods log cabin that probably predated Daniel Boone. Because of the pine trees all around, casting enormous shadows now that the sun was setting, the place had a sinister appearance. The instant I shut off the motor, Cooke hurled himself over the seat and crouched down on the floor in back. We saw why at once: a horde of large mongrel dogs attacked the car. Rolling up the windows, I gritted my teeth as I watched the destruction of a paint job that had cost me a hundred bucks. Then the dogs fled, and about fifteen men came piling out of the cabin, surrounding the car with the now familiar shotgun barrels.

With a bravery that I marvel at to this day, I lowered my window and announced that I wanted to see Lemm Shepard. The request aroused hoots of laughter, and a spokesman for the group said damned if they'd turn Lemm over to any —— —— revenue agents. I assured them we were Marines, not revenue agents, showed them a picture of myself in uniform, showed them my identification tag, all to no avail. I don't know why they finally decided to believe me—maybe it was the way I stuck to my story—but all of a sudden we were invited to come up on the porch and "set a spell." Cooke refused, so Horsefly and I went without him, taking the car keys. Each of us was given a jug of moonshine, and my first swallow of that matchless brew almost burned my insides out.

Then a man came out of the cabin and asked what the hell we wanted with him. A sociable type, Lemm Shepard. I told him we were professional divers, in town to dive for the gold, but he immediately cut me off, launching into a long monologue about his chickens, dogs, and other nonsense. When he showed no signs of stopping, I slammed down my jug and said I didn't give a damn about his chickens or his dogs and, since he was obviously more interested in them than in getting rich, we would work only with Blackstone, who also knew where the gold was. That did the trick. Instead of declaring war, Lemm shook our hands and he said he was the man to lead us to the gold for a half-share. At this point Cooke poked his head out of the car window and reminded us that we had promised *him* a half-share. Then all the other clan members began shouting that they wanted half-shares too. The thing was turning into a problem in higher mathematics. I assured them all that no one would come out a loser if we found the gold, and they quieted down. Then Lemm told us his version of the treasure story, which agreed in every detail with Blackstone's, and gave us very explicit information about the location of the gold. Horsefly and I promised to bring the gold directly to the cabin as soon as we found it. We shook hands all around, and the parting was far more amicable than the meeting.

It was pitch dark by the time we got back to town. As soon as we hit Main Street, Cooke jumped out of the car, assuring us he would meet us in the morning and accompany us on the hunt. Rejoicing in our freedom, Horsefly and I took great gulps of pure, fresh air, and realized we were hungry. We headed once more for the general store. As we approached it, the lights inside went out suddenly, and all our pounding on the door wouldn't get anybody to let us in. There didn't seem to be a restaurant in the town, and Horsefly swore he would rather starve than go back to Blackstone's and eat anything he might give us, so we simply tightened our belts.

Sleeping was another problem. It was the middle of December and too cold to camp out in the car. Though we had misgivings, we went to the place that had "Rooms to Let" on the sign outside. The old woman who opened the door refused us food, claiming she didn't serve meals, but agreed to take us in for the night—reluctantly, as though the dump were the Waldorf and we were a couple of tramps. We got sore, but we knew better than to challenge the local ground rules by this time, and handed over the five dollars she demanded without protest. She led us up two flights of crumbling stairs into a large, cold room that contained a rickety double bed and a bureau covered with dust. Lighting an oil lamp, she withdrew quickly. I didn't blame her: I would have cut out, too, if there had been anywhere to go. However, a bed was a bed, even if the sheets were made of old flour sacks, and the quilts would keep us warm. Not daring to make a closer inspection, we flopped down on the bed and fell asleep at once.

We were awakened a few minutes later by a knock. As the door swung open outward, we both sat up. I don't know what we expected to see—the Raven, maybe. A frail old man came in and started jabbering about ghosts. We tried to tell him we weren't true believers, but he refused to leave until we repeated an incantation guaranteed to drive away all evil spirits. Feeling like damn fools, we did as he asked to get rid of him. Then we tried to get back to sleep. It was no use. During the night we had two more visitors, both of whom begged us to forget about the cursed gold and leave while there was still time.

We managed a couple of hours of sleep (it couldn't have been more than that) before being awakened by a furious stamping and shouting. It was Cooke, standing at the foot of the bed and swearing at us. What a sight to wake up to! He was cold sober and much less friendly, snarling at us to get a move on. We wanted to get some breakfast, but he told us it was no use trying because it was Sunday and the general store was closed. Tightening our belts another notch, we got in the car and headed for the river.

The temperature was close to freezing, and there were strong gusts of wind blowing down the mountainside. We felt cold in the car even with the heater going full blast: we had to leave a window open because of the smell. I expressed some doubt about whether we would be able to dive, but Cooke assured me that the river never froze over because the rapids half a mile upstream broke up the ice. Then he refused to say another word, muttering curses under his breath. I noticed a bulge in his coat, and didn't like the looks of it. Casually, I asked him for a drink from the bottle he had hidden under his coat. He said he didn't have a bottle or anything else under his coat—an obvious lie. Suddenly Horsefly pulled his coat open: the treasure he was concealing was a pistol. When I demanded an explanation, he said he was carrying it to make sure nobody robbed us of the gold. Plausible enough, but I began to suspect that Cooke had a notion to keep all the gold for himself. I was sure we wouldn't be able to trust him.

We parked in almost the same spot we had parked the day before—Shepard's directions indicated it was the right spot—and planned strategy. I had not tested the regulator that had been caught in the pipe in Winston-Salem and I was reluctant to take a chance with it, so that left us with one regulator and one air tank. We decided that I would dive, while Horsefly stood on shore and handled a line tied around my waist. The line was necessary because the broken ice swept down from the rapids made the river swift and dangerous; also, it could be used to haul in the pot, if and when I found it. With my teeth chattering, I put on my rubber suit. Horsefly put on his, too, in case I got into trouble and he had to enter the freezing water.

The river along this stretch was only about fifty yards wide and bushes grew along the banks, hanging over into the water in places. The depth varied from ten to fifteen feet because the bottom was strewn with boulders, some as high as six feet. The water was very clear and trout abounded in it. I figured that if the trout could take the temperature, so could I. The minute I submerged, the pressure of the water tightened against the thin rubber of my suit, and I felt as though I would turn into an ice cube in seconds. My teeth were chattering so badly I could hardly grip the mouthpiece of my air regulator. As soon as I was numb enough to breathe properly, I scanned the river bottom, looking for the ledge mentioned by the two boys. I didn't find it, but I did find countless wagon wheels and other carriage parts: more substantiation for the part of the tale about Angus's sideline.

I surfaced to get my bearings. As long as I live I'll never forget the sight that greeted my eyes when my head first rose above water. Sitting on both sides of the river, half hidden by the foliage, were no fewer than twenty men. I recognized Lemm Shepard and members of his clan, but others I hadn't seen before. For people who were supposedly scared to death of ghosts, they sure as hell looked brave enough as they stared at me over their shotgun barrels. I shouted "Good morning" to Lemm, but he didn't acknowledge it. Deciding that underwater was the safest place for me, I was ready to dive back down again, when suddenly my safety line went slack and the current started carrying me downstream at a fast clip. I headed straight for the bottom and grabbed hold of a rock, then crawled from rock to rock, working my way back upstream, surfacing occasionally to get my bearings.

After what seemed ages I reached the point I had started from. Horsefly apologized for letting go of the rope, which had slipped from his hand as he stooped for a rock to throw at Cooke. Apparently my greeting to Lemm Shepard had convinced our trusty ally that a ghost was speaking, and he had fled, taking his pistol with him. I showed Horsefly the spectators in the foliage, who now emerged from their camouflage and approached us. I thought I would have time for one more dive before they closed in. I had already used most of my air crawling upstream to give Horsefly the end of my safety line, but I wanted to find that ledge before my air gave out completely.

I went down again, passed the wheels, and bore left about twenty feet. Right there, I saw the ledge and the deeper water beyond: it was just as the boys had said. I slipped over the ledge and continued to the left, toward the side of the river where the large tree and the site of the old inn were. After a few minutes, I ran out of air. I'm sure I couldn't have been more than a few feet from the gold—if there was gold. Frustrating to have to surface without finding out, but that's the way things went on this expedition. One lucky break after another.

As I climbed up on the river bank, dozens of hands reached for me, and in a minute I found myself in the middle of a circle, facing the wrong end of a gun any way I chose to turn. My teeth were chattering so hard now that I couldn't speak (in pulling me out of the water they had torn my rubber suit, and the cold was seeping in). I'm sure the mountaineers thought I was trembling with terror.

Lemm Shepard took a menacing step toward me. "We want our share."

I couldn't believe my ears. It was obvious I hadn't brought up any gold, so how did those idiots think I could divide it? Maybe they thought it was invisible. Or maybe they thought I had swallowed it. I tried to tell them what I thought of them, but I couldn't get my chattering teeth apart.

Suddenly Horsefly broke through the circle, grabbed my arm, and led me to the car. To my amazement—I expected them to shoot us in the back—they didn't interfere. The car motor was running, the heater was on, and the car seemed like the warmest place in the world. Climbing into the back seat, I stripped off the rubber suit. Horsefly coated me with lanolin grease, wrapped me in blankets, and turned to face the mountaineers. They were ringed around the car, watching these strange rites with open mouths. Horsefly lit into them with language I had never heard from him before: he used every obscenity I knew and a few more, which I suspect he invented for the occasion.

They weren't a bit fazed. Lemm Shepard said they wanted their gold, and if we had any notions of sneaking back when they weren't around and keeping it all for ourselves, we should forget them. They weren't dumb. Not by a long shot. No city slickers were going to make fools of them. I was going back into the water to bring up that gold right then and there—or else.

I climbed out of the car, feeling like Big Chief Sitting Bull in those blankets, and explained that I couldn't go back in the water because my tank was empty. There was an air compressor in the trunk of the car, but I didn't tell them that: by now I was sure that if I ever brought up the pot of gold, I wouldn't live another two minutes. In what I hoped was a friendly, conversational voice, I assured them we would return with more tanks the very next day.

It didn't work. Their faces became more ornery than ever, and I could see those trigger fingers starting to itch.

Then Horsefly had his brainstorm. He told them that our commanding officer at the base knew exactly where we were and, if we didn't get back safely, he would send the entire U.S. Marine Corps into Willisville. Worse than that—here he paused for emphasis, and his face looked even meaner than Lemm Shepard's—the Marines would bring revenue agents with them.

That rocked them on their pins. They all looked at Lemm, who stroked his beard like somebody trying to live up to his role as clan leader and source of wisdom. A moment later, after some deep thinking, he nodded and said we could go—if we promised to return the next day.

We said we would and climbed into the car.

Suddenly two members of the clan took out knives and marked the doors of the car with the letter X. A curse? A way of sealing the bargain? We didn't delay to ask questions. Horsefly gunned the motor. As the car took off, he shouted some sweet words—too tender and personal to repeat here.

We didn't slow down until we reached Charlotte, which seemed like the height of civilization to us. There, piling some welcome food into our stomachs, we had a good laugh over the whole adventure. Needless to say, we didn't go back the next day. Or any other day. The gold—if there is gold—can sit at the bottom of that river till doomsday, for all of me. I'll risk my neck against the elements, wild animals, even sharks, but I draw a line at moonshiners, and I don't care who knows it. When I think about that particular treasure hunt (and believe me, I don't think about it very often), I like to imagine there's a bearded man with a shotgun guarding the river bank twenty-four hours a day, waiting for us to return. Better still, I like to imagine they had ideas of bringing the gold up themselves, and drowned one by one. Not a very charitable thought, I guess, but honestly, it couldn't happen to a more deserving bunch of guys.

Chapter Three

•

Gringo Loco

•

I had been sold on the Caribbean long before I ever entered the Marine Corps. A glance at any hydrographic chart of the area will show why. The thousands of treacherous coral reefs that dot the Caribbean are still a hazard to modern-day sailors, but in the old days before accurate charts, they must have been the downfall of many a Spanish treasure galleon and merchantman, as well as the Dutch, English, and French pirate ships that preyed on them. Of course Cape Hatteras was full of wrecks, too, but I needed only one dive in the warm, clear waters off the island of Vieques, Puerto Rico, where I was assigned to set up a Marine Corps diving school, to convince me that the Caribbean, and not Hatteras or anyplace else in the northern Atlantic, would be my wreck-hunting grounds. Instead of five-foot visibility, I could spot a brightly colored coral head fifty yards away; and instead of bone-chilling temperatures that set your teeth chattering after ten minutes even in July, I could dive for hours in only a bathing suit, any month in the year.

My only problem was deciding whether to head straight

back to the Caribbean after I finished my hitch in the Marine Corps, or finish college first. College won out as soon as I started to think about all the fascinating subjects—archaeology, history, geology, navigation—I could study. So I returned to Los Angeles in September 1956 and enrolled for day courses at Los Angeles City College and a full schedule of night classes at UCLA. I had already accumulated two years of college credits from courses I had taken before enlisting, as well as University of Maryland extension courses during my time in the Marine Corps, and I was determined to finish the next two years in one.

I had been afraid I would have trouble keeping up with all my classes on this heavy schedule. That was a laugh. In most of my courses we didn't get past the first twenty-five pages of a textbook. Not that it made much difference, since everyone seemed to be catching up on lost sleep during class anyway. I became friendly with one of the professors, who taught archaeology and anthropology at Los Angeles City College, and he was so happy to find someone actually interested in his lectures that he spent hours of his own time each week giving me a one-man seminar, from which I learned more in three months than I would have in four years of regular classes.

We talked about many of the ancient civilizations, but the one that really fired my imagination was the Maya, the pre-Columbian culture that had flourished long before the arrival of the Spaniards in southern Mexico, Honduras, and Guatemala. What especially interested me as a diver were the hundreds of *cenotes,* or large sinkholes, dotting the peninsula of Yucatan, which the ancient Maya held sacred. In Yucatan, rainwater seeps quickly through the porous limestone rock, forming subterranean streams that carve out channels and caverns, and when the roof of one of these caverns collapses, a natural well or *cenote* is formed. *Cenotes* are still the only source of water in most of Yucatan, and after running out of water myself on several occasions in that scrubby jungle, without a river, lake, or spring within a hundred miles, I can well understand how the Maya came to regard these *cenotes* as sacred.

The most famous of these *cenotes* is located at the great ceremonial center of Chichén Itzá near the northern tip of Yucatan. A young American archaeologist named Edward Thompson rediscovered Chichén Itzá at the turn of this century, and during the years he spent clearing the site (which he bought for the princely sum of $25) and gathering data for the Harvard University Peabody Museum, he was intrigued by legends the early Spanish missionaries had recorded about the large *cenote* nearby. This *cenote* was especially sacred to the Maya, who believed that it was the home of their rain god, Chac. Whenever they suffered one of the frequent droughts that occur in Yucatan, and their staple maize crops were withering away, they would try to coax Chac into sending rain by throwing gifts of jade and gold, ceremonial vessels, and figurines into the *cenote*. Sometimes they also resorted to a form of human sacrifice: the Maya priests would cast a young maiden into the *cenote* as messenger to the rain god, and although a few of them managed to survive both the sixty-foot drop to the water's surface and many hours of immersion (the walls are almost vertical without a ledge or niche to hold on to) to bring back the occasional message from Chac, the vast majority simply joined Chac in his watery home.

Thompson reasoned that if these legends were true, the bottom of the *cenote* must be a storehouse of valuable artifacts. He rigged a dredge from the high rim and even went down himself in a helmet suit with a Greek sponge diver assisting him. His hunch paid off. Out of the slimy sediment they eventually recovered one of the richest archaeological hauls of the century —delicately wrought gold disks and bells, beads and idols carved out of jade (more precious to the Maya than gold), numerous clay figurines and vessels, and the only fragments of Maya cloth yet to be found.

After reading Thompson's own account of his work and everything else I could find on the Maya, I became convinced that there was still plenty of work to be done where Thompson had left off. Chichén Itzá was only one, even if so far the most famous, of hundreds of *cenotes* in Yucatan, and maybe there were still many artifacts Thompson had missed at Chichén. As far as I knew no one had even thought of making a new search using aqualungs and a modern airlift, and I was burning to try. My archaeology professor didn't know it, but all those books on the Maya he had been lending me were about to bring my college career to a premature end.

It was during midterm vacation, early in January 1957, that I happened to run into an old friend at the Marineland of the Pacific—Dr. Nelson Mathieson (known as "Doc" to the diving world), a pioneer of skin diving in the United States in the 1930s like my other good friend, Captain Legge. After shooting the breeze for a while, Doc casually announced, "I'm heading for Yucatan in a couple of days to make some topside and underwater movies. Want to come along?"

"Yucatan," I echoed, my eyes popping. "You're not kidding me, are you?" He wasn't, and three days later we landed at Mérida, the capital of Yucatan.

Easygoing Doc led the film-making crew. I was the youngest, driving everyone crazy, or so they let me know, with an endless stream of talk about the Maya, especially that sacred *cenote* at Chichén Itzá. There was Rupe Gates, one of the best divers I've ever known, but looking more like a physics professor than anything else; Mel Fisher, a flashy southern Californian and also a very good diver; and about six or seven others Doc had assembled from among his many diving cronies in the Los Angeles area.

That evening, while sitting around the hotel bar working out our shooting schedule, we met an American archaeologist from Tulane University, Dr. Wyllys Andrews, whom I quickly cornered and started pumping about the sacred *cenote*. He told me he doubted that any foreigners would be permitted to dive at Chichén Itzá, since the Mexican government was still smarting from the loss of all the artifacts Thompson had carted away to the Peabody Museum (in fact, three years after this, a good portion of the treasure was returned to Mexico to help re-establish good relations). Seeing how disappointed I was, Dr. Andrews said, "Come out tomorrow and see the ruins I'm excavating. We've a *cenote* you can dive in there. Who knows? You might find something."

Doc thought it was a great idea, and early the next morning we drove out to the site of Dzibilchaltún, which dates from about 200 B.C. and contains some of the earliest Maya buildings on the Yucatan Peninsula. At that time, however, excavations had barely started, and except for one temple wall the Indian workmen were beginning to uncover, all we could see were brush-covered mounds of earth of varying sizes.

After a brief tour of the site, Dr. Andrews led us to the largest of the several *cenotes* in the area. It was about seventy-five feet in diameter and, unlike the *cenote* at Chichén Itzá, the water level rose almost to the rim. Four of us—Doc, Mel, Rupe, and I—donned aqualungs, slipped in, and drifted slowly down the funnel-shaped well. The water was so clear that we could see our air bubbles rise high overhead and catch on the sloping wall like blobs of mercury. After we reached the bottom, about 150 feet down, we spread out and started up again, searching in the muddy sediment of the lower wall for a fake Chinese statue Mel had thrown in before to play a joke on Dr. Andrews (not that he would have been fooled for more than three seconds, if that).

Probing at arm's length in the mud, I felt something round and smooth, which I pulled out and saw was a human skull. Immediately my mind started racing: maybe this was another sacred *cenote,* and the skull was from a victim to the rain god Chac; then there had to be other artifacts down here, too. I probed deeper and deeper until I was practicaly buried in the mud, when suddenly my air was cut off. The fine silt had jammed the regulator valve, and I wiggled free, wondering if I could make it to the surface a hundred feet above. But luckily Rupe Gates was nearby and, with that sixth sense a good diver has, he realized I was in trouble. He rushed over, holding out his mouthpiece for me to take a breath and we ascended together, sharing Rupe's air supply.

After grabbing a new tank and regulator, I returned to another spot about halfway down the wall and began to probe again—this time more cautiously. After about a quarter of an hour I felt something round and smooth again, but too large to be a skull. Pulling it gently from the mud, I could see in the *cenote's* clear water that it was a large clay pot in perfect condition; the protecting layer of silt had preserved its vivid blue wash, with vertical bands of darker blue (blue was the Maya color of sacrifice) almost like new. Cradling the pot in one arm, I probed again and found another one, almost a twin, nearby and then surfaced.

Dr. Andrews beamed with delight when I handed him the two pots, which he identified as dating from a very early Maya period, perhaps from the first century A.D. This really excited the rest of our team also, and we decided to spend a week at Dzibilchaltún to see if we could find any more goodies for Dr. Andrews. At times all ten of us were searching in the sediment at once. We recovered many human and animal bones, some jade beads, and stacks of potsherds, but no more intact vessels like the two I had recovered the first day. The following year Dr. Andrews and the National Geographic Society organized a three-month dive at Dzibilchaltún led by Luis Marden, *National Geographic's* senior photographer. They recovered many interesting artifacts, including an ancient clay flute, but the expedition almost ended in tragedy when Luis Marden and another diver, Bates Littlehales, suffered severe attacks of the bends and had to be rushed to a makeshift decompression chamber in Mérida.

After spending two more weeks shooting sequences and diving in different *cenotes* around Mérida (finding a large cache of old rifles in one *cenote,* probably from some long-forgotten revolution), our team finally moved on to Chichén Itzá. Although not as old a site as Dzibilchaltún, Chichén Itzá was much more impressive, with a huge pyramid temple visible for miles around the flat plain, palaces and lesser temples, acres of stone columns, and even a ball court where the young Maya used to play an ancient version of basketball.

While we were wandering around the site, Doc had a bright idea. "OK, Marx," he said, "you've been driving us nuts for weeks with this sacred *cenote* of yours. We'll shoot a sacrifice scene, and since you're so hipped on the *cenote*, you can play the Maya virgin sacrificed to the rain god."

I didn't exactly look the part of a Maya virgin—or anything else Maya—with my lanky six feet and blonde hair, but we did our best. I had to shave off a fine mustache I had been cultivating—Doc even insisted I shave my legs—and wear a black wig and a white nightgown thing Maya women still wear today. Rupe and Mel, both dressed as Maya priests, or as close as we could get with a few moth-eaten jaguar skins and some bangles, stood on the edge and tossed me out into the middle of the *cenote*. I tumbled over and over, losing my wig and landing on my back on the cement-hard surface of the water sixty feet down.

Doc yelled over the edge as I surfaced, "Come on back up, virgin, we'll have to do that again."

Someone threw over a rope and I climbed back up, my body aching all over, regretting I had ever mentioned that *cenote* to Doc.

All went well on the second try, that is, until I got halfway up the rope. I bumped into a wasps' nest on the wall of the *cenote*, and in seconds was being attacked from head to toe: they even managed to get under that damned wig. Losing hold of the rope, I fell back into the water, gashing my head on a rock on my way down, but Rupe came to the rescue again, jumping in to help me, while the ring of Indians who had gathered around the

edge to watch grinned broadly; they probably thought I had
gotten what I deserved for desecrating the home of the rain
god.

We spent several months shooting different travelogues
around Yucatan and other sites on the Mexican mainland, then
headed for our final location, the island of Cozumel off the
eastern coast of the peninsula, to shoot some underwater scenes.
Even before we landed I had fallen in love with the island. It
was almost completely surrounded by white sandy beaches. The
water was so clear that I could see the sharp outlines of the reefs
even hundreds of feet below the surface, and only the faintest
blue-green color indicated where the beach ended and the water
began. The village of San Miguel, the island's capital, had a
population of about two thousand, and with its simple, limestone
block houses, roofed with palm thatch, it looked very much the
way it must have appeared to Hernán Cortés, when he stopped
at Cozumel five centuries before on his way from Cuba to the
historic conquest of Mexico. The rest of the thirty-mile-long
island was almost completely unpopulated, except for thousands
of brightly colored parrots.

I liked everything about Cozumel: the climate; the easygoing way of life; the people, who are the friendliest and most
generous I have ever met. My plan had been to return to college
in Los Angeles after we finished shooting and wait to see if the
Mexican government would give me permission to work in the
sacred *cenote* at Chichén Itzá, but the longer I stayed in
Cozumel the less attractive this plan seemed. Then one day, out
spearfishing for an underwater sequence, I happened to notice a
large anchor half embedded in the coral, not far from the beach.
It had obviously been there a long time, although I didn't know
just how long (it was not until later that I found the remains of
the seventeenth-century Spanish warship it had belonged to).
Finding that anchor set me off again. That evening I spent hours
talking to the local fishermen in my halting Spanish. They had
all seen the anchor and told me there were many more like it in

those waters, and cannons too. Hell, I thought, why go back to school? I had some money saved and I might as well stay on that beautiful island and maybe find "millions in gold" while I was waiting to hear from the Mexican government.

All the other members of the crew thought I was completely crazy when I announced my plan, especially Mel Fisher. "Only nuts search for treasure, Marx," he scoffed. I wonder if he still thinks so. He and Rupe Gates went searching for treasure a few years ago in Florida and have so far recovered an estimated $4 million worth of gold and silver from a Spanish treasure fleet wrecked off the Florida coast in 1715.

After Doc and the rest of the team had left I settled down to a peaceful routine on Cozumel. I spent most of the day searching for old wrecks and spearing fish, which I bartered for meals, and the cooler evening hours wandering inland to search for Maya ruins. Sometimes I would take off for days, heading back only when my water supply ran low. I found many different temples half hidden in the thick undergrowth—Cozumel was an important ceremonial center for the Maya before the Spaniards arrived—and even the remains of what must be the oldest church in Mexico, one Cortés ordered built over the main Maya temple. But I stupidly talked about the find, which wasn't far from the village, and had barely hacked away the brush before someone decided to cart off all the stones to build a house. Whoever it was only followed Cortés's lead, since he had taken the stones from the Maya temple in the first place.

I spent most of my time underwater, even when I wasn't looking for wrecks. Cozumel is, or was, a diver's paradise. In all my years of diving—along the Pacific Coast from Seattle down to Colombia, the whole eastern coast of the United States, the Mediterranean, and off every island in the Caribbean larger than a kitchen table—I've yet to find water as clear as around Cozumel. A diver feels he's suspended in mid-air, and the only limit to visibility is the range of his own eyesight. At that time, little or no spearfishing had been done around the island. There were so many fish that I could have several dugouts almost overflowing in less than an hour. But it was too easy and I soon tapered off to spearing only enough to eat myself and to barter. I had already noticed around Puerto Rico and the Virgin Islands how quickly reefs become depopulated after spearfishermen move in (not only the fish that are actually speared; the rest seem to get wary and move away to safer grounds). So I kept some of the reefs as fish reserves, where I would spend hours at a time making friends with the local population. Some of them, especially the groupers, got so tame that they would come out of their caves when I jumped in and swim over to gulp some tidbit I always brought.

Even the sharks around Cozumel were friendly, or at least not aggressive, perhaps because there was so much other food around. One of the reefs we called "Shark Reef," an area where the shallow water suddenly drops off into what looks like blue infinity and where there were always dozens of big hammerheads, blues, and tiger sharks cruising around. But for some reason none of them ever bothered me, even if I grabbed hold of one's fin for a ride. I got to the point where I decided that all the talk about shark attacks was a big myth. In my opinion, a shark was a stupid, harmless animal (and also one of the most graceful in the sea); inquisitive, perhaps, but all you had to do was poke him in the snout and he would swim away. This notion I developed about sharks from my Cozumel experience was to suffer drastic modification later—but that's another story.

Even though the sharks never bothered me, I never grew exactly fond of them and preferred the intelligent porpoises that often came to investigate this strange, two-legged fish. One day I was approaching the beach near Shark Reef to roast some lobster for lunch, when I sighted a baby porpoise floating in the waves. It must have gotten separated from its mother and been attacked by sharks, for it was bleeding badly from several wounds. I could see that it was having trouble staying afloat to breathe, and I waded over to hold it up. When after several hours the porpoise didn't seem much better, I wrapped it in some wet sacks and took it back to the village. I persuaded some of my friends to help me fill an abandoned cistern with sea water, in which we placed the porpoise, which by that time I had named "Oscar." For the next four days and nights we took turns in the cistern lifting Oscar's head every few minutes so that he could breathe. Finally he was able to breathe on his own, but I kept him there and fed him until his wounds were healed and then put him back in the sea, feeling a little sad as I watched him roll away out of sight.

The next day I was out diving and had just speared a juicy little margate, when something nudged my back. I whirled around in panic expecting to see some hungry-looking shark (this was before I had formulated my sharks-are-sissies theory), but it was only Oscar, waiting for a handout. I gave him the margate and some more fish I had in the boat, and from then on Oscar was a steady customer. No matter where I entered the water for the first day's dive, whether ten miles north of the village or ten miles south, Oscar was there waiting for a snack or just wanting to play. This lasted for about six months, and then one morning he just didn't appear. I never saw him again, but by that time he had grown to a good size and was, I hope, well able to take care of himself against the sharks.

It was only a question of time before someone would think of "discovering" Cozumel for the tourist trade. It had a large airstrip built by the United States during World War II, excellent beaches, and warm, clear water—everything but a hotel (there was only a small guesthouse). One day about three months after I arrived, three brothers of Lebanese descent, the Joaquins, who were the local tycoons and owned everything from the bakery to the small bank, came to me with a proposition. They decided to start a hotel and wanted me to help them run it. I didn't know anything about the hotel business, but since I was low on funds, having sunk most of my savings into a sturdy little island schooner I was having built there, I agreed to help—provided it didn't cut too deeply into my diving and digging time. The Joaquins rented the largest building on the island, a former governor's palace where I had been slinging my hammock, and we set to work turning it into a hotel. I could see why they had asked me to help. I didn't know much about hotels, but I could at least solve the mystery of how to put a bed together (i.e., the mattress goes on top, not underneath), while the Joaquins, like everyone else in Cozumel and most of Yucatan, had never slept in anything but a hammock, which is much more suitable to that climate anyway.

The tourists began to arrive by the planeload almost before the paint was dry. I hadn't been very happy at the thought of hordes of tourists invading what I already considered my island, but the people who came to Cozumel in those days weren't typical tourists. They knew that Cozumel was no Monte Carlo or Miami Beach, and most of them were keen sportsmen who wanted to fish or dive. I found that my little schooner *Aguilucho* ("Eagle") couldn't handle all the people who asked me to take them diving. I had to go into partnership with the Joaquins, who added two more boats, the *Clipper* and the *Bluebird,* and I soon found myself with a thriving business, taking parties on diving or fishing trips and later on visits to the nearby mainland also to hunt wild game and explore some of the Maya ruins.

Most of the islanders were excellent sailors, and my boatmen were the best of the lot. Cappy, my first mate, was a retired sea captain of indeterminable age who could take a schooner through a maze of reefs that would daunt a barracuda without so much as a scratch in the paint. Cappy would usually handle the fishing and sailing parties on the *Aguilucho* and *Bluebird,* while I took out diving groups on the *Clipper,* that is, if I wasn't off searching for some wreck or wandering around the mainland jungle.

Some of the tourists were already experienced divers, and neither they nor the many beginners I taught from scratch gave me much worry, but once in a while there would come along

what I called a "YMCA pool diver." There is nothing wrong
with the YMCA courses on lung diving, but too many people
think that after three lessons in a swimming pool they are ready
to challenge Hans Keller or Captain Cousteau. I had a hard time
keeping these types from drowning themselves. One man, after I
had warned the whole diving party about a large moray eel that
lived in a cave near where we were anchored, decided to impress
us. He speared the eel, an eight-footer, in the tail, and it naturally
went after him. I was finally able to get a spear through the eel's
head and extricate the man, but not before he had lost three
fingers.

One of these so-called divers nearly succeeded in drowning
me as well as himself. I returned to the hotel one afternoon with
a party of beginners I had been giving aqualung lessons and
came upon a group of tourists being held spellbound by a heavy-
set, middle-aged American who was telling of his exploits in the
Navy UDT during World War II (the number of ex-UDT
divers I have come across over the years easily exceeds the
number of men in the entire wartime Navy). Then he asked one
of the beginners how deep I had taken them, which was fifty
feet. He proclaimed that six-year-old kids could dive that deep on
their own breath, and that no one could consider himself a diver
unless he had been down at least two hundred feet. All that
evening and the next day he hounded me to let him take one of
my triple-tank sets for a deep dive. I normally didn't let any but
the most experienced divers use even a double tank, but I
finally agreed to take him on a two hundred foot dive, as long as
he followed me down and didn't try anything stupid. I took him
to Shark Reef, where the bottom drops off sharply, expecting
that the sharks would soon send him topside, but I later learned
that he was so nearsighted he couldn't have seen them anyway.

Moments after we jumped over the side, the man's wife
panicked and told all the other people in the boat that her
husband had never been a Navy frogman, in fact had never even
used an aqualung before. But they had no way of telling me, nor

did I suspect anything, since he looked quite calm as we started down. At 100 feet all the bright colors of the reef had turned to an eerie blue, getting darker and darker as we continued down. Everything went fine until 175 feet, when suddenly the man lunged at me and ripped my face mask off. I was still recovering from the shock and trying to adjust my eyes to the salt water, when he charged again and grabbed at my regulator mouthpiece, which I luckily had firmly gripped in my teeth. By this time I realized he must be suffering from nitrogen narcosis, a serious peril to divers caused by the high concentration of nitrogen in the brain cells when diving at great depths. It is also called "raptures of the deep," because the diver loses his senses, and some have been known to tear off their diving gear, thinking they were fish themselves and didn't need it. This was apparently the hallucination my little pal was suffering, only with a slight variation: he thought *I* was a fish. When he made the second swipe at my mouthpiece, I had to give him a kick in the groin, and as he doubled up I grabbed him by the hair and pulled him to the surface. Back on board the boat I had to explain why his groin hurt—he didn't remember anything that had happened below—and when I learned the whole story from the other people in the boat, I felt like letting him take another deep dive—alone, with an anchor around his neck. Well, at least I didn't have to hear any more of his stories about defeating the Japanese Navy single-handed.

Of all the tourists I met during my three years on Cozumel, the one who really sticks in my memory is Lawrence Spence, or "Larry Mills," as we knew him. I'm sure that the FBI and several other law-enforcement agencies in the United States and Mexico remember him, too. Larry arrived on the island during the spring of 1958, accompanied by two odd-looking characters, one a seedy Englishman and the other a plump little Belgian wearing a heavy coat with a fur collar, which he never took off, even though the average temperature on Cozumel is 80 degrees. Larry's two pals were very obnoxious, always insulting the other hotel guests, and I had to ask them all to leave after a few days. They rented a cottage nearby and continued to spend every evening at the hotel bar, as obnoxious as ever, but the Joaquins decided that the heavy bar bills they ran up more than compensated.

Larry began to go out for morning and afternoon diving lessons, and being an athletic type anyway, he soon became a very good diver. We became pretty friendly, or as friendly as anyone ever got with Larry, who was very close-mouthed, and now that I think back, he hardly ever spoke a word to anyone but me, not even his two pals. Then one morning, when we were all in the water diving, one of my boatmen was clearing a space on the deck to set out lunch and happened to pick up the paratrooper trousers Larry always wore. They were very heavy and in each of the two large pockets the boatman found a .45 automatic. The boatman told me about his discovery when we got back to Cozumel, and I thought it was strange—one .45 maybe, but two of them seemed a bit excessive. A few days later I was looking at a month-old edition of a Mexico City newspaper and came across a story about a certain Lawrence Spence, known as the "Flying Bank Robber," number one on the FBI's wanted list for bank robbery and murder. The photo of Lawrence Spence showed a clean-shaven man with wavy blonde hair, but a few strokes of the pencil and there was Larry Mills, with a dyed-black crewcut and mustache.

According to the story, Larry had been serving a prison sentence for armed robbery when he was connected with a murder, tried again, and sentenced to life imprisonment on top of the thirty years on the robbery charge. On the way back to prison after the trial, Larry, who was a huge, muscular man, somehow overpowered his two guards, strangling one of them, and escaped. In the next few days he managed to rob three different banks, hundreds of miles apart. He then stole a plane in Texas, and a week later the plane was found crashed in the mountains near Veracruz, Mexico, without any sign of either

Larry or the bank money. The FBI and the Mexican police had been cooperating in a large-scale manhunt, but so far no leads had turned up.

At first I thought of playing hero and bringing Larry in myself, but then I thought of those two .45 automatics and vetoed that plan. There was no point informing the local police; they couldn't even handle the local drunks on Saturday night. Instead I sent a message to the American consul in Mérida with a tourist taking the next morning's flight, and started to count my reward money. Larry came out diving the following day as usual, wearing the same paratrooper trousers and carrying the two .45's, still loaded, according to the boatman, who had checked again while we were diving. As we were approaching the pier that afternoon I noticed a large U.S. Air Force plane coming in to land. My message had started wheels turning much faster than I had expected.

Even before the boat was tied up, I took off running for the hotel to get my pistol, not wanting to be left out of the action. Larry called after me, "Where you running to, Marx, to meet some dame?" I didn't stop to answer, and after getting my pistol I grabbed a bicycle from some startled tourist and charged off to the airport. Milling around the airport were about twenty high-ranking police officers from Mexico City and two American FBI agents, who were very relieved when I found them, since they wanted me to point Larry out so that they could nab him before their Mexican colleagues did. During the flight, they said, the officers had been getting more and more excited, with the help of some tequila, about helping their good *amigos* from the "Effay Bee Eee" (FBI, in Mexican) to catch this *bandido,* and the agents were afraid Larry might get shot before they had a chance to question him.

Then the general of the Mexican air force wing stationed on Cozumel decided to get into the act and insisted on sending forty of his men along, some of them armed with bazookas. When we finally started out, our motor caravan numbered four jeeps, six trucks, and about a dozen cars. I was in the lead jeep with the two FBI agents, who were getting more nervous by the minute as the police officers, who were enjoying themselves thoroughly, kept waving pistols and yelling to the tourists and islanders along the road about how they were going to make mincemeat out of some *gringo bandido*. Then I spotted Larry coming out of the bar next to the pier, where he always stopped for a few drinks after a day's diving, and one of the agents had our driver speed ahead of the others. When Larry saw us bearing down on him, plus the long caravan behind bristling with pistols, rifles, and bazookas, he stopped dead, calmly put up his hands and waited. In a matter of seconds the two agents had him disarmed, handcuffed, and wedged in the jeep between them.

Meanwhile Larry's two pals, the Belgian and Englishman, had been standing with a group of tourists alongside the road, looking as amazed as the rest of the onlookers. Some of the soldiers in the vehicles to the rear recognized them, leaped down, flung them to the ground and started to pound them with rifle butts. One of the FBI agents fired a shot over their heads to stop them, and this resulted in complete pandemonium, since other soldiers and the police officers, who by that time had all arrived on the scene, heard the shots and started firing too. The spectators ran for cover, with some terrified tourist screaming, "It's a revolution! It's a revolution!" but fortunately no one was hit, and in the confusion the agent was able to rescue the two battered men from the soldiers and hustle them into the jeep along with Larry.

We drove to Larry's cottage, where the agents started to question all three. The Belgian and the Englishman looked truly bewildered, said they knew nothing, and Larry confirmed that he had only met them in Mérida. But that was all they got out of him. I had to admire his cool nerve, the way he had just stood calmly in the road with his hands up, and now sat there very relaxed, refusing to say anything during hours of questioning, except "Go to hell" every once in a while. The Mexican officials tore apart the cottage and even had the whole garden dug up, finding only $5,000 that had been stashed in the thatched roof. They were all for giving Larry a good working over to make him tell where the rest of the stolen bank money was, and the two agents probably felt like it themselves, but I guess the FBI has very strict rules.

I finally got bored, went back to the hotel for supper, and then returned with some food for the two agents, Larry, and his pals. Larry munched away, looking as unconcerned as if he were dining on the hotel terrace. When he finished he turned to me and said, "Thanks for the chow, Marx. By the way, you're always talking about finding a treasure. Try looking under the keel of that modern wreck we visited last week—you might find something interesting."

He refused to say anything more, but then it hardly needed spelling out. I ran to get the *Clipper* ready and with one of the FBI agents and several Mexican police officers aboard, headed for the wreck. It was already dark when we started and the wreck was about a two-hour run to the north of San Miguel. I don't like diving at night, which is "gobbler," or shark-feeding, time in my book, but, as I said, the sharks around Cozumel don't seem to go for human meat, and even if they did there was that reward money to think of. I put on an aqualung and went down with an underwater light, which naturally refused to function, so that I had to search along the bottom of the wreck by feel. Starting at the bow, I worked my way aft, finding nothing but a large spiny sea urchin that went straight through my glove, until I was almost at the stern. There, partly buried in a sand pocket under the keel, was a large wicker basket, which I remembered having seen Larry carry on board the *Clipper* a few weeks before. As soon as I surfaced, a dozen eager hands grabbed the basket and eagerly ripped it open. It wasn't the sort of sunken treasure I'd always dreamed of—no chest full of gold doubloons, but neat packets of bills wrapped in waterproof plastic bags. The FBI agent quickly counted the bills, which totaled slightly over $100,000, all the rest of the bank money except for a few thousand Larry had already spent.

As soon as we reached the village, Larry, his two companions, and the recovered loot were hustled aboard the plane, and Cozumel returned to its sleepy existence. Before boarding, the two FBI men shook hands with me and said: "Nice work there, you'll be hearing from us." I did, but only a letter thanking me for my "outstanding contribution to law enforcement," or some such jazz, without any mention of a reward. I never did hear what happened to Larry, either. I suppose he got a stiff sentence, and it's a shame in a way, because he would have made a great diving buddy with that cool nerve of his.

This thief-catching episode was typical of all my get-rich-quick schemes on Cozumel. I was making a good living from my diving and hunting excursions, thanks mainly to Cappy and my other boatmen who ran it for me. Half the time I was away looking for wrecks or exploring the Yucatan mainland, and the other half, when I was on Cozumel, I had the bad habit of forgetting to collect the fees from the people I took out. Even so, the money was rolling in, and it's too bad I couldn't be content with that. I soon decided that making money was such a cinch that I might as well branch out into other lines.

My first scheme was parrots. The island was covered with parrots; they had discovered that Cozumel, unlike the mainland, had no snakes or other animals that preyed on birds' eggs, and they came there by the thousands to nest. One I found with a tag on its leg had come all the way from Ecuador. The boys on the island snared them, selling them for less than ten cents apiece, while the friends I wrote to in the States assured me that parrots sold for as much as $50 each there—a pretty good profit in any business.

I enlisted a small army of local boys, offering the vast sum of twenty-five cents a parrot, and in less than three weeks they had brought me nearly eight hundred birds. I arranged for a cargo plane, which flew right over the island on bi-weekly runs between Miami and Guatemala, to stop at Cozumel, and I rode up to Miami with my cargo, already figuring what I would do with my first million. But moments after landing, a U.S. Health Department officer came aboard to spray the plane, and as soon as he saw the dozens of cages full of squawking parrots, he started yelling something about parrot fever and threatened to put the pilot, the co-pilot, and me in jail. My friends had been right about the high prices parrots fetch in the U.S., but they had neglected to mention the reason why: there is a very strict law prohibiting the importation of parrots into the United States because of some disease they carry called parrot fever.

The health officer calmed down a bit when he realized I really didn't know about this law: anyone planning on smuggling parrots could hardly have hoped to conceal a shipment of eight hundred. But we had to take off again immediately or face a very stiff fine. I had already spent all my money on parrots, cages, and the air freight, and couldn't begin to pay for chartering the plane back to Cozumel, so the only thing to do was let all the parrots loose as soon as we reached international waters. They probably flew to nearby Cuba, and if they went in the other direction to Florida, well, there aren't any laws against parrots' *migrating* to the United States.

The parrot fiasco didn't faze me at all. I soon had several thousand dollars saved again and started to search around for another export product. Almost everyone who visited the island remarked that the pineapples grown there were the sweetest and juiciest they had ever tasted. After checking carefully into laws on importing pineapples into the United States, I had fifty thousand of them planted, and as soon as they reached a good size I arranged for a freighter, which ran between British Honduras and Tampa, Florida, to pick them up. I even had a buyer ready in Tampa to take the whole shipment and confidently wired him to expect the pineapples in a few days. But instead of heading straight for Tampa, the freighter captain received orders from his home office a few hours after leaving

Cozumel to change course and pick up some more cargo in Curaçao, off the coast of Venezuela. The freighter wasn't re-frigerated, since it normally carried only sisal, so that by the time my pineapples reached Tampa a few weeks later they were fit only to be sold for pig fodder.

Almost two years passed before I hit upon another sure-fire scheme to make a million. I learned that a new craze for salt-water tropical fish had hit the States, since someone had recently developed a convenient food for them—a dehydrated form of brine shrimp. There was a big demand for the small, brightly colored ones, and one species, called "Moorish Idol," was so rare that a pair of them sold for $500. If there was one thing Cozumel had more of than parrots it was tropical fish, and I had even seen some of those rare Moorish Idols on the reefs around the island. The little fish were easier to catch than butterflies, with a net I improvised out of a sawed-off broom handle, some wire, and part of a lady's stocking. I also set out Coke bottles baited with bits of sea urchin glop; when a fish swam in, all I had to do was stick my thumb over the top and haul it up. I soon had the hotel's salt-water swimming pool full of thousands of glittering little fish, looking like a huge show window at Tiffany's.

In the meantime I had contacted a friend in the States who had an old surplus B-25 from World War II, which we over-hauled and fitted out with large plastic tanks for transporting the fish. Expense was no worry—I had already collected a small fortune in Moorish Idols alone. The big day arrived. We filled the tanks with sea water and fish, while all my island friends stood around making wisecracks about the "big *gringo* capitalist" and betting me a hundred to one that I'd lose my shirt again. I felt bad as my partner took off, thinking of all the hard-earned money they would have to pay me.

After several days had passed without any word from my partner, I began to worry that he had made off with my share of the profits. Then I received a telegram: *"Fish all dead on arrival.*

Seasick." Seasick! He must take me for a first-class idiot to swallow that one, I thought. I took the next plane to Miami for a showdown, but my partner turned out to be on the level: the fish had been dead when he touched down at Miami Airport. The plane had hit turbulent weather all the way to Miami, which caused the water to slosh around in the tanks, but the electric current to the tank aerators had shorted also, and no doubt the fish died mainly from suffocation. Whatever the reason, that was the end of my tropical fish business, and I returned to Cozumel to pay off all my bets. At least the odds had been a hundred to one in my favor.

That did it. I finally realized I didn't have the Midas touch, a conclusion anyone else would have reached long before, but I'm a slow learner. And I can't really say I admitted defeat even then. I still had many more money-losing ideas that I toyed with—frozen lobster tails, a cottage industry of Yucatecan hammocks for export, training porpoises for shark patrol off bathing beaches. There was no end to the possibilities, but I never got around to trying any of them. I was convinced I would eventually find a sunken treasure anyway, and in the meantime there were a lot more interesting things to do than fool around with parrots and pineapples. For one thing, there was the whole east coast of the Yucatan Peninsula to explore.

Chapter
Four
*
Land
of the
Plumed
Serpent
*

On sixteenth-century Spanish maps, the eastern half of the Yucatan Peninsula appears as a huge empty space, with a few names of bays and capes inked next to the shore line. Today it looks much the same, except that the territory has a name, Quintana Roo, in honor of a minor hero of Mexican independence.

For over three hundred miles of coast line, from Cape Catoche in the north down to Chetumal, the capital of the territory, on the British Honduras border, there are less than ten villages, none of which contains more than twenty families. But the coast is densely populated in comparison to the area inland, where there isn't another settlement marked for fifty, sometimes a hundred miles from the coast.

Quintana Roo is pretty well isolated from the outside world.

With a total population of a thousand (except for Chetumal) scattered over an area of twenty thousand square miles, there is little demand for an airstrip, and the three dirt roads that lead into the territory from the states of Campeche and Yucatan are passable only in the dry season. Sea communications are little better. Cozumel is separated from the Quintana Roo coast by a narrow channel only twelve miles wide, but few of the islanders would venture across in the small local sailboats for fear of being swept away by the strong northerly current that runs through the channel on its way to join the Gulf Stream. There were a few turtle fishermen who worked over on the mainland at times and several smuggling boats that occasionally went there for a load of copra to take to British Honduras, but it was not until the *Aguilucho* and then the *Clipper* and the *Bluebird* were put into use that anything like steady communications started between Cozumel and the nearby mainland coast.

Quintana Roo is not only one of the least accessible regions in the Western Hemisphere—it is also one of the most hostile. But I was totally ignorant of this when I decided to take the *Aguilucho* over for a short reconnaissance trip several months after settling on Cozumel. All that the islanders could tell me was that no one lived over there but a few Indians and one or two families who owned copra plantations. I suppose I expected just a bigger version of Cozumel, but I was in for a shock, and so were the four attractive young schoolteachers staying at the hotel who persuaded me to take them along. Even before we anchored the *Aguilucho* offshore I could see that there was a big difference. Cozumel had lush vegetation, but this was a real jungle, which started right at the thin strip of beach and became higher and denser the farther inland it went. Then we rowed to shore and were immediately greeted by swarms of sand flies and mosquitoes, which had obviously not had a square meal in a year. We had, of course, come without any insect repellent, but we decided that a few thousand insects wouldn't faze us and set about building a thatched lean-to for our campsite. My two boatmen were smarter; it occurred to them that the *Aguilucho's* anchor might drag during the night, and they decided they had better sleep on board.

After we had eaten supper I set off for a stroll down the beach with one of the teachers. Not far from the campsite, we spotted a four hundred pound loggerhead turtle scooping a hole in the sand and sat down to watch her lay her eggs. My companion kept saying, "I feel someone is watching us watch the turtle." And she became so insistent that I finally climbed a high sand dune behind us to have a look. I saw nothing but the long strip of beach reflecting the bright moonlight, with the dark bush behind, and was starting back when something charged out of the bush right past me, heading for the beach. It was a large jaguar, its mottled gold-and-black coat unmistakable even though I had never seen a live one before. Within seconds it had pounced on the loggerhead's neck, sending up a jet of blood that splurted on the petrified girl who sat only twenty-five feet away.

I was totally unarmed; in fact the only weapons I had brought along on this lark were spearguns for underwater fishing, and they were back at the campsite. Picking up a piece of driftwood—not that it would have been of much more use than a matchstick—I ran past the jaguar, grabbed the girl around the waist, and sprinted down the beach without stopping until we reached the campsite. She was in hysterics by then, and the other three joined in as soon as they caught sight of her, spattered with blood from the decapitated turtle. I don't know which was worse, the jaguar or four screaming women, but for a few minutes I felt like going back to join the jaguar. I yelled for my two boatmen to come and help, but even with three of us we could hardly hold down the hysterical girl, who was screaming and thrashing around in a frenzy, and I finally had to knock her out. The other three calmed down as soon as I could explain that their friend wasn't wounded, only frightened, but they started up again as soon as they heard the word "jaguar," convinced it would come down the beach to attack our camp. I was sure the loggerhead was a big enough meal to satisfy a couple of jaguars, but I had the boatmen build four bonfires around the lean-to, and the three of us sat up on guard duty all night armed with spearguns. No one would have been able to sleep anyway, since a steady parade of land crabs, lizards, frogs, and snakes crawled all over us and even inside the sleeping bags.

With the first light of dawn the expedition, which had been planned to last a week, was over by silent consent. Exhausted, swollen with insect bites, and thoroughly shaken, we broke camp and headed for Cozumel.

My next trip to the mainland was in the way of a badly needed apprenticeship with one of the best hunters in Quintana Roo, Miguel López, who runs a chicle enterprise in the northern part of the territory. I had taught Miguel how to dive on Cozumel and I decided to take him up on his invitation to go hunting with him. It was obvious from that fiasco of a first expedition, in which we hadn't even left the beach, that I had a lot to learn before I could go exploring the Quintana Roo backlands.

I could have been in New York in one tenth the time it took me to reach Miguel's main chicle depot at Leona Vicario, located about twenty-five miles from the coast on one of Quintana Roo's "highways." First I had to go to another island north of Cozumel, called *Isla Mujeres* (or "Island of Women," so-called because of the thousands of Maya statues, all of women, the Spanish conquistadors found there in the early sixteenth century). The weekly boat, the *Cisne*—I can't think of a less appropriate name for that tub than *Swan*—managed to make Isla Mujeres without breaking down more than twice, which is a record, and then continued across to the small fishing village of Puerto Juárez on the coast, where Miguel was waiting to meet me.

As we jolted along the road to Leona Vicario, Miguel told me I had come at a good time, since he had been planning to take supplies to one of his camps in the jungle and bring out the chicle the men had collected for him. (Chicle, the base of chewing gum, is made from the sap of a tree that grows wild all over the rain forests of Central America.) Expecting that we would have to walk, I was surprised the next morning to see that we were traveling first class—by narrow-gauge railroad. We rode an open flatcar pulled by two mules and loaded with supplies, including two large sea turtles Miguel had bought in Puerto Juárez; flipped over so that they wouldn't suffocate from their own weight, they made good backrests. Several Indians walked along the track in front, cutting away just enough of the under-growth to let the mules and flatcar pass. The jungle was so thick on each side and overhead that we seemed to be going through a never-ending green tunnel.

Twice the mules acted strange, and I thought there might be a jaguar lurking nearby, but both times Miguel grabbed his rifle, bounded off into the bush, and returned with a type of wild boar called *jabalí*. We talked a lot about hunting in general and jaguars in particular, and Miguel told me that jaguars often kill turtles when they come up to the beach to lay their eggs, but that they rarely attack humans unless cornered. If I was so interested in jaguars, he would make sure I got a crack at one before I went back to Cozumel.

By evening we had reached an Indian settlement of several huts, where we were to spend the night. It looked as if the life of these people had hardly changed since the time when their Maya ancestors were building temples at Dzibilchaltún and Chichén Itzá. They still made their *milpas,* or corn patches, by burning a clearing in the jungle, and they still planted the corn by digging a little hole with a fire-hardened stick. Their huts were no more than thatched roofs on poles, although one of them, it must have been the headman's, had sides on it as well. Aside from the few cows and the dozens of half-wild, skinny dogs slinking around—animals brought originally from Europe —there was little to indicate that the Spaniards had arrived at all.

Miguel, who is half Maya himself and understands the

language, learned that a big jaguar had been bothering the village. It had killed several cows and even attacked one of the men, who was badly mauled but survived. Miguel decided to lay a trap for the jaguar that night. He had a dog tied to a stake in the center of a low-fenced corral, with a piece of raw meat just out of reach so that it howled and barked incessantly. Then he placed us, nine men in all, around the corral. I thought this was a bit dangerous, since someone might shoot the person opposite, but then Miguel was the hunter. He gave me his own good rifle and used one of the primitive shotguns the Indians make themselves (another European innovation). Their ammunition is also homemade, and they use the cartridges over and over, simply refilling them with scraps of metal and glass mixed with powder. Oddly enough, they work.

It was agonizing to stand absolutely still for hours, not even able to swat at the millions of mosquitoes gorging themselves on us. I was beginning to regret ever mentioning my desire to shoot a jaguar to Miguel, when the dog suddenly stopped yapping— our long-awaited visitor had arrived. A tense minute or so passed, during which it dawned on me that the jaguar would have to get past us to reach the dog. I was wondering if it would find one of the sentries more interesting than the bait, when the animal made a tremendous leap from the bush right over the corral between Miguel and one of the villagers. Eight cannon seemed to explode, drowning out my rifle crack, while the jaguar was still in flight, and it fell dead right on top of the startled dog. Its body was riddled, and I looked carefully for signs of my rifle bullet, finally finding it in the left hind paw—a great shot.

"Never mind," Miguel said. "*Tigres* move fast. You'll know to compensate next time."

I hoped so, for the next time I might not have eight homemade bazookas to help out.

We started out on the jungle express the next morning and late in the afternoon reached the camp, a clearing containing about twenty huts and a high windmill for drawing fresh water up from a *cenote*. I noticed that all the supplies we were unloading, except for the turtles and a few sacks of rice and beans, were cases of tequila. Miguel explained that the *chicleros* were good hunters, and tequila was what they wanted from the outside, not food.

By nightfall most of the fifty or so *chicleros* had returned from their rounds. They were a tough bunch, untalkative even after downing astonishing quantities of tequila: arguments were settled quickly, and privately, with long-bladed hunting knives. The only group I can think of comparable to the *chicleros* are the sixteenth-century *boucaniers* (not their successors, the buccaneers) who lived half wild on the deserted north coast of Hispaniola selling *boucan,* or smoked meat, to passing ships. Like them, the *chicleros* are a mixture of escaped convicts and men who are not lawbreakers but simply prefer complete freedom, even with incredible hardships, to the restrictions of society. Out there in the jungle nobody bothered them. In fact, except for Miguel and his two Indian helpers, I was the only outsider that had ever visited the camp.

For the next two weeks Miguel and I hunted nearly twelve hours every day. Miguel is as much at home in the jungle as I am underwater. He seemed to glide through invisible openings in the bush, while I, only two steps behind, would become enmeshed in a tangle of vines. To me, the noise in the jungle was just noise—birds screeching and monkeys chattering and howling just for the hell of it. But Miguel showed me how the sounds change and can mean, for one thing, the presence of a jaguar or ocelot, the same way that underwater the reactions of the smaller fish often signal the approach of a shark. But Miguel tracks game mainly by smell. I eventually got so that I could smell out a jaguar also; there's no mistaking that pungent, musky odor, and if you ever skin a dead jaguar it almost knocks you out. However, on this trip we never got closer than the smell, although we feasted royally on the small, succulent Yucatan deer, pheasant, and *jabalí*, a leaner, more tasty version of domestic pork.

One day we were tracking a jaguar that Miguel had "smelled out," when we heard a shot nearby. We rushed in the direction of the shot, cursing our luck that someone else had gotten the jaguar first, and then stopped dead at the scene before us. One of the *chicleros* was lying with a bullet in his head and both hands neatly severed at the wrist, and another *chiclero* was calmly nailing the dead man's hands to a tree. The dead man, the *chiclero* explained, had been stealing chicle from his area for months, and he had finally caught him in the act; the thief's hands were nailed up as a warning to other would-be thieves. Miguel did not look at all shocked. "The *chicleros* have their own jungle justice," he said, "brutal, but effective. Just forget the whole thing. The police don't dare show their faces around here anyway." No one in the camp ever mentioned the dead man's absence, and that was the end of it.

At the end of two weeks I decided I had to get back to Cozumel, jaguar pelt or no jaguar pelt, and asked Miguel if I could borrow a mule to ride back to Leona Vicario. But he said that we could both take the "train" the next day, since he was out of supplies and had to return also.

Sometime in the middle of the night we were awakened by heavy pounding on the door of the thatched hut that nearly shook us out of our hammocks. Miguel went to the door and found several very drunk *chicleros* who had run out of tequila and wanted more. He told them he was completely out of supplies, and when they kept insisting, he slammed the door shut. As he turned away, a machete blade sliced through the door, missing him by inches. More *chicleros* congregated outside, shouting demands for tequila and accusing Miguel of holding out on them. After awhile, someone said, "Let's burn Miguel's house down. We'll teach him not to play games with us." At this Miguel threw me his pistol, grabbed his rifle and machete and quietly cut an opening in the rear wall, through which we crawled.

In seconds the flimsy hut was ablaze; in minutes there was nothing left but a small pile of smoldering ashes. We spent the rest of the night hiding far back in the jungle, and the next morning, after the *chicleros* had gone out on their rounds, we grabbed two mules and rode back to civilization, if you could call Leona Vicario civilization. Miguel not only refused to report the incident to the police (nor would he report the murder), but also planned to go right back to the camp with another load of supplies, assuring me that he would be in no danger as long as he was careful not to run out of tequila again.

From then on I spent more time on the mainland than I did on Cozumel. The *Aguilucho* could make the trip straight across in two hours; I would cruise down the coast looking for a likely spot, hop ashore, and tell my boatmen to come back for me in a week. At first I concentrated on hunting, but now that I was armed with both a pistol and a good all-purpose 30-06, the jaguars were making a point of avoiding me. I ran into everything else—deer, packs of *jabalí*, a few anteaters, which look dangerous with their long clawlike nails but are completely harmless, and monkeys by the thousands. I found that the general rule about jaguars not attacking unless cornered doesn't apply to their smaller cousins, the ocelots. They try to compensate for lack of size by being extra vicious and have a nasty habit of leaping down from overhanging branches. My guess is that an ocelot could not kill a man unless it fastened on his throat, but they can certainly leave some healthy scratches before you can shake them off your back.

When I finally tracked down my first jaguar, it was almost too easy. He was polishing off the last of a *jabalí*—I had heard the rest of the pack squealing as they crashed through the bush—and I was able to get close enough for a good head shot. He was a young male, only about six feet from nose to tail, but with a fine pelt. I got two of the men from the small Indian village on the coast to show me how to skin him properly and cure the hide, which they do by stretching it on a frame, scraping the inside and rubbing it with salt. Hunting soon lost any excitement for me after that. I began to take over small groups of tourists, four to five men to a party (no women, after that first fiasco), but when I was alone, as long as the animals didn't bother me, I didn't bother them, except for the occasional deer or *jabalí* for food. I was much more interested in another quarry—Maya ruins.

On one of my first expeditions I had come across the ancient walled city of Tulum, perched on a cliff overlooking the sea across from the southern tip of Cozumel. A team from the Carnegie Institution had partially restored the ruins in 1922, but they had become almost completely overgrown with bush again, except for the bleached limestone walls on the seaward side. Tulum had been the capital of almost all the eastern coast of Yucatan at the time the Spaniards arrived, before the long wars of conquest eventually left the region almost depopulated. There were several smaller ruins scattered along the coast, and I had already found one small temple not far inland, literally stumbling upon it, since it lay hidden in a tangle of undergrowth. I was sure that the dense jungle farther inland concealed other remains of the Maya civilization, unknown to anyone, since the Spaniards had not settled in that part of Yucatan, and few of the Indians survived.

The first three hunting parties I took to the mainland stayed fairly close to the coast, but my fourth group was a rougher bunch of men, game to go anywhere with me. We decided to travel as far inland as we could go for four days and then work our way back to the coast leisurely, hunting along the way. On the morning of the fourth day, when I figured that we were about twenty miles inland and should head back soon, we came upon a slightly clearer patch in the jungle, which was probably the remains of an old Maya corn patch. The thin soil had become so exhausted from years of burning off and cultivation that even centuries later the vegetation growing there was not as dense and high as the surrounding jungle. In the center the undergrowth rose in a slightly elevated mound that I knew from experience must conceal some ruin. Hit by one of the sudden cloudbursts that are so frequent in Quintana Roo (except when one is lost, out of water, and dying of thirst), we made a dive for the mound, hacked away the tangle of vines covering the entrance, and crawled inside a small, dark room.

After awhile our eyes had become accustomed to the darkness, and one of the men exclaimed, "It's a damned shame I didn't bring my camera and flash attachments. It would be great to photograph these colored drawings."

Looking up at the wall he was pointing to, I could scarcely believe my eyes: there were frescoes depicting three vessels that looked like Greek or Roman galleys, each of them with dozens of men standing with shields, spears, and long-handled swords in their hands. I knew that the Maya were supposed to have made very large dugouts, in which they traveled as far as the Greater Antilles and Nicaragua, but these were no dugouts by any stretch of the imagination. After brushing away some of the cobwebs and mold covering the paintings, I saw that the men in the vessels had light reddish hair and beards and certainly did not look like Maya or any other indigenous American race.

Only a few months before I had been at Chichén Itzá as the guest of Don Fernando Barbachano, who runs both that site and another famous Maya city, Uxmal, and probably knows more about the ancient Maya than anyone in Mexico. We were wandering around the ruins one morning discussing my plans for diving in the sacred *cenote,* if I could get the government's permission, when Don Fernando stopped at a stone column and pointed to the carvings, which depicted a series of bearded men with straight noses and deep-set eyes—very un-Maya-like. I remembered Fernando's saying: "Roberto, these men here are not Indians. Look at the features and the beards. You know that neither the Maya nor any other pure-blooded Indian in Mexico has facial hair, or at least not enough for a beard."

"Then, who do you think they are?" I asked.

"For years I have been thinking about this, and I am convinced that there was some sort of contact between the Old World and America, or at least Mexico, before the Spaniards arrived. But when I bring this up with the different archaeologists who come here, they just say I'm crazy."

"Then we're both crazy," I exclaimed. "I think you're right." For a long time I had been skeptical of Columbus's so-called discovery of America. His voyage was highly publicized and came at a time when Europe was ready to expand on a large scale, but that did not mean it was the first. This is not to belittle his feat; it was extraordinary in many ways. But if the printing press had not been developed, and if the Europeans had not settled permanently in America but had disappeared the way the Vikings did at Newfoundland, we might know even less about Columbus than we do about Leif Ericson.

For days afterward Fernando and I talked about our theory of pre-Columbian voyages to the New World. I had read a lot about ocean currents, early methods of navigation, and what little is known of the ships and voyages made by the Phoenicians, Carthaginians, and other ancient Mediterranean peoples and thought that such voyages were more than possible. But the discussion always ended with Fernando's insisting that no one would ever take us seriously. "People are conservative," he would say. "Look how long it took them to accept Copernicus, or Darwin. But maybe someone will find some irrefutable proof. Maybe you, Roberto, with all your diving in these waters, will find the remains of a Phoenician or Greek ship. That certainly would be proof enough."

I never imagined I would strike pay dirt so soon after Fernando had inspired me to search for clues: I was now straining my eyes at what looked like three ancient Mediterranean ships (whether Phoenician, Cretan, Greek, Roman, or what, I couldn't tell), all bearing bearded men. Without any means to photograph the find, I knew that I would have to make sure I could find the site again. I estimated that we were about twenty miles inland, but it is so difficult to judge distances traveled in the jungle, since one never walks a straight line, that it could just as easily have been ten or forty miles. I climbed the highest tree in the area, hoping to spot some distinguishing feature, or perhaps the coast, but I could see nothing but the perpetual haze that hangs over the Quintana Roo jungle and beneath, a solid carpet of green.

I had a hard time convincing my trigger-happy team of the importance of the find, but they finally agreed to forego hunting for the next few days and help me clear the area around the ruin. Late the next afternoon I was hacking away at some stubborn undergrowth about thirty yards from what we thought was the only ruin, when one of the men yelled to me from the other side: "Hey, White Hunter, I found some horses we can use to ride out of this damned jungle."

From the beginning this man had been particularly skeptical of "all this fuss over some old paintings," as he put it, and at first I thought that this was his idea of a joke. But as I approached he started to crawl into a small hole in the bushes that turned out to be the entrance to another temple he had discovered only thirty-five feet from the first one. It was no more than six feet by six feet and four and a half feet high, and so well concealed that the rest of us had overlooked it completely.

I rushed over and squeezed my way inside the tiny room, already crowded with three other men. The ceiling and two of the walls were covered with a thick calcareous deposit, but visible on the other two walls was another series of frescoes, this time with horses—dozens of them, grazing, frolicking, and running, and some with riders. Again I was pop-eyed in amazement. According to historians and paleontologists, there were no horses in America (except the small ancestor of the horse, which became extinct before man appeared) until the Spaniards brought them over in the sixteenth century. Yet from what I knew of Maya architecture and history, this building, which was little more than a Maya hut reproduced in limestone, had been built and probably abandoned long before the Spaniards ever arrived.

One of the men, seeing how excited I was over this second find, joked: "Boy, you're going to commit suicide when we get back and find out that some jerk came over here and painted these things a few years ago."

I didn't find it very likely that some unsung Michelangelo had been wandering around the Quintana Roo jungle recently with his little paint box. No, those frescoes were old; the only question was how old. Either they had been painted soon after the Spaniards arrived—although none of the riders wore armor, which is how horsemen always appear in the few post-conquest codices that survive—or, as I believed, dated from a considerably earlier period. What I had to do was get some photographs of the buildings and the paintings, so that experts on the Maya civilization could tell me.

By this time we were getting low on food and water, and since I was not exactly sure of our location, I decided that we had to head back the next morning. We had already cleared an area of about 100 by 150 feet with the larger of the two ruins in the middle, but the bush grows back almost overnight in Quintana Roo. To be on the safe side, I took my yellow rain poncho, which would be easy to spot from the air, and stretched it across the flat roof of the larger ruin, weighting down the corners with boulders. Then I climbed four high trees on each side of the rectangular clearing and hung the red canvas door-flap of a pup tent and other brightly colored pieces of cloth.

The next morning, after a quick breakfast of dehydrated foods, we broke camp and set off on a compass course that I estimated to be the most direct route to where the *Clipper* was waiting for us offshore. Three days later we stumbled out on the beach, completely exhausted, even though I calculated, by carefully counting my paces on the return trek, that the site was only ten, rather than twenty miles inland. After so long in the almost sunless jungle, the bright reflection off the white sand blinded us, and we did not realize at first that we were only a half a mile from where the *Clipper* lay at anchor. The first thing we did when we reached the boat—that is, after drinking gallons of water—was to throw all our stinking clothes overboard and dive in ourselves to wash off some of the nine days' accumulation of filth. The salt-water bath didn't loosen the hold of the hundreds of ticks embedded in our skin, though, and we entertained ourselves during most of the trip across the channel by extracting them with lighted cigarettes.

I knew I had to act fast or the path we had chopped on our way out would be completely overgrown, making it more difficult to find the site again. I couldn't entice any of the men from the hunting party to go back—I couldn't really blame them, since they had come for a vacation, not an ordeal—and after all the harrowing stories they told around the hotel bar, none of the other tourists was interested in helping me relocate the "fresco site." And since none of the islanders was willing to go either, no matter what salary I offered, I decided to go alone.

After a few days' resting and writing to different archaeologists who I knew would be interested in the find, I set off again with my best camera equipment. During the crossing to the mainland, I managed to persuade one of my crewmen to accompany me inland. He wasn't at all enthusiastic but he finally consented when I offered him a daily salary equivalent to what he earned per week.

I had the boat drop us off at the same spot we had come out of the jungle before and told the remaining crewmen to take the boat back to Cozumel, since the hotel was full and all three boats would be needed for fishing parties, and then return to pick us up in seven days. Actually I expected we would be back in about four days at the most, since on the way out I had marked our trail by chopping every third or fourth tree trunk, and the two of us alone could travel much faster than the hunting party.

At first it was easy going. The jungle is not as thick close to the sea as inland, and the path, besides being marked already, was still fairly clear from our machete work on the way out. A few hours from the coast a heavy cloudburst hit us, and we headed for the shelter of a large tree to be sure that my camera gear stayed dry. These cloudbursts stop as suddenly as they start, and soon thin rays of sunlight began filtering through the thick foliage overhead. The only trouble was that we couldn't find the narrow trail again. This probably would not have happened to someone more experienced in jungle travel, but after searching for several hours I had to admit that we were lost.

Taole, my companion, suggested that we backtrack all the way to the coast and go along the beach until we found the beginning of the trail again. This was certainly the only sensible suggestion, but I don't make any claims to being sensible, and I hated the thought of losing a whole day to get more or less right back where we were then. I was sure I could find the ruins by following the compass heading and blazing a new trail, and even if we were off by a mile on either side, I could always spot those brightly colored markers I had left by climbing any high tree.

As soon as darkness approached, we found a small clearing and pitched camp for the night. We were both exhausted and after a quick meal of canned beans we dropped off to a sound sleep. Awaking the next morning to the playful chattering of the monkeys, my first movement after unwrapping myself from a cocoon of mosquito netting was to reach under the folded blanket beneath my head for my pistol. It was gone. Then I noticed that my rifle, which had been lying on the floor of the tent between Taole and me, was gone too. I shook Taole awake and we made a rapid inventory of our gear and supplies: the two sacks full of canned rations, which Taole had been carrying, were missing, as well as a five-gallon plastic water container; my pack, which contained more food, was still there, but only because Taole had been using it as a pillow; my camera bag was there, since it had no value to the thief or thieves, but it was open, and cameras, lenses, batteries—everything—were drenched in dew. The only water we had left was the four canteens on my web belt, which I had hung on a branch. Our nocturnal visitors had missed that and our two machetes also, stuck in the same tree.

Taole and I rushed over, grabbed the machetes, and started to charge into the bush after the thieves, but then we came to our senses, realizing that they could have covered a mile just while we were checking our losses. We returned to the campsite and sat dejectedly, not saying anything to one another, but mumbling curses at the robbers, ourselves, and everything in general.

Anyone in his right mind would have said, "That's the breaks. You've had bad luck, so give up for now." But, unfortunately for Taole and myself, my mind never works that way, especially when I'm obsessed with some goal, like photographing those frescoes. We broke camp, and I led the way, blazing a trail that pointed inland instead of seaward. I was working up nerve to tell my plan to Taole, who had been muttering to himself since we started that we were headed the wrong way, or so it seemed to him, when the truth dawned on him.

"Eh, *Capitán*," he said, "are you crazy? The sea is in the opposite direction."

"*Hombre,* are we going to let a little thing like the loss of our guns and part of our supplies force us to give up?"

"You *gringo loco!*" yelled Taole. "Everyone on Cozumel says you are crazy and they are right. How do we fight the *tigres* if they attack us? What do we do when we have no more food and water?"

I showed him that my pack was full of dehydrated food, enough to last, if we ate only two small meals a day, for four or five days. The water was a more serious problem, but I was sure we could catch a supply of rain water with my poncho when we reached the site. I also offered to double his already astronomical salary, but the clincher was my agreeing to give him one of my best suits, with all the accessories. His eyes shone, imagining himself the best-dressed seadog on Cozumel, although I am a full eight inches taller than Taole.

The next morning I was sure we would find the ruins before the day was over. After a few hours photographing the frescoes, we could head back on the good trail the hunting party had helped me clear and reach the coast in less than three days. Just to be on the safe side I climbed a high tree to see if I could spot my markers, but there was nothing except the usual un-ending carpet of green under the same bluish haze.

During the next two days, as we climbed dozens of other trees, this view was to be repeated over and over again, always looking exactly the same as our last sighting. We spent the next two days criss-crossing the area, hoping to find either the site or the marked trail, and then on the third, I told Taole that we had better start back to the coast immediately, since we had barely a day's supply of food left and absolutely no water. Taole said that would be foolish. It would take us several days at the minimum, and it would be better to keep heading inland, since we were already near the road that ran down the peninsula from Mérida to Chetumal. My maps had been in one of the stolen sacks, and I couldn't check on the road, but I knew there was one and Taole's suggestions had certainly been more sensible than mine from the start. So we headed inland.

Each day, convinced, or at least hoping, that we would reach the road before nightfall, we stumbled on, catching iguanas to roast—until the matches ran out and we had to eat them raw—and drinking what little water we could find in rock crevices. By our seventh day in the jungle, we were both so weak we had to rest an hour for every half hour we spent hacking the bush, and our palms were so blistered we had to use both hands to swing a machete. By this time the insects were having a hard time finding any place on our bodies that hadn't been bitten, but that didn't seem to daunt them. I don't know how many times a day one or both of us climbed a tree, feeling certain we would sight the road. There was nothing, nothing, nothing. I do know I vowed on the average of once every five minutes never to set foot in the jungle again or even look at a photograph of it.

That evening, as we kept up a steady conversation to forget our empty stomachs, I casually asked Taole how he knew about that road. He said he had once taken a bus trip on it from Mérida to Chetumal that had an overnight stop at Peto.

"Peto!" I screamed. "Peto is in the very center of the peninsula, at least a hundred miles from where we started on the coast!" I was not sure how far we had traveled so far, but even if we had been moving in a straight line we couldn't be much more than thirty miles inland, and that left seventy more miles to go.

My mind had not been working very well for the last few days, imagining all sorts of wild fantasies as we stumbled along. In fact, I could not remember exactly what I was supposed to be doing on this expedition. But this sudden revelation must have shocked me back to my senses, such as they are, and I realized that our only chance was to head due east until we reached the sea, or until we dropped. Taole was already asleep, and I joined him, stretched out on the bare ground, since we had already discarded our heavy bedrolls and tent, and my camera bag, somewhere along the way.

When I tried to rouse Taole the next morning, he refused to budge, protesting that he just wanted to lie there and die, but after I smacked him across the face a few times he seemed to come out of his trance and got up. Then I discovered that I did not have my compass, nor could either of us remember when I had last used it. Using the sun as our guide, which we had constantly to climb trees to sight, we set out on what I believed to be an easterly course, but which I later calculated must have been more like a southeasterly one.

For the next three days we kept on as steadily as our weakened condition would allow, our only nourishment being the liquid we wrung out of different vines Miguel had told me were not poisonous (and some I wasn't sure about). Then during the afternoon of the third day we stumbled upon a *sacbe,* one of the elevated causeways the ancient Maya built to connect their different cities and ceremonial centers. According to all the books on the Maya, none was known to exist in this unexplored section of the peninsula, but I wasn't exactly elated over our discovery—my only thoughts were on food and water. The *sacbe* ran in the same direction we were headed (which I thought was due east) and we decided to use it, since the vegetation covering it was not as thick as the rest of the jungle.

About two or three hours later, with archaeology and history the farthest things from my mind, we almost tripped over what turned out to be one of four large stone wheels that lay strewn over the *sacbe.* They were all perfect in shape, about three feet in diameter, and made of some kind of hard rock that was not limestone, the one rock normally found in that area. Again I knew this was an important find, since it was a commonly accepted fact that none of the pre-Columbian civilizations in America either knew or used the wheel. This had been another topic in my long talks with Fernando Barbachano. He disagreed with this theory, since wheel-like objects were depicted in several Maya frescoes and carvings, and several pre-Columbian toys had recently been excavated that had functioning wheels. Again there was no proof that these four stone wheels had not been made after the Spanish conquest, although this part of the peninsula had not been populated since around the thirteenth century. But we could not afford to stop, wheels or no wheels, and started off down the *sacbe* after a few minutes.

The following morning, the eleventh since the boat had dropped us off, we were trudging along the *sacbe* when it abruptly ended at the edge of a large lake, one of the few in the entire peninsula. The water was cloudy and tasted stale, but we didn't care about taste and foolishly drank so much water and so quickly that in moments we were both rolling on the ground with severe cramps and vomiting. Then we started all over again, taking small sips. We were relieved to find that our swollen tongues returned to almost their normal size, but were furious with ourselves for having discarded all our empty canteens, which meant that we could not carry any of the water with us. We started to walk around the lake, which was several miles in circumference, and soon sighted an Indian hut on the other side. Even though we ran the whole way, the short twilight had turned to pitch black by the time we neared the hut. I had learned a few words in Maya from the local missionary—Taole, although a full-blooded Maya himself, lived on Cozumel and knew even less—which I shouted out in greeting, but the Indians must have thought we were evil spirits, since they all took off screaming into the jungle. We were too hungry to worry about them and quickly gorged ourselves on green bananas growing around the hut and a clay jar full of dried-out tortillas.

Afraid the Indians might decide we were thieves instead of spirits, we thought it best to get plenty of distance between us and the hut. We took all the tortillas, several dozen bananas, a few husks of corn, and two gourds filled with water, leaving behind in payment our only possessions: my good wristwatch and Taole's gold chain, minus the holy medal, which had broken off and been lost sometime during our trek.

With our bellies full for the first time in days, we kept going all that night and the following day, stopping only to climb trees for a sun sight. By the evening of the thirteenth day, we were out of water again and had not a drop of saliva to chew and swallow the remaining raw corn and dried tortillas (my idea of what a wooden house shingle would taste like, only worse). But that night, as we lay down to sleep, I told Taole I could smell the sea and was sure we would reach it the next day. Early the next

morning we both climbed a tree for a sun sight, and when we
saw a flock of pelicans fly overhead, even the skeptical Taole had
to agree that the sea was very near.

Before starting out we had to tear up the rag hanging on my
back, which had once been a shirt, to tie around Taole's feet. He
had started out on this venture wearing sandals, which had fallen
apart after a few days, and the clumsy moccasins he had made
from a piece of deerskin we found in the hut did the same. I
could hardly look at his feet without getting sick. We had tried
taking turns with my boots, but he couldn't keep them on since
my feet are twice the size of his.

Around noon on the fourteenth day we detected the unmistakable sound of voices through the usual jungle din. People,
and that meant food and water! Whooping with joy, Taole and I
dashed in the direction of the voices and burst into a large
clearing containing a number of huts, obviously a *chiclero* camp.
But one of the *chicleros,* who was standing about ten yards from
the edge of the clearing, suddenly pulled out a pistol. We
stopped dead and dove for the ground as six shots zoomed
overhead. Perhaps the *chiclero* thought we were bandits, I
reasoned, and as soon as the firing stopped, I cautiously raised
my hands to show we were unarmed—we had even thrown away
our machetes as we dashed to the clearing. Taole would not even
move, but lay flat on the ground with his eyes squeezed shut and
praying very rapidly out loud.

We were soon surrounded by about twenty ruffians who
looked like characters from a Pancho Villa movie. Every one of
them was carrying some sort of weapon, ranging from semi-
automatic rifles to antique blunderbusses that should have been
in a museum. They fell back at the approach of a burly shirtless
man with a mat of black hair, who resembled a gorilla more than
anything human. He walked over to me—Taole was still prone,
praying more fervently than ever—grabbed me by the hair with
one hand, and proceeded to smash me across the face with the
other. He stopped as suddenly as he had started and walked

away. Meanwhile several men had grabbed Taole and, after giving him a few knocks, dragged us both to what appeared to be a large birdcage, but which I later learned had held a pet jaguar belonging to the gorilla (who I also learned went by the name of Barbanegra, or Blackbeard). He had shot the beast just recently when it scratched his face, adding a few more scars to his collection.

Even in my half-dazed state I was beginning to suspect that this was no *chiclero* camp; we had, as it turned out, stumbled upon the base of a well-known group of *bandidos,* who were about the only authority in that part of Quintana Roo. But this I did not learn until later, and at that point my main concern was over what these characters, whoever they were, intended to do with us. We were given no food or water, and since the "bird-cage" was unprotected by any trees, we roasted in the sun for the rest of the day and then shivered that night after being soaked by a heavy rain shower.

The *bandidos* apparently made their own booze, which I think was fermented heart of coconut palm, and drank steadily all day. I don't know whether they were celebrating our capture or whether this was routine, but by nightfall many of them had fallen into a drunken stupor, including Barbanegra, obviously the gang's leader. At first Taole and I were too frightened to sleep, but we must have dozed off. We awoke some time later to find our cage moving: four drunks were carrying it toward a fire blazing in the middle of the clearing and yelling for everyone to come and watch the show. Inserting a long pole through the cage, they started to swing us over the fire—not very close at first; they obviously enjoyed our screams as the heat blistered our bare feet (Barbanegra had appropriated my boots) and wanted to prolong the fun.

But their fun was cut short by several shots. The four drunks almost dropped the cage but fortunately set it down away from the fire, as Barbanegra lurched toward us, waving a still smoking pistol. He smashed one of our tormentors across the face with his pistol and another with the flat of his long hunting knife, but the other two took off for the jungle before Barbanegra could reach them. He dispersed the onlookers, threatening to skin alive the next man who acted without his orders (the unauthorized entertainment was, apparently, the reason for his rage, since I'm sure he had nothing against a little torture in itself), and had our cage moved next to his hut for safekeeping.

The camp was soon quiet, except for the snores from Barbanegra's hut. Neither Taole nor I could sleep with our feet so badly blistered. I heard something move outside the cage and poked Taole, sure that our tormentors had returned, but instead the face of a young girl appeared out of the dark. At first I thought I was dreaming, since we had seen no sign of any women in the camp that day, nor did she look like any of the local Indians. Motioning to us to be quiet, she handed in a gourd filled with coconut water and two pieces of salted venison which we quickly devoured.

Speaking in a low whisper, since Barbanegra's hammock was only fifteen feet away, she told us that her father was the headman of a small village about fifteen miles inland from the coastal ruins of Tulum. That explained her appearance, since I knew the village, and most of its inhabitants are descended from Chinese laborers who were brought over to British Honduras in the nineteenth century after the Negro slaves were emancipated and had escaped to settle in Quintana Roo. This same gang of *bandidos*, the girl explained, had raided her village two years before and, after killing several of the men and raping most of the women, had stripped the village bare and carried her off as a hostage for tribute payments. She lived as Barbanegra's concubine and was going to have a child soon. She broke her story off, as Barbanegra snorted and stopped snoring altogether, and after grabbing the now empty gourd, quickly disappeared into the hut again.

Taole and I felt almost as sorry for the girl as we did for ourselves. She had told us that her father could not help her because Barbanegra had threatened to kill her if the police were told of the raid or her capture. But even if he decided to take the chance, I knew that the nearest police force, except for the two-man contingent on Cozumel, was at Chetumal, over 150 miles away, and, besides, probably no one knew exactly where the bandits had their camp.

The next morning it almost seemed as if we were waking from a bad dream. We were let out of our cage and even given a big breakfast of tortillas, black beans, and cocoa. When we finished, Barbanegra appeared, sat down with us, and began firing questions in such rapid Spanish that I could barely understand him, since I was used to the slow, singsong accents of the people on Cozumel and the rest of Yucatan. After awhile I learned that he thought we were some kind of spies sent by the police to locate his camp. He finally decided that with my accent I had to be a *gringo* tourist, but he would not believe the story about looking for ruins, or that Taole was a seaman. He kept pulling Taole's nose and saying the only noses he had ever seen like that were on policemen. The questioning abruptly ended when Barbanegra stood up and said it didn't matter who we were, because we knew the location of his camp, and he would have to kill us.

For the rest of the day we were completely ignored and even left to wander around the camp, well aware that we would be shot at the first move we made for the clearing. Taole and I mostly sat around nursing our blistered feet and trying to stay inconspicuous. There was no reason to think that Barbanegra had not been serious about having to kill us (in his position, I certainly would have felt the same), and our only consolation was that he did not seem to be in any particular hurry.

We were given a fish head each and some more beans and tortillas for supper and then tied to a large tree for the night, a decided improvement over the cage, which was too small for us either to lie down or stand up in. By sundown everyone was drunk again; the majority had passed out, leaving only a few playing dominoes and practicing knife-throwing, at which they were experts even when dead drunk.

For hours Taole and I twisted and rubbed the half-inch hemp rope holding our arms and legs to the tree, but it would not loosen. We had not seen the Chinese girl all day and feared that she might have been observed talking to us the night before, but sometime around midnight she appeared again, moving silently out of the bushes behind the tree. She quickly cut the ropes and handed us a gourd of water and a rag bundle containing venison and tortillas, then slipped off into the darkness. I knew she hoped we would be able to help her return to her village somehow, and I promised myself we would not let her down.

The ropes had been so tight around our legs that we had to crawl into the bush. Then I remembered the rope, which the *bandidos* would be able to tell had been cut by a knife, so I crawled back, retrieved the pieces and rejoined Taole. Once we were about fifty yards from the camp, both of us broke into a run and crashed through the bush until we fell panting to the ground. While lying there trying to catch my breath, I came to my senses: we were both weak, almost naked, with blistered, bleeding feet and only a small amount of food and water; in our condition we couldn't last more than a few days in the jungle, even if the bandits did not track us down immediately. I was sure we were near the sea—the salt-water fish heads we had been given for supper seemed to confirm that—and decided our best chance lay in heading for the coast. Taole disagreed, saying that was exactly what the bandits would expect us to do, but not wanting to waste time arguing, I got up and started to backtrack in order to work my way around the camp and head for what I figured was east. Looking back, I saw Taole following.

We passed within a hundred yards of the camp and froze in our tracks when the camp's pack of mangy dogs broke out in a chorus of barking, but one of the *bandidos* yelled to quiet them down and we continued on, soon running into a narrow path that led in the direction we were headed. The going was easier, and we were able to keep up a fairly steady trot for several hours. Fortunately my sense of direction had not been off. After what seemed like twenty miles, but which I later learned was only two, we reached the coast, or really the shore of a deeply indented bay called Bahía del Espíritu Santo.

We turned north along the shore, but after a few minutes spotted a thatched hut up the beach. If we turned back, the closest settlement would be more than a hundred miles to the south, so we would have to sneak around the hut. When we crept closer, we saw with relief that it was only a roof thatch covering four dugout canoes. Checking that no one was about, we rushed out of the bush and started to launch one of the dugouts. Then I realized it would be insane to leave the other three behind for our pursuers and had to waste precious minutes searching for vines strong enough to tow them with—bashing in the bottoms with rocks was ruled out because of the noise. We tied them in a line behind ours and started paddling furiously down the middle of the bay for the open sea.

In less than a quarter of an hour the sun rose in a blazing ball of fire in front of us, and I knew that the bandits would notice our disappearance then, if they had not already done so. The other three dugouts slowed us down considerably, since, aside from the weight, they swayed continually from side to side, creating extra drag. But the tide was coming in and they would have drifted ashore in no time if we had cast them loose. There was, of course, the chance that we had missed seeing other dugouts on the beach, but there was little we could do about that.

By noon I estimated that we had covered almost half the twenty miles to the mouth of the bay. We cast off the other dugouts, which increased our speed threefold, even though we had to rest more than we paddled. By about four that afternoon we were only a short distance from the bay's entrance, but the closer we got, the stronger the force of the northerly current, which runs along the Quintana Roo coast. I was afraid we could not clear the bay before we were pushed on to its northern shore, since we were drifting sideways faster than we could paddle forward. Taole and I must have both dropped off to sleep from sheer exhaustion soon afterward. Suddenly we were both in the water; something, probably one of the many alligators that live in the bay, must have come up under the dugout and flipped it over. Whatever it was, it did us a big favor, for I heard rifle shots and noticed that we had drifted north to within half a mile of the shore. The bandits had followed us, heading around the bay by land, and were firing at us from the beach. We grabbed for the two paddles floating nearby and, holding on to the dugout's carved keel with the other hand, kicked frantically away from the shore.

Either we made poor targets in the water or the bandits were bad shots, but fortunately the bullets splashed pretty wide. About an hour later it began to get dark, and we figured it was safe to turn the dugout over. We didn't stop paddling until we were a mile out from the bay, where the two-knot current began to carry us north without any further effort on our part. We had another stroke of luck besides that timely heave from the alligator. This canoe would undoubtedly have foundered in any seas over a foot high, but there was a flat calm, and we drifted along scarcely aware we were moving.

Taole and I had both dropped off to sleep again as soon as we realized we were safely out to sea and did not wake until sunrise. We were about a mile from shore and had already drifted to within several miles south of Tulum. The sea was still calm and Taole suggested that we try to take the dugout all the way to Cozumel, the southern tip of which is almost directly across the channel from Tulum. I vetoed this plan when dark storm clouds started to line the horizon, signaling the approach of a squall. Tulum was uninhabited, but there was a large copra plantation, named *Tancah,* located only five miles north, and Taole said he knew the González brothers who owned it.

While the current carried us north we also paddled toward shore, but the squall hit us before we could reach the opening in the reef in front of Tancah. Swamped by the heavy seas, we clung to the overturned dugout and were soon thrown over the reef by a large comber which left us unhurt in the calm, waist-deep waters of the lagoon. Several Indians came out in another dugout and helped us ashore, where we were met by the González brothers. They were astonished to see us alive: my boat had been cruising up and down the coast for the last ten days after we failed to appear at the rendezvous point, and only the day before it had left Tancah for Cozumel, having given us up for dead.

The two brothers were hospitable in the best Mexican tradition. Not only did they clothe us, but seeing what a sorry state we were in, they had their wives and maids give us the best nursing care they could. We could not keep down solid food and were fed broth every hour or so while the women tried to clean and medicate the hundred and one cuts, scratches, and burns covering us.

I felt more exhausted than I ever thought possible, but neither Taole nor I could sleep soundly all that day. Tancah was only thirty miles as the crow flies from the spot where the *bandidos* had been firing at us the evening before, and we were sure they would follow us. Late that afternoon we sat on the wide verandah with the two brothers and over a few tequilas told them what we could remember of our experiences at the time. They did not show the least surprise at our story about the *bandido* camp, and seeing that we were really serious in our fears that we would be followed to Tancah, they finally admitted that they paid a large monthly tribute in money, bullets, and cigarettes to Barbanegra in return for his keeping his hands off the plantation—the classic protection racket, Yucatan style. That was little comfort to us, since I could hardly expect Barbanegra to honor the agreement in our case, especially after we were told that no one else knew the location of their camp.

Everything else about Barbanegra was well known in the district. The brothers told us that he had been a famous guerrilla leader in the mountains around Veracruz during the Mexican Revolution, which started in 1910 and lasted in some areas through the 1930s. Even after the revolution triumphed, he continued the fighting, having fallen out with the new leaders of the republic. After all of his followers had either deserted or been killed, he made a long trek overland to Quintana Roo, where he was joined by malcontents and criminals from all over southern Mexico, and he virtually ruled the district.

When I told them about the Chinese girl who had helped us escape, they verified her story. Her name was Lola Lung, they said, and she had actually been betrothed to one of their nephews when she was taken hostage. I could hardly believe that all these things were such common knowledge, yet no one had done anything about them.

"There is nothing anyone can do," one of the brothers commented bitterly. The government knew about the bandits and their activities, he explained, but was unable to control them. Ten years before a twenty-four man force of policemen had been sent to round them up. Ten of the twenty-four had been found by their companions in the jungle, beheaded, and the rest of the force never succeeded in finding even a trace of the bandits. Since then no further efforts had been made.

Exhaustion won out over curiosity, and Taole and I fell asleep before we could learn any more about Barbanegra and his crew. The next morning one of the brothers announced that a plane would be coming to pick us up. I thought it was a joke, but he said that they had a rough airstrip located halfway between their house and the ruins of Tulum, and the plane they had radioed to Mérida for the evening before would be arriving soon. After a fast breakfast, several Indians half carried us to a jeep, and we were driven at a lunatic speed through the coconut grove along the beach to a clearing they called an airstrip but which bore a closer resemblance to a rock quarry.

We sat there nervously scanning the sky for signs of the plane, half expecting the bandits to burst out of the jungle that surrounded the strip. Before long, a twin-engined Beechcraft made a pass over us, banked, and then made one of the bumpiest landings I have ever seen. We thanked the González brothers as they hoisted us aboard, and moments later we were on our way to Mérida. Below us for the first hour was a solid floor of dark green without a road or hut, exactly as it had looked from the countless treetops Taole and I had climbed in the last two weeks.

On landing in Mérida, we were met by several police officers to whom we gave a brief account of our experience in the bandit camp with as precise a location as possible. Then the American consul appeared and rushed Taole and me to a hospital, where we were to stay for more than a month. I had lost over forty pounds during our seventeen-day ordeal, and Taole only slightly less. We were both suffering badly from dysentery, which in my case was compounded by malaria, although I had probably contracted it on a previous expedition.

About two weeks after we had reached Mérida, several hundred soldiers were landed on the shore of the Bay of Espíritu Santo, but when they reached the camp they found it deserted, except for a few barking dogs that had chosen to remain behind. I didn't find out whether the camp had been hastily abandoned at the soldiers' approach or whether Barbanegra had decided to move soon after we escaped, but the force spent several weeks combing the area without finding a trace of the bandits.

After only a few days in the Mérida hospital my recent experiences began to seem less like an ordeal and more like just another interesting adventure. I completely forgot about the many vows I had made never to set foot in the jungle again and was already thinking of those frescoes and the four stone wheels we had found on the *sacbe*. Brief mention of my finds reached even the European press, but most comments were skeptical—understandably so, I suppose, in view of the absence of any proof—and this only made me more determined to return and obtain photographs. I also heard from friends and different scholars I kept in correspondence with, and they all reminded me that "a photograph is worth a thousand words."

The most encouragement came from Professor John Goggin, professor of anthropology at the University of Florida. Goggin, a kindly older man, whom I had met in Mérida during one of his digs on a Spanish colonial site, had taken me under his wing. As soon as I returned from my first expedition I had written to him about the frescoes, and even sent him several potsherds, plus pieces of the two wooden lintels from the entrance to the two ruins, so that he could date the site. He offered me his full support, promising to come down and make a thorough study of the ruins as soon as I had a foolproof way of locating the site.

By the time I finally returned to Cozumel, nearly two months had passed since we had originally stumbled upon the "fresco ruins," but with Goggin's encouragement, I decided to make another attempt to locate them. I knew that finding the wheels would be easy—simply a question of starting out from that lake along the *sacbe*—but the frescoes were another matter. Dreading the thought of spending weeks, or even months, wandering all over the jungle again, I decided to search by air, which is what I should have done the moment I returned to Cozumel after first discovering the ruins. Once sighted from a plane and marked on the map, they would be much easier to locate from the ground.

I knew all the pilots in the Mexican Air Force wing stationed at Cozumel, and I often hitched rides on the four or five T-6's, pre-World War II training planes the United States had generously donated to Mexico after our Air Force had declared them unfit for service. I contacted my friend Chucho, whom I considered the best of the pilots, and he agreed to fly me over the mainland the next day.

Rushing out to the airfield shortly after sunrise—the best

time for searching over the jungle, before the haze gets thick—I found that Chucho had not yet recovered from a heavy bout with tequila the night before. I chewed him out for letting me down.

"Roberto, my friend," he slurred, leaning heavily on my shoulder, "you know I wouldn't let you down. I have arranged for the best pilot in the whole Mexican Air Force to fly you. Paco," he yelled, "take the *señor* and fly him where he wants to go."

Paco, a kid dressed in greasy overalls, looked scared to death, and I found out later that he had good reason to be. He was the plane's mechanic and had only a few hours' flying time under his belt, none of them solo. I should have suspected something was wrong when Paco kept crossing himself and murmuring Hail Mary's all the way to the plane.

A startled chicken flew out of the aft cockpit as I climbed in, and then I tied myself in with a frayed rope that served as a safety belt, while Paco climbed down again from the forward cockpit, spouting a stream of Mexican obscenities because the batteries were dead. When the engine would not turn over even after he smashed the fuselage a few times with a heavy wrench, he called several men over to prime the prop by hand. Without waiting for it to warm up, Paco gunned the throttle and charged down the runway.

I had taken off all the badly scratched plexiglass windows for better visibility, and the moment we started down the runway I was bathed in gasoline. It was flying out of one of the wing tanks which I noticed had not been closed properly, and I leaned forward, tapping Paco on the head, and pointed to the problem. There was still half of the two-mile runway ahead of us, but, instead of slowing down gradually, Paco cut the engine off, slamming down both foot brakes at the same time. Naturally the plane flipped up on its nose, sending sparks flying, and skidded to a stop on the grass apron skirting the runway. We jumped out and ran like hell, expecting the plane to explode, but it didn't, and except for my bloody nose we both got off without a scratch.

Chucho was grounded for a month by the general (Paco, I think, was demoted to private), but as soon as he could fly again, he came to beg me to forgive him for his little joke and to offer to carry out his original promise. Since I was obsessed with finding those ruins, and since Chucho was really the best pilot on Cozumel—when he was sober—I accepted. This time, however, I carefully inspected the plane, especially the caps on the fuel tanks, while Chucho strapped on his set of pearl-handled pistols and tied a five-foot yellow scarf around his neck, so that his girl in San Miguel would recognize him when we flew over.

Chucho made a perfect takeoff, and after buzzing the town a few times, we headed across the channel. We flew over the jungle at treetop level for about an hour, then went up to 200, 500, and finally to 1,000 feet, but there were no signs of a clearing, the yellow rain poncho, or anything but unbroken jungle. After four hours we had to give up the search and head for Cozumel. Although the fuel gauge already registered empty, Chucho spent another ten minutes buzzing the town until his girl finally stuck her head out of a window and waved. Just then the engine started to cough, and he headed for the nearby airfield, but the landing gear would not go down. "Diver, we're going for a dive," he yelled back to me, and moments later we landed on the shallow inland lagoon just north of the town, settling gently on the soft mud bottom. It was a perfect landing, and it should have been, since Chucho confessed that it was the fourth time he had landed there. In less than two weeks the plane had been salvaged, and Chucho was flying again.

I made several more air searches over the jungle (with tourists who had come down to Cozumel in their own planes, not with Chucho), but all with the same results. I was beginning to wonder if I had imagined those "fresco ruins," but if I had it must have been mass hallucination, for some of the men who had been with me when we first stumbled across the site were still writing to ask me if I had relocated it yet. The only solution was to search for the site again by land, although more than a year was to pass before I was able to mount another expedition. My interest in the "fresco ruins" did not fade, but the tourist business was becoming busier and busier as Cozumel developed into a popular resort island, and any spare time I did have was devoted to my main interest: the old wrecks around Cozumel and on the Quintana Roo coast.

During that year I became more and more convinced that there was something to the theory of pre-Columbian voyages to Mexico that Don Fernando Barbachano and I had discussed. First, Goggin had the potsherds from the "fresco site" analyzed by several different experts, who all dated them around the twelfth century, which also agreed with the results of the radio-carbon dating of the two wooden lintels. I had also conducted trial digs around different ruins on both Cozumel and the Quintana Roo mainland, sending potsherds and photographs of pottery I could not identify to different museums. Several items were identified as being European and pre-Columbian in date.

Then one day, while leading a boatload of tourists around Tulum, I noticed that one of the walls of the largest temples had crumbled and fallen down since my last visit. On inspecting the damage, I discovered that the plaster covering the wall next to it had also fallen, revealing a large carving of a bull. Like horses, cattle were supposedly unknown in America until imported by the Spaniards. Tulum was inhabited when Cortes visited Cozumel in 1519, but it was abandoned shortly later; yet here was an unmistakable carving of a bull. The fact that it had been plastered over indicated that it dated from early in the city's history, for the Maya and other pre-Columbian peoples often rebuilt their temples. Worship of sacred bulls, like the Minotaur of Crete, was well known in early Mediterranean cultures. By itself the carving could be passed off as a minor mystery; but the evidence, even if still circumstantial, was beginning to mount up.

I had not abandoned my idea of exploring the Yucatan *cenotes*. They might produce more of the clues I was seeking, and, in any case, as Goggin constintly reminded me in his letters, the most interesting and best preserved Maya artifacts to date had come out of *cenotes*. But I had still received no answer to my petition to the Mexican government to dive at Chichén Itzá, even though it had Fernando Barbachano's full support. I decided to fly over to Mérida and check on the progress of my application and also to see Goggin, who was due down shortly to resume his study of Spanish colonial sites.

After landing in Mérida and checking into the hotel, I went directly to the office of the government archaeologist—let's call him Dr. Ricardo López—in charge of all pre-Columbian monuments and excavations in Yucatan. Dr. López was very cool when I entered his office; he asked me to excuse him for a few minutes and disappeared into another room. I wasn't particularly surprised by his lack of cordiality: not only had I been pestering the man for over a year about my diving permission, but also on my previous trip to Mérida, I had made some salty comments about bureaucratic efficiency in Mexico, with particular reference to Dr. López's department.

While I was waiting, however, one of his assistants, whom I knew fairly well, passed through the room and greeted me with: *"Qué hubo, gran ladrón de antigüedades mexicanas,"* which translates roughly into: "Well, if it isn't the great thief of Mexican antiquities." And when Dr. López still failed to appear after twenty minutes, it began to occur to me that something was up. I was just rising to leave, when in rushed four policemen, who grabbed me and hustled me out to a waiting patrol car. Something definitely was up but exactly what I could not find out. The four policemen just told me to shut up every time I asked what was going on. I was given no explanation, when after a short drive to the outskirts of town, I was taken to a large, windowless building—apparently the local prison—frisked, and deposited inside a foul-smelling room with about fifty other prisoners.

Looking around me after my eyes had become accustomed to the dim light, I spotted one of the *bandidos* from Barbanegra's camp. At first he refused to speak to me, claiming he had never seen me before, but after I started sharing my pack of cigarettes with him, he became positively friendly. It was fascinating to hear what had happened after Taole and I escaped. The bandits had decided to move their camp farther inland even before the soldiers arrived. They apparently never suspected that Lola, the Chinese girl, had helped us escape, but I was sad to hear that she had died a few months later in childbirth. Barbanegra himself died shortly after from some fever, probably malaria, and then the gang broke up. This *bandido*, whose name was Gervasio, and two others became highwaymen. It was a very good line, he confided, although every once in a while some dope tried to play hero, and he did not really like shooting people.

Gervasio was awaiting trial on four charges of murder, which did not seem to bother him very much. What did bother him was the way he had been caught. A girl he had fallen for, the daughter of a white Mexican who was the fence for their stolen goods, had been sent off to a convent in nearby Valladolid, and Gervasio had gone to "release" her. It was bad enough that they had refused to let him in, even after he fired off a few shots, threatened to burn down the whole convent and the church, and told them who he, Gervasio, was. But those nuns had actually turned him in, and he had always been very religious, had even once gone on a pilgrimage to Chalma. When he went back after spending a few hours in the local bar, the police were waiting in ambush and grabbed him before he could even draw his pistol.

I sympathized with Gervasio. It must be very embarrassing for a self-respecting *bandido* to have to confess that he was undone by a bunch of nuns.

But at least Gervasio knew why he was in prison. Not

knowing why I had been arrested or how long I would be there was worse than the prison itself, which was pretty foul. We slept on vermin-ridden piles of straw and were fed some indescribable mess twice a day that made pig slops a delicacy in comparison. Then, on the afternoon of the sixth day, I was suddenly released with no more explanation than when I had been brought there, and they even returned my watch and wallet.

Waiting outside the gate were the American consul and John Goggin. Good old Goggin. I probably would have rotted away in there if it had not been for him. He arrived in Mérida two days after I was arrested and, paying the customary courtesy call on Dr. López, had learned that I was being held for several "serious offenses," which Dr. López was not at liberty to disclose. After failing to persuade Dr. López to have me released and obtaining the same results from the governor of Yucatan and other local authorities, Goggin remembered my having mentioned in one of my letters that I had been teaching the son of the president of Mexico to dive, and that we had become good friends. Unable to reach him by telephone, Goggin had flown to Mexico City, where he finally located him. A few well-placed phone calls and a letter Goggin brought back to Mérida did the trick.

But we still did not know why I had been arrested in the first place, and without even stopping at my hotel for a badly needed shower and change of clothes, the three of us drove directly to Dr. López's office to find out. Dr. López was all smiles and handshakes this time—and apologies.

His explanation was so absurd it had to be true. About a month before, an American yacht had arrived at an island, called *Isla de Sacrificios,* an important pre-Columbian ceremonial center off Veracruz, where the Spaniards first came upon the practice of human sacrifice in Mexico. The Americans produced fake documents authorizing them to conduct archaeological excavations there, and the caretaker, who probably could not read anyway, let them go ahead. After three weeks, the island looked as if it had been blitzed; they even used dynamite and demolished several of the temples. Then they disappeared, carting off tons of priceless artifacts, many of which were already on sale in different cities in the United States. The furor in Mexico over this act of vandalism was tremendous, and the government archaeologists, who had been caught napping, were pressed to take some action. As an American well known for my interest in pre-Columbian artifacts, I "naturally" came under suspicion.

The logic was almost irrefutable. "What do you mean, 'naturally'?" I yelled. "I haven't been off Cozumel in six months, except across to the coast, and you know it. Everyone knows I poke around ruins there, but keep me out of this other business!"

"Yes, of course," he apologized. "It has been a very grave mistake, but I am sure that you understand my position."

We left on friendly terms. I did not really hold it against him, although I hoped that the next time the politicians were screaming for his head, he would find another scapegoat. He even promised to hurry along the matter of my petition to dive in the sacred *cenote* at Chichén Itzá. But that was a laugh. When I eventually left Mexico three years after requesting permission, I still had not heard one way or the other.

I spent two valuable weeks helping Goggin on his colonial excavations in Mérida. Goggin was an authority on sixteenth- to eighteen-century Spanish pottery—the amphoralike olive jars, "blue-on-blue" tiles, Talavera ware, and other items that would help me date the Spanish wrecks I was finding off Quintana Roo. The Yucatan sun was hot, and we used to cool off in the evenings at the hotel bar, finding my recent run-in with the authorities more hilarious with every round of drinks. Goggin would shake his head at me in mock solemnity: "Bob, I was pretty wild in my younger days, but at least I never dynamited any ruins!"

I got an unexpected chance to dive in a *cenote* on that trip, but it was a dive that cooled my enthusiasm for *cenotes* for a long time. I ran into the American Maryknoll missionary from

Cozumel, who was over in Mérida buying supplies, and he suggested I visit the new priest who had just taken over their mission at Peto. Remembering that there were supposed to be some interesting ruins around Peto, one of the few sites in Yucatan I had not yet visited, I decided to go.

Peto is in nearly dead center of the peninsula, and the day-long bus trip was typical of public transport in rural Mexico. More than one hundred people, in addition to a few dozen chickens and three pigs, crammed into an ancient vehicle designed to seat about forty, with the overflow clinging to the back, the luggage rack overhead, and the hood, completely blocking the driver's view. All the other passengers were Indians, friendly and generous like all the Maya, who produced a continual supply of highly spiced delicacies wrapped in banana leaves which they pressed on the poor *gringo* who was obviously dying of malnutrition—I was very thin in those days.

Father Hubert, the young missionary at Peto, was glad to see me, especially since my visit gave him a chance to relax into English after having struggled along in Spanish or, mostly, Maya, ever since he had arrived at his new post. The next morning he had to ride over to another village to visit some sick woman, but he arranged for one of the local Indians to show me the different ruins around Peto.

About two miles from the village, on the way to one of the sites, I spotted a small hole, which on investigation turned out to be the top of an unusual *cenote*. Most *cenotes* drop almost straight down, but this one was like a crater in reverse, the sides sloping sharply away from a diameter of eight feet at the top to one of over two hundred feet at the water level sixty feet down. My Maya guide knew no Spanish, and my knowledge of Maya was not much greater, but using sign language to indicate that this was a very bad spot, he insisted upon moving on.

Back in Peto that day, I inquired about the *cenote*. It was supposed to be haunted by spirits guarding a treasure, I was told, and at the word "treasure" my ears perked up. Legend had it that in the early days—apparently at the time of the conquest—some holy men were fleeing from the Spaniards with precious things from a temple which they flung into this *cenote*. When the Spaniards caught up with them soon afterward, they too were flung into the *cenote* to drown.

Remembering what Thompson had found by following a legend connected with the sacred *cenote* at Chichén Itzá, I decided to have a look. The only problem was that I had brought no diving gear, and there was naturally none to be found in Peto, a hundred miles from the sea. I finally managed to obtain goggles—tinted ones belonging to the blacksmith; they had holes in the frames for ventilation, but that was fixed with a few pieces of Scotch tape from Father Hubert's little office.

My guide agreed very reluctantly to return to the *cenote* with me. With the goggles hung around my neck and a metal bar for probing in the *cenote*'s bottom tied to my belt, I started cautiously down a strong hemp line we had tied to a tree several feet from the edge. I had not gone down ten feet when I was suddenly flying down to the water another fifty feet below, along with half the overhead roof which had collapsed from my weight. Unable to determine the depth of the water from above, I had kept on my heavy boots, in case it turned out to be only a few feet deep. I have no idea just how deep it was, but weighted down by the metal bar and the boots, I plummeted down for what seemed like a hundred feet, after hitting the surface with a painful belly smack.

I remember in the Marine Corps some medic telling me my lungs were too large. Well, these "distended lungs," as he called them, came in handy in the *cenote*. Normally, in free diving I could stay under a little over three minutes without any strain, but it must have taken me twice as long to get rid of that bar, unlace my boots, and fight my way to the surface again, and that without any hyper-ventilation. After a good gulp of air, I quickly jettisoned my pants and shirt, which were also weighting me down, and began to shout for the guide. There was no sign

of him above, and when I saw how much of the roof had come
away, I decided that he must have fallen in also and probably
drowned. As it turned out, he had not, and after seeing that I did
not surface, he figured that the *cenote* had claimed another
victim and went back to Peto—with my watch and wallet—to
announce my death.

Meanwhile, I began to feel I knew how those Maya priests
must have felt when the Spaniards threw them in. I was
accustomed to swimming in the much more buoyant salt water
and found that I could not keep afloat without treading water
constantly. I swam around the *cenote* several times looking for
some kind of ledge, but the sides were smooth. All I could do
was alternately hang on to one of the small crevices until the icy
water started to cramp my legs, go back to treading water until I
was exhausted, and then hang on again for awhile. The worst of
it was the many water snakes both in the *cenote* and on the walls.
I did not know whether they were poisonous or not, and when it
got dark I could only feel them slithering around me.

Somehow I managed to keep from sinking that night and
the next day, until, about five in the afternoon, I saw Father
Hubert's anxious face peering over the edge. He looked surprised when I shouted up. He had remained an extra day to bury
the woman, who had died soon after he arrived, and had
returned to Peto only an hour before to find the guide and half
the village mourning (or celebrating) my death over large
quantities of *mezcal* paid for with the money in my wallet.

The only trouble was that Father Hubert had rushed
straight out to the *cenote*, forgetting to bring more rope, but he
shouted down encouragements for the hour it took someone to
run to Peto and back. They then tied the new line to a tree, but
at a safe distance from the rim, and when they saw I could
barely raise my arms, let alone climb sixty feet up a rope, they
lowered down one of the boys who had come along to watch. He
tied the line under my arms and they pulled me up slowly, since
everyone, especially me, feared that more of the roof would cave

in. A few pieces did fall, but they weren't very large, and none of them hit me. By the time I was safely on the surface, I had spent more than twenty-four hours in the icy water of that *cenote* and cared little if the treasure from every Maya temple in Yucatan were down there.

Back in Mérida, Goggin and I had another good laugh over my latest misadventure. After failing to persuade him to leave his dig and come to help me look for the "fresco site" (Goggin prudently insisted that I find the place again first), I returned to Cozumel.

It was another American archaeologist, Dr. Lowell Hemming, who joined me in the search for the "fresco site." Hemming, who had spent a month every year for the past twenty years exploring Yucatan, had shown great interest in the frescoes, and I invited him along on my next expedition.

This expedition was much better equipped than my little jaunt with Taole: Hemming brought most of the equipment from the States, while I contributed one of my boats, which would stay over on the coast during the full month we had set aside for the search, as well as food supplies. In fact the expedition was too well-equipped. When I saw the mountain of gear Hemming arrived with, including everything from surveying equipment to a large direction-finder radio for marking the site precisely on the map, I realized that we would have to hire Indians to help us carry it. I asked my friend Father Bob, the Catholic missionary stationed on Cozumel, to help us, since I knew that he was widely respected by the Indians, who ordinarily will not work for anyone. He agreed, especially since this would give him a chance to visit some of the villages on the mainland, which he had not been to for months. Communications were so bad that Father Bob rarely got to visit his mainland territory, which extended along two hundred miles of coastline, starting at the island of Holbox in the north, around past Cape Catoche, and down to Tulum, unless I took him. Hemming became very excited when Father Bob told him that the whole coast was dotted with ruins, and we decided to make a run along the coast before starting the main expedition.

We headed directly for Holbox, where almost the entire village crowded into dugouts to lead Father Bob ashore. Most of the people in his mission territory had never even seen a priest until the American Maryknollers started their mission work in Yucatan a few years before, yet they had retained a deep devotion to their religion. Every village had its catechist, usually the most influential man there, who somehow kept Catholicism alive from generation to generation, although, as Father Bob would indulgently point out, not in a form easily recognizable to any North American Catholic. We stayed there several days, while Father Bob performed several baptisms and one marriage, and then headed south for Isla Mujeres, where the same routine was repeated.

The next stop was the island of Contoy, which has a thriving population of about ten families. We were surprised when no dugouts came out to meet us and more surprised when the usual swarm of children failed to flock around as we stepped ashore. Hemming took off to the other end of the island to photograph some ruins we had passed coming in, and Father Bob and I headed for the village. At first sight it seemed to be completely deserted, but entering one of the huts, we were met by the grisly sight of an old man lying in a pool of blood with a large piece of wood piercing straight through his chest directly under the shoulder blade. We thought he was dead, and he should have been, considering the amount of blood he had lost, but there was still a feeble pulse beat.

As Father Bob knelt to administer the last rites, I went to look for the other villagers and in the very next hut found another problem: a very pregnant woman who was moaning and thrashing around on a straw mat. Luckily she spoke a little Spanish and I was able to learn that the other villagers, including the local *comadrona,* or midwife, had gone to the mainland the day before for a fiesta and would not be back for a few more days. The old man was her father. He had been chopping down a tree that fell the wrong way, and one of the branches had impaled him; she had not been able to do much to help him and thought that he had probably died already.

I ran back to the other hut where Father Bob was still praying and announced my new discovery. "You'll have to handle that, Bob," he said. "You probably know as much about obstetrics as I do."

I flipped and threatened to run off and leave him with the job, but he conned me into it, saying that it would be inappropriate for him, a priest, to deliver a baby as long as there was someone else around. Five hours later, during which I drank all the homemade booze I could locate in her hut, the woman gave birth to a baby boy, in excellent condition, if I may say so. Maya women are very hardy and brave, and this one seemed to fare better from the ordeal than her "midwife"; she hoisted herself up and started to wash the baby, while I went outside to collapse.

By this time Hemming had returned. We carried the old man, who was unconscious but still alive, the woman, and her wailing baby out to the boat and headed back to Isla Mujeres, which has a small airstrip. The old man was flown out to Mérida within an hour after we landed and I learned that they managed to save his life. Mexican doctors are well trained; there simply aren't enough of them.

Two days later we dropped anchor off the mainland village called Playa Carmen. Before going ashore Father Bob said, "Let's pray that everything will be normal here." It wasn't. There had been a feud raging between two families for some time, and only two days before one side had decided to put an end to it by burying alive four members of the opposing faction. Father Bob ordered the bodies uncovered and gave them a proper Christian burial, which all the villagers attended, including the culprits. They looked very repentant after the severe dressing-down they had received from Father Bob, who had also told them they must cultivate the dead men's fields until their sons grew up. I know they obeyed, too, for Father Bob's word was law among the Indians.

After the burial service a woman asked Father Bob to see her son, who was sick. The boy had a raging fever, and Father Bob suspected a ruptured appendix (he was right, as we found out). We rushed him aboard and headed for Cozumel, abandoning our plans to visit the rest of the settlements and ruins down to Tulum.

This particular mission tour was longer but not much more eventful than the many others I accompanied Father Bob on during my three years on Cozumel. The Indians accept suffering and premature death as a matter of course, very grateful for help but never expecting it. Father Bob and I (to a much lesser extent) did what we could, but the problems were overwhelming. Malnutrition, for one thing. I thought the Indians could diversify their crops, and I sent up soil samples from around some of the villages to a friend of mine who owns one of the largest fertilizer companies in the world. His lab's verdict: a miracle that anything grew on that soil at all.

Hemming and I spent several days on Cozumel loading up with provisions and headed back to the mainland to find my "fresco site." Father Bob had to stay behind on Cozumel this time, but he gave us a letter to the headman of Inah, the village closest to the spot from which I thought we should start our trek inland.

Glancing around while the headman translated the letter from Spanish to Maya for the other villagers, I noticed a bright patch of yellow in one of the huts. My curiosity was aroused, since there is usually nothing to relieve the uniform drabness of the Indians' huts, and I walked over to have a look. My heart sank: inside was the yellow rain poncho I had stretched across the roof of the main temple at the "fresco site," being used as a tablecloth. I grabbed it and ran out, shouting my discovery to Hemming. The villagers thought at first that I was accusing them of stealing it and would tell me nothing, but I was finally able to convince them that I only wanted to know how it came to be in the village.

The headman explained. He had been hunting deer with bow and arrow and, after wounding a large stag, had followed it for more than a day before finally giving up the chase. On his way back to the coast, he stumbled across our ruins, and seeing the colored markers tied to the trees, as well as the poncho, he had taken them all home. He then showed me the other pieces of cloth, which his wife had sewn together to make a dress. I learned that he had done this about the time that Taole and I were starting out on our trek, so that it was no longer a mystery why we had been unable to spot the markers during any of our treetop surveys. By the time I went searching from the air, two months had passed, and the clearing must have become completely overgrown by then.

There was one consolation. The Indian claimed he could find the site again easily, and he not only agreed to lead us there but also persuaded three of the other villagers to come along. We found, however, that even with four Indians helping us, we had much more than we could carry, and we had to leave behind Hemming's surveying gear plus a large part of our provisions. Although the headman, who was named Chumn, assured us that we would reach the site in a day, with each of the Indians taking turns blazing the trail, I made sure that we had at least a week's supply of food and water.

This expedition, as I said, was much more carefully planned than Taole's and my fiasco, but it did not really make much difference. I am convinced that Yankee efficiency and organization, without either luck or the experience gained from being born and raised in that environment, is just not worth a damn in the Quintana Roo jungle. The first and second days, then the third and fourth, passed without any sign of the "fresco ruins." Every time I questioned Chumn he was the picture of confidence, assuring us repeatedly that we would reach there in no time. Not that Hemming and I were exactly disappointed.

On each of these four days we came upon a different set of ruins; the first three contained only a few buildings each, but the fourth was a real metropolis. We counted at least thirty buildings, most of which were merely bush-covered mounds, but several were large, stepped pyramids, topped by temples, whose outlines were only partially obscured by the undergrowth. We knew that these temples had not been visited by any recent explorers, probably not even by the Spaniards, because undisturbed artifacts of pottery, jade, and stone lay scattered all over the site, and on the altars in two of the temples we found large, beautifully decorated incense burners still containing the *copal* the ancient Maya used for incense.

Although it was still early in the afternoon of the fourth day when we found this large site, we decided to camp there for the night and spend the rest of the day exploring and photographing the ruins. Our first move was to set up the radio direction-finder to plot the site's position on the map: either Chumn was leading us on a wild goose chase or I had been completely off in my estimate of the fresco site's location, for it turned out that we were now at least fifteen miles from where I thought that site should be.

While we photographed individual ruins, we had the four Indians clear as much of the area as possible so that we could get shots of the temple groupings. One of the Indians was bitten on the ankle by a fer-de-lance, a small but venomous snake, for which there was no antidote, or at least none we knew of. All we could do was make an incision over the bite and suck out the blood and, hopefully, the venom too. The man was soon unconscious despite our efforts, and since we had only a few days' rations of food and water left, I decided we had all better start back for Inah. Chumn insisted that the other two men could make better time alone, and when they reached Inah they could get a few of the other villagers to help them bring back more supplies. I agreed to this rather reluctantly. We would keep searching for the fresco ruins, but I had Chumn tell the other two Indians to follow the trail we would blaze from there and as a further safeguard, if either we or they got lost, to make the present site the rendezvous point.

Two long saplings and one of the pup tents made an excellent litter, and before dark the two Indians left at a trot carrying the unconscious snake-bite victim. We learned later that they reached Inah in less than twenty-four hours, following the trail we had blazed, but the man was dead when they arrived.

We regretted having to leave this important site so quickly, but the fresco ruins were our goal. We set out early the next morning, leaving behind the supplies we were unable to carry at the site that was to be our base camp. Around noon we came out into a large clearing, which I recognized as one I had spotted from the air and marked on the map as being many miles from the fresco site. I told Hemming this, and we agreed that we were wasting our time; Chumn was too stubborn or too proud to admit that he no longer had the slightest idea where he had originally found that yellow poncho. We decided that we would return to the coast and try to find the site ourselves by using my original compass bearings. As was often the case, this clearing contained several mounds—three small ruins—and after pitching camp, we spent the rest of the day poking around the ruins, finding a few figurines and potsherds.

The following morning, while searching for dry wood for a fire, Chumn discovered the entrance to a cave on one side of the clearing. He would not go in himself, since Indians are afraid of "cave spirits," but he led us there, and Hemming and I entered with flashlights. As usual, the bats went berserk from the sudden bright light, careening all around the cave and smashing into us in the process, but after they settled down we started to move farther back and found that the cave was much larger than we had originally thought. The floor was littered with goodies— intact clay pots of all sizes and shapes and at least twenty complete human skeletons. Mixed in with the bones we found nearly two hundred green jade beads, some of them from necklaces that had adorned the corpses, as well as many larger ones and earplugs of white jade, which the Maya prized very highly. There was also an assortment of ornately carved knives and axeheads of obsidian, a volcanic rock the Yucatan Maya must have obtained in trade from the highland Indians.

From the vast assortment of potsherds we found all over the cave, dating from different periods, we surmised that it had been in use for many centuries. Hemming found some charcoal which he started to collect for radio-carbon dating, while I walked back flashing my light along the walls to see if there were any frescoes. Suddenly my light was reflected off two emerald-green eyes, belonging to a large jaguar (all jaguars seem large at a distance of ten feet) which was crouched on the floor of the cave. I was so startled I dropped my flashlight and only felt the animal brush past me as it headed for the entrance to the cave.

I picked up the flashlight and when I found that it would not work I yelled to Hemming to flash his light over my way, so that I could get back without stepping on any of the delicate clay pots that littered the floor. But there was no answer from Hemming. I rushed over, pots or no pots, and found him lying unconscious on the cave floor. Dragging his 220-pound frame outside into the light, I could detect no injuries. He was breathing, and I loosened his shirt so that he could breathe more easily. Other than that I did not have any idea what I could do for him, except get him back to a doctor. But there was no sign of Chumn, whom we had left waiting outside the cave. By myself I could barely support Hemming, much less carry him (since I had arrived in Yucatan, malaria and amoebic dysentery had brought me down from my usual 190 pounds to 130). At first I thought of setting out alone for Inah to bring back help, but ruled out this plan when I realized that, if the jaguar or anything else came nosing around, Hemming would be totally defenseless.

I sat there feeling pretty helpless, or useless, myself, until Hemming finally came out of his coma four hours later. All he knew was that something had knocked him down—when I explained about the jaguar and its headlong flight out of the cave, he almost went back into his coma—and he figured he had then had a heart attack, since he had already suffered two others in recent years. He was very weak and barely able to stand, even with a crutch I made him from a tree limb and with my support on the other side. I had to leave everything behind but my machete and a few canteens of water, wrapping our rifles and cameras in a tent and burying them under a mound of bat guano in the cave, and hoping to reach our base camp with the rest of our supplies in a day's time.

From then on it was almost a repeat performance of Taole's and my ordeal eighteen months before, only worse this time, because now I had to half carry, half drag poor Hemming. Even though we went on all that night, stopping only briefly to rest at hourly intervals, we did not reach the base camp until late the following afternoon, and then only to find that all the supplies we had left were gone—another mysterious jungle thief, since Chumn swore later that neither he nor the other villagers had taken them.

Hemming by this time had lapsed into semi-consciousness. I was so worn out I simply dragged him up the steps to one of the low temples and fell asleep myself next to the altar. The next morning I found some of the vines Taole and I had quenched our thirst from with no apparent ill effects. I forced some of the liquid down Hemming's throat, drank some myself, and started out again.

I remember little of what occurred during the next four days and nights it took to reach Inah, except Hemming's dead weight. He would awaken on and off, but mostly he was unconscious, and the last two days I was so weak myself that I had to drag him by the arms. It is a wonder that this alone didn't kill the man, and in fact he did end up with a dislocated shoulder, but it was either that or leave him behind in the jungle.

I had hoped to throw Hemming on board my boat as soon

as we reached Inah and head straight for Cozumel, but when we emerged from the jungle, I was startled to see the boat lying heeled over half up on the beach, with neither of my two boatmen in sight. Instead I headed for the village, still dragging poor Hemming after me. The first person to see us was Chumn's wife, who took one look and ran off shrieking. Eyes peeped cautiously out of huts, but no one would come out until some brave soul sneaked up behind me to poke me cautiously with a machete, and when I jumped, it was decided I was not a ghost. Chumn, it seems, had seen the jaguar come flying out of the cave and had fled immediately, telling everyone in the village that the jaguar had eaten both of us and letting his imagination supply the details of the gory scene in the cave.

While I attacked some beans and tortillas, Chumn explained what had happened to my boat, and I wish it had been as fictitious as his tale about the jaguar. Soon after we left, my two boatmen broke into one of the lockers they knew contained a good supply of Scotch and brandy and started on a roaring drunk that lasted five days. During that time they made several raids to carry two of the village women back to the boat, all unsuccessful. Each time the Indian men had driven them back with machetes, and the last battle had ended in total defeat, after one drunken boatman lost his left ear by a machete stroke and the other shot himself in the foot with one of my spearguns.

The Indians did not know what to do with their captives, fearing reprisals from Cozumel if they killed the men, and finally decided to send them back to Cozumel via a boat that was loading copra from the nearby plantation of Acumal. The two Indians had returned with the dead snake-bite victim in the middle of the war, and in the excitement they had forgotten all about taking the rest of the supplies back to the base camp. The village simply returned to normal—that is, until Chumn came running in a few days later with the story of our being devoured by the jaguar. With this news they all set about stripping my boat bare, even to the portholes and parts of the engine. They also took the anchors, leaving the boat tied to a hunk of coral, so that when a squall hit the coast the next night, the wind and heavy seas threw her up on the beach.

Chumn and his villagers were basically honest—maddeningly unreliable, but not thieves. They had taken property which they thought no longer had an owner, and while I slept they worked the whole night putting everything back. Not a thing was missing the next morning but the contents of the liquor chest my boatmen had stolen. They then helped me refloat her and get Hemming aboard, considering themselves generously paid with the food supplies I left. The engine of course was a dead loss, at least for the time being; the Indians had replaced all the parts but without remembering which parts went where, and I am not much better as a mechanic myself. I hoisted sail, and with a favorable wind we actually made it across to Cozumel in less time than is usual even under motor power.

Hemming had regained consciousness before we left and was even able to talk. He was in pain from his dislocated shoulder but considered that a much lesser evil than being left back in the jungle. He was flown out to Mérida, where he spent the next few weeks in a hospital. There was nothing wrong with me that a few good nights' sleep and some solid food could not cure. A week later I headed back to the cave, before the trail became completely overgrown again. For a change, nothing went wrong. The jaguar had probably decided the neighborhood was getting crowded, and I retrieved the rifles and cameras, and also collected some charcoal as well as artifacts from both sites for dating, all without incident.

During the next twelve months before I left Cozumel for good, I made five other expeditions to search for the "fresco site," all without mishap but also without any success. That part of Yucatan must have been very densely populated at one time, for on each of the expeditions I came across at least one site of ruins, sometimes two or three, but not the one I was looking for. The jungle had swallowed it up again, apparently without a trace. Like the wreck of the *Monitor,* I always planned to go back and search again for the "fresco site," and perhaps some day I will.

Chapter Five
•
Underwater Eldorado
•

Glancing over a chart one day, a few months after settling on Cozumel, I noticed a place on the Quintana Roo coast directly opposite the island, called *Punta Matancero,* which translates roughly as "Slaughter Point." Perhaps some sort of slaughter or massacre had taken place there. But none of the old chronicles mentioned any Spanish settlement anywhere near there. Or could a ship have been wrecked there and the survivors massacred by Indians when they reached the shore?

No one on Cozumel had any idea how the place had gotten its name. But soon after my curiosity had first been aroused, I ran into an old sea captain, Algimiro Argüelles, who, besides running a two-masted trading schooner between Cozumel and British Honduras, owned a large copra plantation at Acumal, which includes Punta Matancero. Argüelles did not know why it was called Slaughter Point, but he did have some interesting information about its recent history. There was a large cannon lying at the water's edge, and very often after heavy storms old shoe buckles, buttons, and small brass crucifixes had been found on the beach nearby.

Only a few years before, he went on to relate, one of the Indians who worked for him had found three gold coins on the same beach, and this discovery had caused him so much trouble that he had to forbid his plantation hands ever to set foot on Punta Matancero again. The Indian kept his find a secret even from Captain Argüelles, but one day he went over to Cozumel and started to quench his thirst at one of the local cantinas. His few *pesos* soon ran out, but he was still thirsty and, pulling out his three gold coins, he asked the barman if he would accept them in payment for more tequila. The word quickly spread, reaching the general who was the island's civil governor as well as its military commander, and the gold rush was on. Within two hours the general had extracted the story from the Indian, commandeered Argüelles's schooner, *Cozumel,* which was lying in port, and started out for Punta Matancero with twenty-seven relatives and servants and nearly a hundred soldiers armed with rifles and shovels.

Guards were posted around the area to keep off curious visitors from Cozumel and Acumal, and for six weeks the soldiers dug up the beach while the general supervised from his headquarters at Acumal. Not only were Captain Argüelles and his family forced to move out of their house to some Indian huts, but they also had to provide food for the entire expedition.

"Over one hundred head of beef, I don't know how many pigs, and every ounce of rice, beans, maize, bananas, and pineapples we had on hand," Argüelles recalled indignantly. "And all without one *peso* in payment." I could well understand why the old captain, who had spent most of his long life carving that plantation out of the Quintana Roo wilderness, was unable to see the funny side of this wacky treasure hunt.

"That old thief would have stayed forever," he continued. "But the fact is there was nothing left to eat. He found his just reward waiting for him when he returned to Cozumel—again on my boat; which he had kept waiting to carry out the gold. His chief in the capital had gotten wind of the little expedition. The

Señor General was demoted to captain and transferred off the island."

"But did they find anything?" I asked.

"Nothing but some old nails, bits of broken pottery, and a few other worthless items. I've been back there myself since then and found more of the same—always after a heavy storm—but so far no more gold coins."

Captain Argüelles did not try to hide his own interest in Punta Matancero, and I soon found out why he chose to confide in me. "I have heard about your miraculous money machine," he said. "Does it really work?" I stared at him blankly for a minute and then realized he meant my metal detector, which some of the islanders had seen me testing around the hotel. As a matter of fact, the detector, one of the early models and a real lemon, was not working at the time. But I thought he might be wasting his time on the beach anyway and asked if he had seen any signs of a wreck underwater.

He had not—but he had not looked either. Argüelles thought there had probably been a small Spanish fort on the shore that some hurricane had destroyed, and that the winds and waves during heavy storms stirred up the sand on the beach, uncovering the artifacts. I argued that they could just as easily be from a wreck washed up on the shore during storms, which would explain why so few things had been found even by digging deep into the sand. Argüelles ended the discussion by inviting me to spend a few days with him at Acumal to explore the area myself.

Punta Matancero turned out to be more of a bump on the Quintana Roo coast line than a sharply defined point. As we approached in Captain Argüelles's schooner *Cozumel,* I could see that it was certainly not a very likely site for a fort. The shore was unusually flat and desolate even for Quintana Roo, and far from having a good anchorage, it was fronted by a solid coral reef 250 yards wide that started right at the beach and extended another sixty yards out from shore. The jagged surface of the reef slopes gradually from almost water level down to a depth of thirty feet where the deeper sandy bottom begins off shore. But luckily the sea was almost flat calm that day, and Captain Argüelles (the old man, who must have been at least seventy-five then, was acknowledged by everyone, including Cappy, as the best sea dog in the territory of Quintana Roo) was able to ease his seventy-foot schooner fairly close into shore before dropping anchor.

The water was clear—almost but not quite as clear as around Cozumel—and I jumped in wearing only snorkling equipment. As soon as the foam and bubbles had cleared, I looked down and almost directly below the *Cozumel's* hull were the outlines of two coral-encrusted cannons. They were both about six feet long, similar in size and shape to the one Captain Argüelles had pointed out at the water's edge. Closer inspection revealed that they were both firmly cemented to the reef.

It seemed unlikely that cannons from a shore battery would have been carried that far out even in a severe hurricane, and I soon located two fifteen-foot anchors, as well as six more cannons, all in a relatively small area of the reef. The anchors were indisputable proof that a ship had been there, but were they necessarily proof of a shipwreck?

At this time very little was known about early wooden wrecks. (There were a few old-timers working in Caribbean waters who had located and perhaps even salvaged old shipwrecks, but they understandably were not eager to share their knowledge with other divers.) By then I knew better than to expect to find a completely intact ship with a skeleton at the wheel, as portrayed in some of the books and movies that had held me spellbound at age twelve; one could guess that the hull of any wooden ship run aground on a reef would eventually break up and that much of it would be destroyed by wood-eating marine worms called *teredos*. But I did expect to find some signs of a wreck—at least a pile of ballast stones and some of the less perishable cargo and ships' stores. Yet I covered the entire reef without finding anything more than the eight cannons and two anchors.

Back aboard the *Cozumel,* I told Captain Argüelles of my finds. "So there wasn't a fort there after all," he concluded. "A ship must have run aground here, and they cast over the cannon and anchors to lighten her. It looks like they succeeded in getting her off, too, since there are no signs of a wreck."

"But what about the coins and other things found on the beach?" I asked.

"Well maybe a few chests stowed on deck got lost overboard and washed up on shore later." Captain Argüelles's hypothesis seemed to provide the only possible explanation, and I returned to Cozumel in a few days to forget all about Punta Matancero— that is, until an accidental discovery completely transformed my ideas about the anatomy of old wreck-sites.

Several months after Argüelles and I had dismissed the possibility of a wreck at Punta Matancero, I received a letter from a friend, Dr. José Lima, a retired government official then living on Isla Mujeres, inviting me to come and investigate some cannons recently spotted by a local fisherman. Dr. Lima's two sons led me to the site, which was actually on the coast directly opposite Isla Mujeres, and we located these cannons easily in the clear shallow water close to shore. It was an exciting find: a richly decorated bronze cannon in perfect condition (bronze being highly resistant to corrosion) and seven iron lombards, a rare, very early type of cannon, its long slim barrel ringed by reinforcing bands. We raised the bronze cannon and two of the lombards but a survey of the surrounding reef produced the same results as on Punta Matancero—nothing. It looked like another case of a vessel's having run aground, cast over the heavy cannons, and pulled off again.

I lay awake that night thinking about the day's finds. The bronze cannon puzzled me. I knew from my reading that the Spaniards valued bronze cannons so highly that they generally would attempt to salvage them from wrecks even before a treasure. I finally fell asleep having decided not to return to Cozumel next morning but to go back and search that reef more thoroughly. That decision opened up a whole new chapter in underwater archaeology for me, and perhaps for other people as well. Although the water was only ten feet deep, I borrowed several aqualung tanks from my friend so that I could hug the bottom closely. The first thing I noticed was what looked like a large ring fastened to the reef. Chipping away some of the coral with a small crowbar to loosen it, I found that the "ring" was really the muzzle of another lombard, completely embedded in the reef. I continued my search, this time with my face plate barely inches from the bottom, and spotted two more cannons, only minute parts visible above the coral. Most of my finds were not visible at all. Hacking away chunks of coral I found pieces of ceramic and pottery, iron and brass nails, and other pieces of metal under the surface. In one spot I noticed that the normally whitish limestone under the multicolored reef surface was stained black. Remembering this same discoloration around corroded iron cannons (from the iron oxide), I dug farther, and three feet under the surface found an old sword. Almost everywhere I hacked there was something, even a wooden pulley block from the ship's rigging: there was a wreck after all, but all of it completely buried under the coral. Dr. Lima later sent photographs of the cannons and the items I found to several Mexican historians. From the type of cannons and their location, they identified the wreck as the *Nicolasa*, a caravel that had wrecked on that coast in 1526 during a bad storm, en route from Cuba to Veracruz with supplies for Cortés.

All the way back to Cozumel, I kept thinking about the way the reef had completely concealed the signs of a shipwreck. Why not at Punta Matancero also? Remembering that parts of the Matancero reef had been oddly discolored also, I became convinced that Captain Argüelles and I had been wrong.

Meanwhile, I had been writing to my old friend from the *Monitor* days, Clay Blair, suggesting that he come down for a skin-diving vacation. He finally accepted my invitation just about the time I returned from Isla Mujeres, and a few weeks later, around the end of September 1957, he arrived on Cozumel with a close friend of his, Wally Bennett, a staff photographer for *Time* magazine. I had never met Wally but I had heard of him from Doc Mathieson and other skin-diving "greats" in California, for Wally had been a member of that original group that had started the sport of skin diving in the U.S. right after World War II. Wally, an excellent photographer, both underwater and topside, as well as being an experienced diver, was a definite asset to any diving expedition.

I briefed Wally and Clay on Punta Matancero and on my reasons for thinking that there might be a wreck there. Both of them were eager to have a look and help me check out my theory. Wally said, "Hell, at the worst, we could get some good photographs of the cannons and anchors."

I saw that Wally was in excellent shape, probably because he worked out daily in a gymnasium at home in Washington, D.C., but Clay had gained a lot of weight, besides not having had much diving experience except for his brief baptism at Hatteras and a few practice sessions in swimming pools. It had been unusually calm the day I had been at Punta Matancero, but I knew that the diving conditions there were usually very rugged, with a heavy surf and strong undertow, and I decided we should stick around Cozumel for a few days and get Clay diving like a pro before we headed for Punta Matancero.

The next day I took them out for some spearfishing. I had been boasting to them about the fabulous abundance of fish around Cozumel and they were not disappointed: a 450-pound jewfish, a 550-pound loggerhead turtle, a six-foot moray eel, fifty lobsters, and about a thousand pounds of assorted smaller fish. My *amigos* on Cozumel ate well that night!

Or at least I thought they were not disappointed until Clay said on the way back, "That spearfishing is dudsville. When are we going to do some real diving?"

Wally looked as surprised as I did, and later when I asked him, he said that he had thought Clay was enjoying himself: he did very well in the water and was even reaching depths of thirty feet on his own breath. After a few rounds of rum that evening, I asked Clay what he had against spearfishing, and he finally came out with it. He knew that blood attracts sharks; spearfishing bloodies up the water, hence spearfishing was dudsville.

At this stage in my life I was still the brash, cocky Marine, unafraid of anything on land, in the air, or under the sea. In fact, I was just plain stupid. I believed that almost all reports of shark attacks were fictitious. Except for the incident years before off southern California, when I had seen those killer sharks devour the herd of sea lions, I had never had any problems with sharks, nor had I known anyone else who had. Only a few weeks before Clay and Wally arrived, I had seen a sixteen-foot hammerhead, which the books claim is a man-eater, lying motionless on the bottom, either resting or asleep—one can't tell, since sharks have no eyelids and sleep with their eyes open. I swam down, tied a line to its tail, with the other end fastened to the skiff, and poked it with my knife. The shark took off like a bat out of hell, pulling the skiff and paying no attention to me on its back. I don't remember whether I speared that one or not—probably by that time I had gotten bored with killing sharks and let it go. The point is that the sharks around Cozumel acted no more ferocious than a St. Bernard, and I was convinced that they were all sissies.

"Sharks don't bite, man," I assured Clay. "They're all cowards. I'll show you tomorrow."

Wally, who had done most of his diving in California waters where sharks are comparatively rare, took it for granted that I knew what I was talking about. Clay, with much coaxing from us both, agreed to the experiment if I promised to have one of my boatmen follow closely behind us in a skiff, in the event that a fast exit was needed.

The next day, in fact for almost a week, we had a ball

riding and spearing sharks. Or at least Wally and I did. Clay was
still leery of them, although he got interested in spearfishing and
shot plenty of his own fish. But Clay's fear of sharks was only the
instinct of self-preservation. Perhaps he carried it to an extreme,
but how I ever survived so long treating sharks as sissies is a
mystery to me today. Either fool's luck or a very well-fed shark
population around Cozumel. In any case, Clay has since been
able to say "I told you so," and my advice on sharks now is: keep
as far away as possible, and never, repeat, never provoke them by
riding, spearing, or even touching them.

Finally we were ready to tackle Punta Matancero, and we
left early one morning aboard the *Aguilucho.* I headed for
Tulum, since neither Clay nor Wally had ever visited any Maya
ruins, and I also wanted to show them the bas-relief sculpture of
the bull on one of the buildings, hoping for new converts to my
theory on pre-Columbian voyages to America. Since it was mid-
afternoon by the time we reached Punta Matancero, we headed
for Acumal, five miles farther up the coast, to anchor for the
night.

That evening, some of the Indians who worked at Acumal
for Captain Argüelles (who was away "trading" in British Honduras) claimed that bad weather was coming and that we should
either plan to weather it out in the reef-protected cove of
Acumal or make a run for Cozumel early in the morning. My
two boatmen agreed, but when I relayed the weather report to
Wally and Clay, Clay said, "Let's stick it out. So what if we
sink? That'll give me good meat for my *Post* article." Since
Wally was all for staying also, and I was eager to see if there was
a wreck at Punta Matancero, we decided to get in at least a day's
diving.

We left Acumal an hour before sunup. It was already
blowing hard, and by the time we reached Punta Matancero it
was definitely boisterous, with large waves breaking all over the
reef. It was so damn rough we had to anchor the *Aguilucho* two
hundred yards from the reef and put out all three anchors. We

had to use snorkling gear, since my air compressor for filling tanks was on one of its frequent strikes, and this meant that we would have to fight the heavy swells and breakers on the surface instead of keeping on the calmer sea bottom.

We were tossed around like corks as soon as we jumped in.

Wally shouted, "Marx, you must be joking. We're not really going in closer to the beach. Those waves are breaking as high as Niagara Falls."

"Hell yes," I answered. "This is calmsville compared to Hatteras."

But at least Hatteras had a sandy bottom. Here each time one of the combers approached, all three of us had to dive and hold on to a piece of coral on the bottom to keep from being swept along and smashed on the rocky beach. During one of these precautionary dives we grabbed hold of one of the cannons. Clay and Wally almost lost their snorkles grinning, and I could see that they felt that the risk was worth it after all.

Wally motioned that he wanted to take a shot of Clay and me holding onto the cannon. As he backed away to get us in his view finder, Clay suddenly shot off along the bottom and then stopped about ten feet away. After surfacing for another gulp of air he dove again and began chopping at something with his knife. Then a large bubble of air started to rise to the surface, and Clay turned holding up the pieces of a green wine bottle, which he had just broken in his haste, releasing the air that had been trapped inside. Wally quickly spotted another intact bottle sticking out of the coral close to Clay, which he left for me to extract. It took about fifty dives to chip away the coral growth, but I finally managed to get the bottle out intact.

Returning from the boat where I had deposited the bottle, Wally yelled, "Get over here quick. Clay's chopping at something else."

I swam over and jack-knifed down, but halfway to the bottom, a high cloud of black, like the ink that an octopus squirts out as camouflage, came floating up past me, followed by

Clay scooting up to the surface for air. Reaching the bottom I saw that Clay had found a teakwood chest (the black cloud, as we learned later, was silver sulfide that had been released when he tried to pry open the chest) which was cemented to a large piece of ship's timber. Now there was no doubt that we were on a wreck.

Rushing back to the boat, I put on the one aqualung tank that was filled and sped back to investigate the area. I found a shiny cut stone, which looked like a diamond of about three carats, then a green one, which looked like an emerald, and within minutes six more diamonds and three more emeralds. I signaled to Clay, who swam down, took the "treasure" in carefully cupped hands, and carried it back to the boat where he hid the stones in his clothes. Next I found a silver buckle, which was almost perfectly preserved, since it was next to an iron nail and the electrolytic field set up by the two different metals had protected them both from the corroding effects of the sea water. Then I returned to the chest, and while I was prying the top with a crowbar Wally had brought to me, a richly carved ivory knife handle fell out. Neither Clay nor Wally was overhead when I looked up for someone to come down for my new find; then I heard the *Aguilucho's* motor start and I knew there was trouble. Surfacing, I ran into Wally who told me that two of the anchor lines had snapped. We would have to make a run for it, since menacing storm clouds were only minutes away, and we were on a lee coast.

The trip back to Cozumel was very exciting. The normal six-hour crossing took us nineteen hours, and we all had to lash ourselves to the mast or helm to keep from being washed overboard. We were so beat we hailed a taxi to take us the two blocks from the pier to the hotel. I knew that my boatmen were no fools and must have realized that we were on a wreck, and before leaving, I swore them both to secrecy.

The next morning the three of us gathered in my room, and after I hung a bedsheet over the window for greater secrecy

The Archives of the Indies in Seville, Spain, where I researched the history of the Spanish fleet for clues to shipwreck sites. The young man on my left is one of the assistants I employed. (*Below*) Captain Robert Legge holds a part of the wooden roof of the cabin of the Civil War blockade runner *Fanny and Jenny*. The coral I'm holding was found near the wreck.

This is one of the Mayan vases I found in the cenote at Dzibilchultun.

(*Opposite*) One of the many Mayan ruins
I discovered during my years in Yucatan.

(*Above*) Divers at work on the Matancero wreck. (*Right*) A gold watch that I found on the Matancero site.

Clay Blair and I on the Matancero wreck. Blair, equipped only with snorkling gear, is holding a wine bottle. I'm helping another diver to extract one of the ship's cannon from its coral grave.

(Above) Some of the artifacts we recovered from the Matancero wreck. (Right) This lobster-hunting skin diver met a white-tipped shark and lost part of his foot in the encounter. He's holding his swim fin from the other foot, which the shark also ripped.

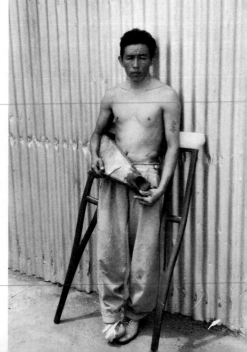

The crew of the *Niña II* after arrival in San Salvador, Bahamas, in front of the Columbus Church. Left to right: Michel, Nicolás (with white beard), myself, Etayo, José (holding a musket), Pepe (his face is partially hidden by the flag), Manolo, and Antonio (standing with the large flag).

(*Above*) My Viking ship as it was when used in *The Long Ships*. (*Right*) The crew of the Viking ship in Tunis after our arrest for entering the port without a pilot and for not having ship's papers. Left to right: myself, Per (wearing a rain jacket), Jumbo (in his goatskin jacket), Knut (holding a plastic container), Bell (hands in pockets), and Bill Holmes.

(probably succeeding only in drawing attention), Clay extracted the stones. We examined them closely, tried scratching a piece of glass with them, and sadly concluded that they were all fakes. However, the knife handle was definitely ivory, and one of the tourists staying in the hotel, a chemist, had identified a black sticky glob I had pulled out of the same teak chest as silver sulfide.

Clay said, "I bet the whole chest is full of ivory-handled silver knives, and maybe some of them deeper down are not so badly corroded."

"Man, you're all wrong," Wally protested. "I'm willing to bet you a thousand to one that chest is full of gold."

Having treasure fever as badly as, if not worse than, the two of them, I agreed with Wally.

Poring over a book I had on old artillery, we decided that the cannons at Punta Matancero dated from the period 1700–1750, but we were not sure about the nationality. Time enough to worry about that after we found the treasure. We then formed an agreement over a bottle of rum that we would work the wreck together and split the treasure evenly. Wally and Clay, who had to return to the States in a few days, would return as soon as possible for a large-scale expedition, and I promised to keep away from the wreck in the meantime to avoid arousing suspicion.

My intentions were good, but neither the *Post* nor *Time* was willing to give Clay or Wally a month's vacation (which we had agreed was the minimum time required for a good salvage attempt) so soon after the last one, and after several months I decided I could not hold off any longer. I made five brief trips back to Punta Matancero, taking every precaution for secrecy. I never took any tourist, and each time I went with the same two boatmen, Elías and Blackfish (a name he had been given while working as a seaman out of British Honduras). What I did not realize was that I was constantly under observation from shore.

The main purpose of the trips was to map out the extent of

the wreck site. That turned out to be easy—it covered the entire reef. No matter where I dug in the coral there were goodies: brass crucifixes and holy medals, silver buckles for shoes and belts, musket and cannon balls, one silver spoon and two silver-plated ones, and a variety of less interesting items like pins, needles, nails, and pieces of rope. I wondered if the ship's powder magazine had caught fire and exploded. Whatever the cause, the cargo was scattered helter-skelter all over the reef without any discernible pattern.

During this same period, while I was waiting for Clay and Wally to return for the big expedition, my weird sense of humor led me into a little prank which was to have serious consequences on our future activities at Punta Matancero.

One day I was spearfishing off the Quintana Roo coast south of Tulum, along one of the barren stretches that run for miles, with the same sandy beach and the same jungle behind, and without a solitary ruin or Indian hut to break the monotony. In short, I do not really know the exact location, nor did it seem to matter at the time. By accident I discovered a nineteenth-century wreck with many lead bars, or pigs, probably the vessel's ballast, scattered on the bottom, and, noticing that some of the pigs were covered with a thick growth of coral, I decided to play a joke on my two boatmen, Cappy and Blackfish. I heaved one of the lead pigs aboard and warned: "Don't either of you sticky-fingered fishwives touch this gold bar, now."

After trolling for dophin down the coast, we decided to anchor for the night and pulled into a small cove where we found one of the turtling boats from Cozumel. Blackfish, whose eyes had been glued to the lead pig all afternoon, rowed over to see his friends, and soon after he returned the turtler left.

Sometime that night, I went topside to check how the anchor line was holding, and after stubbing my toe on the pig for a second time that day I decided the joke had gone far enough and dumped it overboard.

We left for Cozumel at sunrise. I was disappointed that neither Cappy nor Blackfish mentioned the lead pig and decided that they had not been fooled after all. I was wrong. When we reached Cozumel, the turtling boat, which had gone out only a few days before, was tied up and half of the island's population was standing on the pier. Moments later, several police and *Aduana* (customs) officers jumped aboard and demanded to see the "gold bar." I broke out in a fit of laughter. "Hey Cappy, what a good joke, the gold bar. Tell them." Then I noticed that neither Cappy, Blackfish, the *Aduana* officers, nor anyone else was laughing with me. They simply stood there, eying me suspiciously. No sense of humor, I decided, and carefully explained what had happened. Still no laughter.

One of the *Aduana* officers said, "That's a very good story, but we're not interested in stories, just the gold bar."

"This is silly as hell," I protested. "I'll go get the bar for you if you don't believe me." They agreed that I had better get the bar, but they were going with me.

When we reached the cove, I was so sure of picking up the bar in one dive that I jumped in with only a face mask and no fins or snorkel. But instead of finding a hard coral or sandy bottom, I discovered that there were about four or five feet of soft silt, probably from some underground stream that emptied into the cove. The police and *Aduana* officiers waiting on the *Clipper* were not surprised in the least when I announced this bad news, and after spending several hours searching around the bush on shore, they ordered me to take them to the wreck with the other "gold bars."

We weighed anchor and started up the coast, but neither Cappy, Blackfish, nor I could agree on the location of the wreck. We checked all the sites each of us suggested, but by evening we had still found nothing and had to return to Cozumel, since no one had brought any food along. I spent the night in the municipal jail, getting little sleep because no less than a dozen people, including my partners, the Joaquín brothers, came to give me advice on how to handle the situation, all, of course, suggesting first that I cut them in on the "gold."

The rest of the night I spent arguing with the officer on duty, insisting that there was no law against salvaging wrecks anyway. Clay and I had in fact written to several different government ministries in Mexico City inquiring about permission to salvage shipwrecks in Mexican waters, and they had all replied that since there was no law regulating underwater salvage, no special permission was necessary. I relayed this information to the police officer, offering to show him the letters.

"Well, if there isn't any law," he said, "there should be." And on that note of logic the argument ended.

The following morning we started back across the channel again, this time with six of the island's divers along. We spent three whole days searching and discovered two other nineteenth-century wrecks, but not the one with the lead pigs. I was released when we returned to Cozumel and dismissed the episode as simply another one of my jokes that had backfired, although without serious consequences. But by then everyone was convinced that I had found a wreck loaded with "gold bars," had buried one of them someplace, and had bribed my two boatmen to keep quiet.

In May 1958, I finally heard from Clay and Wally that they had obtained their month's vacation and would be down to tackle the wreck at Punta Matancero at the beginning of June. I sent a long list of equipment we would need (luckily, Cozumel at this time was a free port), the main item being two "hookah" units. I had decided that hookahs—which consist of an air compressor that feeds air from the boat through a rubber hose to a regular mouthpiece unit which the diver wears—would be preferable for our purposes in many ways to the aqualung tanks: first, although the diver's range of movement is limited by the length of his air hose, we would actually have no need to wander around the reef, but would be concentrating on specific areas each day, and the diver would not be hampered in his work by a bulky air tank on his back; second, he could stay down indefinitely instead of having to come aboard every forty minutes or so to change tanks; and last, we would not have to spend hours each night refilling empty tanks. The hookah units had some serious drawbacks, but we did not learn this until later.

Wally and Clay arrived as planned on June 1. We spent the day testing the hookah units in the hotel swimming pool and stocking up on fresh food, and early the next morning started to load the *Aguilucho* with our tons of equipment and supplies. Even though it was hours before sunrise, several *Aduana* men were waiting on the pier and made careful note of every item we placed on board. This sudden devotion to duty—the formality of clearing from Cozumel, a free port, to the mainland is usually a breezy *"hasta luego"* to the Captain of the Port—puzzled me. I had forgotten all about the "gold bar" episode, and did not realize that not only the *Aduana* but the whole island thought we were returning to pick up the gold bars.

The trip across the channel was rough and wet, and I remember Wally's remarking over and over, "And Marx claims that in June it's as calm as a lake down here."

After negotiating the narrow cut in the barrier reef fronting Acumal, we dropped anchor close to shore. "You see, Wally," I said, "calm as a lake." Only we were not going to be diving in the placid waters of Acumal's lagoon.

Captain Argüelles's foreman gave us a hut to live in for a rent of two *pesos* (16¢) a day, but it really wasn't the bargain it seemed, considering that it closely resembled the pigsty adjoining it. We spent the morning cleaning it out and storing our supplies off the *Aguilucho*. Just as we were about to sit down for lunch, the *Cozumel* came in through the reef, and I sent word for Captain Argüelles to join us.

I had explained to Clay and Wally that Captain Argüelles owned Punta Matancero, and we agreed it was only fair to tell him that there was a wreck there, which we had come to salvage.

Showing no surprise at all, he pointed to Elías and Blackfish, who were sitting with us: "With those two blabbermouths working for you, news of the wreck and your finds is no secret. In fact, I even heard people talking about it in Belize last month. I've had my people watch you every time you've been to Punta Matancero and have been wondering just how long it would take you to tell me about it." When Blackfish and Elías solemnly protested their innocence, Captain Argüelles, normally soft-spoken, lost his temper: "Are you *hijos de puta* calling me a liar?" They both then slinked away and he continued, "Since you have finally confided in me, I will tell you more about your wreck."

The story he told, which I translated to Wally and Clay, is the kind usually dished out by hack fiction writers for the credulous reader, but the old man had a reputation for un-qualified honesty around Cozumel, and the three of us believed him.

"Some years back," he related, "how many I'm not sure, but at least twenty, since it was before I came to Acumal, a man on Cozumel shot someone in an argument and then fled the island to live among the Indians not far from here. Over the years the Indians came to trust him—he even learned their tongue—and one day they took him to the beach either at or near Punta Matancero and showed him a chest they had dug from the sand. It was full of coins, holy chalices, and other things made of gold. Then they buried the chest again. Years went by and a boat came from Cozumel with word that the president had issued a general amnesty to all escaped convicts and other fugitives, who could return to their normal lives without fear or punishment.

"The man returned to his family on Cozumel, but for years he kept his secret to himself, until he fell seriously ill and before he died he confided in his wife, even drawing a map for her showing exactly where the chest was buried. Now, that was fifteen years ago, but the man's wife is still alive. Two months ago when your two boatmen spread word that you had found gold coins on the wreck, she went to the police claiming that you had really found that chest buried ashore, which she says is her property. I went to her when I heard rumors of this, but she refused to let me use her map to search for the treasure, nor would she say why she had not sent others after it during all these years."

"Why not just find the same Indians and make a deal with them?" I asked.

"*Señor* Marx, do you really imagine I have not thought of that? But that village of Indians has long since disappeared. They stay in one place until the wild game gets scarce and the soil is too exhausted to yield good crops and then move on."

"And when they left they might have carried the treasure away with them," Clay commented.

"That may be so," Captain Argüelles replied. "I have had men digging there all month, and they have found nothing."

There was more to come: "Do you remember that bad storm we had last January? Well, soon after it was over, I took two of my men down to Punta Matancero to dive for conch—there are a lot of them on the sandy bottom near the reef—and when we were ready to get underway again, I found that my anchor was caught. I sent one of the men down to free it, who surfaced telling me it was caught on a large metal 'box.' I ordered him to secure a line to the chest, but he surfaced again reporting that the round handles were stuck to the sides and that the chest was too heavy to move and was half buried in the sand, preventing him from getting a line under it. He also said that there were three other chests, buried even deeper in the sand. The depth there was nearly fifty feet and I marked the position well. I returned with more men a week later, but either I am a bad seaman and did not take good bearings or all four chests sank into the sand, because we could not find them again." (Knowing what a good seaman Argüelles was and remembering my experiences with the *Monitor,* I was pretty sure that shifting sands had covered them.)

All this time I had sat spellbound listening to the old man, and Wally and Clay listened to my translations with the same fascination. We then agreed we would go into partnership with him, dividing any land treasure four ways (if my metal detector was instrumental in locating it) and the same with anything found in the four chests his Indian diver had located. Wally asked eagerly, "Where do we start for our first million, land treasure or sunken treasure?"

The wind had been getting steadily stronger all day. Pointing seaward at the gigantic waves breaking over the barrier reef, I answered, "Landsville, man, unless you want to get killed diving in those seas. It'll be even worse at Punta Matancero."

The four of us set off for Punta Matancero, a five-mile hike down the beach. Captain Argüelles gave us the grand tour of the point, showing us where the soldiers had dug, where his men had dug and were then digging, and where he believed the treasure chest was buried. Since we had not thought to bring the metal detector on the expedition, I knew that our chances of locating that chest were very slim. We could do little more than dig holes at random, which was exactly what a dozen of Captain Argüelles's Indians were doing.

We decided to check the cannon at the water's edge for any markings that might help us identify the wreck. It was lying upside down. "I'll turn it over for you, Marx," Clay said. But he could not budge it, nor could the three of us pushing together. Captain Argüelles, who was sitting nearby laughing at us, called over one of his Indians, who effortlessly flipped it over, using the same principal of leverage his ancestors had used to move the massive building stones for their temples. The three of us felt like fools.

We could find no markings on the badly corroded surface of the cannon, but we took measurements and photographs, and then started back for Acumal, since the brief twilight had already started. The minute the sun disappeared, millions, and I mean millions, of mosquitoes zoomed out of the bush. We ran all the way back to Acumal, collapsing exhausted into our hammocks, while the old Captain, who had set the pace, was not even out of breath.

Wally remarked, "It's that good clean living—seventy-five years without touching a cigarette or a drink."

Gale-force winds lashed the coast for the next three days, and the *Aguilucho* bobbed around on her anchor line even inside the lagoon. We hiked the five miles up to the point and back each day, digging alongside the Indians, who already had excavated an area several acres square. No treasure was found, but we did find many small items that had been washed up on the beach from the wreck; most of them were spikes and nails, which led us to believe that part of the ship had been cast ashore and disintegrated there.

By the morning of the fifth day, the gale had abated. The seas were still high, so high that Captain Argüelles would not take his much larger schooner, *Cozumel*, out to show us where the four chests had been found, but we then had the treasure bug so badly we decided to go anyway. Argüelles gave us the bearings for the chests and sent along the Indian who had spotted them.

Arriving off the reef at Punta Matancero, we dropped all three anchors, and I ordered Blackfish to keep the engine idling, just in case the anchors dragged or their lines parted. If the *Aguilucho* ever got carried on the reef in those seas, it would be the end of her. Guided by the Indian diver, we searched the sandy bottom for hours, covering a large area beyond the reef that corresponded to Argüelles's bearings, but we finally decided that the chests were still covered over with sand and that we should go after the wooden chest and other goodies on the reef.

Letting out more line on the *Aguilucho's* anchors, we dropped back closer to the wreck site, and the closer we got to where the waves were breaking over the reef, the rougher the seas became. I went down alone wearing one of the hookah units, heavy boots instead of fins so that I could walk along the bottom, and a track suit to keep from getting too many cuts and stings (the reef was covered with sharp coral, including "fire coral" which gives a nasty sting). My idea of walking on the bottom was a laugh. The powerful surge and undertow made it impossible to stand erect even with the forty pounds of weights I was wearing around my waist, and I had to crawl along on my hands and knees. Wally and Clay, with safety lines from the boat tied around their waists to prevent them being caught in the gigantic breakers, snorkled overhead, directing me to the teak-wood chest. When they realized it was located exactly where the surf was breaking, we gave up any idea of salvaging it that day, and instead they searched out other lucrative spots for me to work.

Rather than try to extract individual items embedded in the reef, I would hack out chunks of coral about the size of a basketball and throw them into a potato sack. As soon as the sack was filled, I would tie a line around it and Clay and Wally would drag it over the reef to the boat for Elías and Blackfish to haul aboard. It was like trying to mine coal from a roller coaster: every sixth or seventh wave would be larger than the others, lifting me right off the bottom and rolling me over and over toward the line of breakers closer to shore. I would crawl back to where I had been working and manage to get a few more swings of the sledge hammer at the chisel (and usually a few fingers also) before the next big wave would appear and the same would be repeated, every few minutes throughout the day. The track suit protected me from the jagged coral but not from the prickly spines of the sea urchins, which soon spotted my body.

I had already spent three hours in the water searching for the metal chests, and after four more hours on the reef I decided to call it quits for the day. It was lucky I did. I crawled back to the boat and was waiting for someone to lower a weighted line so that I could hoist myself up, when a large wave caught the *Aguilucho* amidships, rolling her over so far that the hookah compressor fell overboard, landing right next to me. What a miserable feeling—no air and loaded down with almost as many weights as a helmet diver. I held my breath, expecting someone to lower a line, and was just about to black out when Clay and Wally, who were still in the water, noticed the predicament I was in and quickly dragged me to the surface. They then retrieved the compressor and we headed back to Acumal.

At Acumal I made another dive, this time right into the hammock, sleeping straight through supper until morning. Clay and Wally were also tired, but they were more excited over the potato sacks full of goodies, and while Blackfish and Elías stripped the hookah compressor down to get it running again, Clay and Wally began breaking apart the chunks of coral. The day's find amounted to several dozen brass crucifixes, about twenty silver buckles, two brass *maravedís* (Spanish coins), plus numerous buttons, glass beads, musket balls, bone handles, pieces of leather and rope, and a large hunk of wax.

The next morning all three of us were awakened by Blackfish's shouts of *"Bonanza, bonanza!"*—flat calm. Looking seaward, I saw that he was right: there wasn't a wave in sight, not even on the barrier reef.

"What the hell are we waiting for?" Wally yelled. Each grabbing a coconut and a handful of leftover tortillas to eat on the way, we ran to the beach, swam out to the *Aguilucho,* and were underway in seconds.

I was to use one of the hookahs, with Clay and Wally alternating on the other one, while one person was to snorkel above us constantly in case anything should happen to the hookah units. Clay came down with me first, a bit leery of this unfamiliar rig that he had tried out only in the swimming pool. He had reason to be, for he had been down only ten minutes when his air was suddenly cut off. I was busily prying the lid off the teakwood chest we had found the year before, too far away to share my air with him, and Wally was back at the boat where I had sent him to get a crowbar for me. Unable to release his weight belt, Clay grabbed his air hose and pulled himself hand-over-hand the fifty yards back to the boat. Luckily, Blackfish had lashed both compressors securely to the decks that day, or Clay would have pulled the compressor into the water instead of pulling himself out. As soon as he had caught his breath on board, he set about trying to figure out why his air supply had stopped, since the compressor was still running. They pulled in the air hose to check for leaks and found instead that Elías had fed it out with a knot in it; the knot became tighter as Clay moved farther from the boat until it closed off his air completely. After unkinking the hose and threatening Elías with a slow, painful death if it ever happened again, Clay went back in the water.

In the meantime I had pried open the chest and found that it was full of ivory handles and the same pulpy black silver sulfide—but none of the treasure we had expected. We spent the rest of the day hacking out more chunks of coral, unhampered by any waves and undertow. The day's find was much the same as the previous day's, with the addition of three pewter plates and two silver spoons, all perfectly preserved and bearing hall-marks, and about twenty beautiful brass holy medals.

The *bonanza,* or flat calm, was short-lived. The next day, Punta Matancero was back to normal, with heavy swells and surf pounding the beach to hell. But we worked steadily, each day finding more goodies than the one before and confident that the next hunk of coral would contain some of the treasure we all knew *had* to be there.

Then, on the afternoon of the expedition's ninth day, Clay snorkled down to where Wally and I were working. Drawing his finger across his throat—our signal for danger—he pointed toward the *Aguilucho,* where I was surprised to see the outline of not one, but two hulls, side by side. We all surfaced and climbed aboard the *Aguilucho* to find three *Aduana* officers from Cozumel lifting the cover off the forward hatch.

"What the hell are you looking for?" I demanded.

"Dynamite and gold," was the answer.

Even though I insisted that we had neither, they searched the boat from stem to stern—finding nothing, of course. Then one of them turned to me, drew himself up to his full height of five-foot-three, patted his pistol at his side, and announced: "You are all under arrest for disturbing an archaeological site. Be so kind as to follow us back to Acumal."

I translated this, and Clay said, "Are they kidding? Those geeks wouldn't know an archaeological site if they saw one. Tell them to go to hell."

"No, man, can't hurt their pride—the shorter they are, the more trigger-happy they are. Just play it coolsville," I cautioned.

In Acumal they searched not only our hut, but all the other huts as well, even the pig pens. As soon as they were satisfied that there was no gold or dynamite around—or perhaps they were just tired—they came back to the *Aguilucho*, where we had been ordered to stay, and told us we would have to return with them to Cozumel. I agreed, but suggested they join us first for a drink and sent Elías ashore to get two bottles of rum from Captain Argüelles.

The rum did the trick, and we soon had the whole story out of them. Everyone on Cozumel was sure we were after the same "gold bars" I had supposedly located before. Someone even swore he had seen us carry several cases of dynamite aboard the *Aguilucho* before we left. A message was sent to Mexico City that we were planning to dynamite some ruins, and the minister of national monuments ordered our arrest on the charge of disturbing an archaeological site.

"That's crazy," I protested. "Why would we waste ten days pulling pieces of junk off Punta Matancero if we had a wreck full of gold bars someplace? And dynamite," I said to one of the officers, "you know damn well you were there when we left and listed every damn thing we carried aboard the boat." Afraid that I would withdraw the second bottle of rum they were working on, the three apologized profusely for the inconvenience they had caused us, protesting that they were merely following orders.

Captain Argüelles came aboard bringing a third bottle of rum and soon had them agreeing that it would be a terrible shame to cut short the vacation of these *simpático* gentlemen. It was decided that the *Aguilucho* had engine trouble, but when it was running in a few days' time, then we would return to Cozumel and immediately report to the *Aduana* office. In the meantime we were only to spearfish and not go near the wreck.

Soon after we had decided that the *Aguilucho's* engine was on the blink, another gale came up that kept all of us storm-bound in Acumal lagoon for three days. But as soon as the *Aduana* cutter disappeared over the horizon after the storm died out, we boarded the *Aguilucho,* having informed Captain Argüelles with a wink that we were going to dive for conch at Punta Matancero.

Actually we only planned to make a brief dive on the wreck site so that Wally could take a few photographs and to pick up several sacks full of goodies we had left behind. But it was so calm when we arrived at the wreck site that we could not resist the temptation. We each spent ten hours feverishly hacking out coral chunks, filling over a dozen sacks, and then we worked even more frantically during the short trip back to Acumal, extracting goodies from the coral. We were able to break apart only a few of the chunks but in them we found over two hundred of the now familiar silver buckles, two silver coins, ten onyx amulets in the shape of a closed fist (still used in Brazil today) and a sixteen-inch gold chain. We all knew that the chain was no fortune in treasure, but it was beautiful, each link as shiny and perfect as the day some goldsmith made it. We hid all the sacks and goodies below deck before anchoring at Acumal and then went ashore, making a big show of cleaning the conchs we had picked up at the end of the day.

We broke camp the next morning, thanked Captain Argüelles for all his help, and headed for Cozumel. Only a few minutes after clearing the lagoon, Wally said, "Marx, are you nuts? They're going to tear this boat to pieces the minute we reach Cozumel and we'll really catch hell when they find all those goodies." Clay then suggested that we bury them on some beach, and we agreed that was the only solution, so I changed course, heading south for a deserted cove I knew near the ruins of Xehla.

Instead of burying the dozen sacks of coral, which would have required an enormous hole, we spent hours chipping out the goodies. We were laying them all out on one of the sails for Wally to photograph, when Elías shouted, "A boat! a boat's heading this way!" Sure enough, there was a boat in sight, heading straight for the cove. We were positive it was the *Aduana* returning to check on us and flew into a panic. Wally and Clay quickly wrapped the goodies in the canvas and dragged them into the bush, while Blackfish, Elías, and I started tossing the broken bits of coral into the water as fast as we could. We were still scurrying around trying to clean up the beach when I suddenly realized that the approaching boat was not the *Aduana's* but our own *Clipper*. End of panic. Cappy stepped ashore grinning—he had been watching the whole show with binoculars—and handed me a note from one of the Joaquín brothers. The note advised me to return to Cozumel immediately, since one of the troublemakers on the island had accused the *Aduana* men of having taken a bribe from us, and had also wired the commander of the Mexican naval base at Isla Mujeres to go after us.

We decided to take this sound advice. But first we had to hide our loot. Sending the others back to the boats, Clay, Wally, and I, in good pirate fashion, carried all the goodies deep into the bush and buried them. Clay even made a treasure map with an "X," which he ripped into three pieces for each of us.

We saw no signs of a navy boat on the voyage back to Cozumel, but on reaching the pier the *Aguilucho* was given a thorough search, as we had anticipated. One of the *Aduana* men even borrowed a face mask and dove under the hull to search there as well. We were then escorted to the local *Aduana* chief, who greeted us with: "Only the gold, gentlemen. No lies, no excuses." I could not help laughing, as I translated this to Wally and Clay, who joined in also. Then the *Aduana* chief slammed his fist down on the desk. We could almost see the smoke curling out of his ears, and quickly became serious again. After several hours I think we finally convinced him that we had not taken any dynamite or recovered any gold bars, but then he came up with a new problem that really stumped us. He claimed that, gold bars or no gold bars, we could not dive on the wreck at Punta Matancero without a permit, yet he had no idea who could issue the permit, nor would he say why he had suddenly decided we needed a permit when only a few weeks before he had told me: "The sea belongs to the fish. I never heard that they demand permits to dive on some old wreck."

As soon as we left the *Aduana* office we composed a long telegram which we sent to six different government departments —the Navy, Fisheries, National Monuments, every one we could think of that might have jurisdiction over wrecks—which we followed up with letters the next day, asking if a permit was necessary, and if so, how we could obtain one. For two weeks we sat waiting for an answer until finally Clay and Wally had to return to the States. We resolved that we would get that permit somehow and then launch an even bigger expedition to Punta Matancero.

The two weeks of waiting dragged on into months, and I became more and more obsessed by the wreck. I think all of us had lost much of our original treasure fever—not that we would have thrown back a chest full of gold doubloons if we had found one, but treasure had taken second place to the wreck itself and the fantastic variety of goodies we were finding. It was impossible to look at buckles, crucifixes, spoons, amulets, and plates without wondering: Where had they come from? Where were they going? How had the ship carrying them ended up on that reef? And when? We knew that the goodies were only a few of the pieces in the giant jigsaw puzzle, and the rest still lay hidden in the reef. We had everything necessary to recover the missing pieces—equipment, know-how—everything, that is, but a permit. The most frustrating thing about our failure to make any headway with the permit was not knowing why. I knew that there was no law covering the subject. That was not surprising, since at the time no one in Mexico (or most other countries, for that matter) had even thought about old shipwrecks, much less requested permission to salvage one. But this did not seem an insurmountable obstacle to me: if there is no law, then make one. I also knew that some articles had appeared in the press soon after Wally and Clay left for the States, denouncing us as "thieves of Mexican antiquities," and as a result a permanent *Aduana* guard had been stationed at Punta Matancero. If the government believed there was a treasure and did not trust us to give the state its share, all they had to do was leave the *Aduana* guard there while we dived. Even so, I reasoned, it might not do any harm to persuade the government and the press that I was not merely a modern-day pirate, only after gold; they might change their minds if I located some important wrecks of purely historical interest that everyone knew did not have even an ounce of treasure on board.

Deciding which wreck to go after was easy: the brigantine *La Gavarra* and the caravel *San Jerónimo,* which in 1527 had carried the expeditionary force of Spanish soldiers, under Francisco de Montejo, to conquer Yucatan. Montejo, who had taken part in the earlier conquest of Mexico, decided to repeat the precaution Cortés had taken in 1519 upon reaching Veracruz: after unloading his ships he set them on fire to prevent his men from deserting and sailing away. They then had no choice but to subdue the Indians or be killed in the attempt. And most of them were killed; in fact, the Maya resisted so fiercely that Yucatan was not completely pacified until 1546, and one Maya group in what is now northern Guatemala held out until 1697.

Locating Montejo's two wrecks was not to be so easy. First I had read all the books I could find referring to his expedition.

They all agreed that Montejo, after a brief stop at Cozumel, sailed across the channel and made a landfall on the mainland coast somewhere near the city of Tulum. Failing to find a suitable anchorage there, he headed north until his pilot sighted a protected lagoon, which the ships entered through a break in the barrier reef; it was here that Montejo burned his ships and then built his first small fort ashore. The trouble was that all the books were very vague about the location of this lagoon. I then sent to Spain for photostatic copies of original documents on the conquest of Yucatan, and found two important clues. One document said that the place they first landed was still within sight of Tulum, and another stated that the brigantine *La Gavarra* drew nine feet of water. This meant that the lagoon could not be more than ten miles north of Tulum, and that they had entered an opening on the reef at least nine feet deep.

The cove at Xehla, where Clay, Wally, and I had buried the goodies from the Punta Matancero wreck, was a protected lagoon north of Tulum, and, as a matter of fact, I had accidently discovered the remains of a small fort there when I returned several months later to dig up the goodies. I even found a few buttons and other relics, which experts had identified as dating from the early sixteenth century, the time of Montejo's expedition. But I was on the wrong track there: the reef opening was too shallow for any vessel drawing over four feet to enter the cove. (As it turned out, this fort was Montejo's, but it was the second one he built as he worked his way north along the coast, and not the first.)

Ever since my hunch about the curious name of Punta Matancero had paid off, I had taken to studying charts more carefully in search of other place names that might lead me to wrecks. There were two points with intriguing names—Punta Cadena and Punta Soliman—each of them forming the extreme end of a crescent-shaped lagoon located about five miles north of Tulum. I knew how Punta Cadena ("Chain Point") got its name: a large vessel, which had run aground there about fifty years before and been refloated, had lost its huge anchor chain which was still lying on the bottom. But Punta Soliman was something else again. I could not find any word resembling "Soliman" in any Maya–Spanish dictionary, nor did it seem likely that a spot in Yucatan would be named after the sixteenth-century Turkish Sultan, Soliman (Suleiman) the Magnificent. The mystery was finally solved when copies of old charts of Yucatan I had sent for from Spain finally arrived. Montejo had named the site of his first fort after his birthplace in Spain, Salamanca, but over the centuries this name had been changed —mainly because of cartographers' spelling mistakes—to Soliman.

I was almost certain then that I had located the site, which I also noticed on modern charts was one of the few places along the coast where a vessel drawing nine feet of water could get over or through the reef. And there was no doubt left after I made a short trip to Punta Soliman. Back in the bush not far from shore I found the crumbled ruins of another small Spanish fort: Montejo's Fort Salamanca.

I knew that any unauthorized wreck-hunting could easily touch off another commotion in the press (this was about six months after Wally and Clay had left, and the heat had died down somewhat, but the *Aduana* guard was still posted at Punta Matancero). Luckily I was able to interest the governor of Quintana Roo in my project, and he gave me written permission to search for Montejo's wrecks, although any excavation had to be authorized from Mexico City. But now that I had pinpointed the site and obtained the permission, I could not find the wrecks. I realized that Montejo would have stripped the ships of cannons and other useful items for his fort before setting them on fire, but he could not remove everything. Yet I made at least a dozen trips, each time bringing large groups of tourists to snorkel up and down the lagoon with me, without finding the slightest sign of a wreck.

I might never have found the Montejo's wrecks without the help of a "mermaid." One afternoon, after spending the whole

day searching for the wrecks inside the lagoon, I decided to shoot
some fish to take back to the hotel. I was snorkeling along the
outside of the barrier reef when I sensed something big nearby. I
spun around warily in a slow circle and nearly had a heart attack
when I saw a huge beast about the size of a whale (well, at least
twenty feet long) swimming toward me. It stopped a short
distance away and hung there motionless staring at me. It looked
like a caricature of a fat old battle-axe with a round whiskery
face, huge breasts, and two stumpy little arms—only it had no
legs.

Not realizing that the beast was a harmless manatee or sea
cow—an aquatic mammal that many believe gave rise to the old
sailors' legends about mermaids—I swam to the skiff Blackfish
was rowing alongside and quickly exchanged my small speargun
for a big bazooka I had for killing sharks and large jewfish. I
returned to the still motionless monster, and placing the end of
the speargun only inches from its head, pulled the trigger,
expecting all hell to break loose. Instead the spear slowly fell out
of the gun, which in my excitement I had forgotten to load, slid
through the manatee's thick whiskers and landed on the sea
floor. The manatee then made a leisurely turn and, flipping its
tail like a porpoise, started off down the reef. I dropped my gun
and took after the monster, losing sight of it quite often but
picking up the trail again by a strange noise it made that
sounded like human laughter.

I must have gone about two miles when the "mermaid"
stopped, turned around giving me a silly grin, and then disappeared into a large underwater cave, from which I could feel a
cold current of fresh water coming out. Taking a big gulp of air,
I followed. The cave, which was full of sardines and large tarpon
hanging in the dark recesses, turned out to be a long tunnel.
Seeing daylight ahead, I raced forward and surfaced in a beautiful fresh-water pond completely surrounded by mangroves,
which were covered with orchids and brightly colored parrots.

I had lost sight of the "mermaid," but sticking my head

underwater again, I heard its "he-he-he-he" and soon found it, along with two other smaller ones. By this time I had decided that the species, whatever it was, was harmless. I swam up to the smallest one and gingerly poked its big spongy head. This made all three of them start laughing: maybe I looked as funny to them as they did to me.

It suddenly dawned on me that Blackfish had seen me enter that cave, or tunnel, more than ten minutes ago and would have decided my number had finally come up. I surfaced to yell to him but the parrots were squawking so loudly I could hardly hear my own voice. I swam back to the cave, escorted by my three jolly friends who were still laughing away, and surfaced outside to find Blackfish kneeling in the bottom of the skiff, wringing his hands and praying for my departed black soul. He was so relieved—and startled—to see me that he nearly fell overboard.

We rowed back to the barrier reef off Punta Soliman to retrieve the speargun I had dropped. When I finally located it, I found that the line had tangled around something on the bottom. It turned out to be a five-fluked anchor shaped like a grappling hook, which I pulled up on the *Aguilucho,* photographed, and then dropped overboard again, since I had promised only to search and not to recover anything.

I knew that this type of anchor was very old, possibly even from Montejo's time. But if it was from Montejo's wrecks, what was it doing on the *outside* of the barrier reef? Returning to the same site, this time with an aqualung, I found spikes, nails, other badly corroded (and unidentifiable) pieces of iron, and many ceramic potsherds, all buried in the coral near the anchor. Then about a hundred yards away I found another wreck, and I knew that all my persistence had finally paid off; for included among the spikes and potsherds and other goodies covering the bottom were small pieces of charred wood.

These had to be Montejo's wrecks, and if I had any lingering doubts, they were soon dispelled. Several experts in

Europe identified my photos of the anchor as being a type used on small vessels in Montejo's time; John Goggin dated some of the ceramic potsherds I sent him as 1500–1540; and a radiocarbon analysis of a piece of the wood placed it as approximately 450 years old.

What had happened—and what I should have figured out long before when I could not find the wrecks inside the reefs—was that both vessels were inside the lagoon when they were set on fire, but they were carried onto the reef either by an outgoing tide or offshore breeze. After burning to their waterlines they eventually broke up in the surf, and the goodies washed down off the reef into the deeper water.

My plan to change the image of "Bob Marx, *thief* of Mexican antiquities" to one of "Bob Marx, *discoverer* of Mexican antiquities" did not exactly backfire—it just fizzled out. I reported my discovery of the Montejo wrecks to the *Aduana,* the police, and to several government departments, but no one seemed particularly interested. In the meantime we were still getting exactly nowhere with our application for a permit to salvage the wreck at Punta Matancero. After eight months had passed without a reply to our inquiries, Clay wrote a detailed letter to the U.S. Ambassador to Mexico, Robert Hill, whom I had met at Cozumel and taught to skin dive. Ambassador Hill placed the matter in the hands of Consul A. B. Horn, who went to a great amount of effort to help us. He investigated all the possibly relevant Mexican laws and even went personally to the different government departments we had written to, but the only answer he could get was that the matter was still being considered.

I was convinced that the problem was a simple one of bureaucratic inefficiency, and it was some consolation to think of all the dusty pending files in Mexico City, in Washington, London, Moscow—all over the world—bulging with petitions like ours that were "under consideration."

But I was wrong. The main problem was that we were not the only ones interested in salvaging the Punta Matancero wreck. Returning to the hotel after a diving trip one evening around the beginning of April 1959, I was told that someone was waiting to see me in my room. There I found a well-dressed, middle-aged man closely examining one of the piles of goodies from the wreck that I had strewn all over the room. I recognized him immediately from Mexican newspaper photos: Pablo Bush Romero, a wealthy Mexican businessman who among other activities had organized the first diving club in Mexico, CEDAM (Club de Exploraciones y Deportes Acuáticos de Mexico). During the same month of June 1958, when Wally, Clay, and I had mounted our short-lived expedition to Punta Matancero, Bush and a handful of divers were carrying out a similar one in Veracruz in search of the wrecks Cortes had burned in 1519.

Without any preliminary, Bush began in perfect English: "Mr. Marx, you are no doubt aware that you could be deported within twenty-four hours for having these artifacts in your possession." He then thrust an official-looking piece of paper into my hand, which verified his statement. Signed by the president of Mexico, it authorized Bush to take any measures he saw fit to prevent foreigners from salvaging wrecks in territorial waters of Mexico.

"But I have no wish to deport you," he continued. "My organization, CEDAM, has obtained official permission to excavate the wreck you discovered at Punta Matancero. I am organizing a large-scale expedition and would be pleased if you would join us, since your experience and skill would be very valuable."

"And just why the hell should I help you or even waste my time talking to you?" I broke in.

"No reason, except that we have the exclusive franchise on Punta Matancero, and either you dive with us or you do not dive at all." Seeing that my face was turning a slow scarlet, he prudently walked out of the room, but stopped outside the door and said: "I will wait for your answer, which I'm sure will be yes."

I was so damned furious that I could have bitten a nail in

two, but after finally calming down, with the aid of several glasses of rum, I wrote to Clay and Wally about the encounter, swearing that I would quit diving and become a Jesuit sooner than dive with that arrogant so-and-so. At first they agreed, but when Consul Horn wrote to us confirming the fact that CEDAM had obtained the franchise on our wreck, we decided to reconsider. As Bush had indicated, we either had to dive with him or not at all, and we were too obsessed with the wreck to let pride keep us away from Punta Matancero. I wrote to Bush, accepting his invitation, but on one condition. I had put a lot of money, work, and time into that wreck and did not intend to invest any more without getting something in return, which would be shared with Wally and Clay too. Much to my surprise, Bush replied, offering me one-half of all the artifacts recovered, except those declared of "intrinsic archaeological value" by the Mexican government.

I thought this offer too good to be true, but soon afterward Bush flew down to visit me again and verified the offer in person. He stayed for several days, during which time we established a cordial friendship and talked over the plans for a large expedition to begin in July, which he wanted Clay, Wally, and me to join.

Bush must really be given credit as a very capable organizer. His CEDAM expedition was a full-scale military maneuver in comparison to our little jaunt the year before. He got a helicopter on loan from the Mexican navy; a C-82 (Flying Boxcar) from PEMEX, the government-owned petroleum company; and jeeps, trucks, generators, compressors, tents, and tons of equipment and supplies from private donors. He even persuaded an American banker from Tennessee, George Clark, to loan his large yacht *Pinch-Hitter* for the duration of the expedition.

Bush had one fault, however: he had too many friends, and the laws of Mexican hospitality demand that you have "open house," even, I suppose on an expedition. At times during the expedition we had as many as two hundred people at the camp—film stars, government officials, television and radio personalities, members of the press, or just plain friends—but less than thirty were divers who actually worked on the wreck, and of these, only three or four really did much of the actual excavation.

On July 15, Pablo arrived at Cozumel with the first wave of divers and "camp followers," and the Joaquín brothers threw a big welcoming fiesta at the hotel. The party was in full swing, and Pablo and I were discussing plans, when someone handed him a telegram. His face turned white. "Oh my God, this couldn't happen," he said, and handed me the telegram. The "Flying Boxcar" had been forced to make a crash landing in the jungle near Campeche after two of its engines conked out. The four members of the crew were unhurt, but the whole plane had exploded soon after they scrambled free, and the cargo was a total loss.

I was not particularly worried about the jeeps and other vehicles, but one item—a specially built, high-speed air compressor that could fill an aqualung tank in less than three minutes—was a serious loss. My two small compressors, which took an hour to fill an aqualung tank, even if run twenty-four hours a day could not meet the demands of the expedition, because all the Mexican divers—unlike Wally, Clay, and myself, who preferred hookahs—had elected to use aqualungs. I rushed off to Isla Mujeres to borrow Dr. Lima's high-speed air compressor, which was very similar to the one lost in the plane accident, while Pablo dispatched the rest of the expedition's armada (which totaled seven vessels in all), full of equipment and supplies, along with twenty of the Mexican divers and fifty camp followers, to set up camp at Acumal.

I expected to find Wally and Clay waiting when I returned with the compressor the next day, but they were stranded in Mérida unable to get plane seats, and in desperation they finally chartered a plane to take them to Cozumel, arriving on July 18. With them they brought two metal detectors, one for land and

one for underwater, that a good friend of mine, John Bender of
Houston, Texas, had designed and built for us to use on the
expedition. The detectors I had been expecting, but not the
detector-operator—an eighteen-year-old kid named Jon Kalb.
Bender, finding it too difficult to explain the operation of both
detectors in writing, had given a quick course of instruction to
his next-door neighbor's son and sent him down to operate them
for us. I was furious. "What does Bender think I am, a damned
baby-sitter?" I shouted at Clay. But young Kalb, or "Momo," as I
later labeled him, turned out to be the hardest worker in the
camp. His job was land treasure-hunting, and by the end of the
expedition he had almost single-handedly demolished the beach
at Punta Matancero.

The following morning the American contingent, which
also included two diving friends from East Lansing, Michigan,
Bob Allen and John Frizzle, and the late-arriving Mexican
expeditioneers boarded the *Pinch-Hitter* for the fast trip across to
Acumal. On the way over, Wally, Clay, and I discussed the final
plans with Pablo, who had put me in charge of all diving and
salvage operations, since he would have to spend most of his time
on Cozumel in the difficult task of logistics and humoring the
press.

Acumal was transformed: tents, pyramids of aqualung tanks
and other diving gear, people scurrying around the beach. Fortunately we had a reservation at the "Acumal Hilton," the same
hut we had used the year before, but which since had had walls
of thatch built on it to keep out the pigs and other unwanted
guests.

It was too late to do any diving by the time we got settled
and acquainted with the other expedition members, but Wally
came up with the brilliant idea of bringing the cannon that was
lying on the beach at Punta Matancero back to Acumal to
decorate the campsite. Captain Argüelles had procured an
antique truck, which he lent us, and with half the camp loaded
in the back (two fell off on the way) we crashed through the

coconut grove to Punta Matancero. It took eighteen men to lift the 1,500-pound cannon, and after we finally had it aboard the overheated truck, whose radiator was still sending up clouds of steam, the driver announced that the engine would not start. We spent the rest of the afternoon pushing the truck the five miles back to camp.

That night everyone gathered around a big bonfire we made on the beach, and Pablo Bush gave a pep talk, explaining the objectives and the rules of the expedition. Then Wally, Clay, and I took over to give a briefing on the wreck site and the method we would use to work it. The site was really the whole reef, 250 yards long by 60 yards wide, and Clay and I had agreed that the first step should be a preliminary survey. Flag markers would be set up on shore, and a series of buoys laid out in a grid pattern covering the site. The divers, spread out in a long line at right angles to the beach, would snorkel along the reef, and as soon as anyone spotted something of particular interest, he would signal for Clay to mark the area on a big chart he had prepared.

We started our survey the next morning. A flotilla of five boats and numerous skiffs carried the divers (who numbered about thirty in total—twenty from CEDAM, the American contingent, and a few local divers from Cozumel I had invited along) to Punta Matancero. The shore markers had been set, and the buoys laid out, and the divers started snorkeling down along the reef. Everything went well for a few minutes. Then the Mexican naval lieutenant who was rowing Clay and his master chart in a skiff ventured too close to shore, and a wave swamped them. The skiff was completely full of water but the lieutenant, who could not swim, kept on trying to row (which drove most of us to fits of laughter) until some of the divers rescued him. That was the end of our carefully planned mapping operation, since Clay's chart had been lost in the breakers.

It was also the end of any semblance of order in the diving.

Everyone started scurrying around the reef looking for goodies to pry loose from the coral. All they could do was snorkel, since we had no tanks full of air (the high-speed compressor I had borrowed needed a fan belt), and only one of the hookahs was working, but one of the divers from Cozumel, Ramón Zapata, made a very interesting discovery, a large double-transomed crucifix, which closely resembled a Cross of Lorraine. Months later I discovered from research in Washington that this type of crucifix is known as a "Caravaca Cross" and was often carried on Spanish vessels in the old days, believed to have special protective powers against storms at sea.

On the way back to Acumal I went over to congratulate Ramón, who, instead of being pleased with his discovery, seemed dejected.

"Roberto," he said, "I feel very stupid. This morning when we were helping you survey the wreck I saw something strange —a large bronze plaque with writing on it. I was trying to signal you when just at that moment the skiff was swamped. I left the spot and went to help that naval officer who appeared unable to swim. Others reached him first, so I went back but I searched all day and even asked some others to help and I could not find that plaque again. But I know I didn't just imagine it."

I promised him that we would all search for it the next morning; maybe it was the ship's name plate and we would finally know the identity of the wreck.

I kept my promise—it was too rough the next day to work close to shore anyway—and we spent the entire day searching the sandy bottom to seaward of the reef, where Ramón claimed he had spotted the plaque. All we found was one pile of cannonballs, but Ramón was so obsessed with finding the plaque, probably because of the terrible ribbing the others gave him, that he spent every available moment during the rest of the expedition in the attempt. I estimate that, between him and the others whose help he enlisted, four hundred diving hours were spent searching for that plaque, which must have been swallowed up by the sand like Captain Argüelles' four metal chests.

One could hardly say that the expedition had gotten off to a roaring start. One diving day was wasted in a fruitless search for Ramón's plaque, the previous day had not been much better, and the following one, July 22, was a total loss—a sea so rough that we could not even think of taking the boats out through the narrow cut in the Acumal reef. To top it all off, the more than sixty people in the camp, only half of whom were divers, were consuming food at a phenomenal rate, and we were almost out of supplies. Around noon that day the *Pinch-Hitter* appeared off Acumal; Bush had brought over badly needed food stores, but it was too rough for the *Pinch-Hitter* to attempt to enter through the reef, nor could we get a boat or skiff out to it. In the end one of the Mexican divers, Alfonso Arnold, and I swam out to the *Pinch-Hitter* and returned with only the badly needed flybelt for the high-speed air compressor and a magneto for one of my hookah units. Alfonso and his brother Reggie soon had both compressors repaired and by evening had all the fifty or so aqualung tanks filled and ready to go.

It was still rough the next morning but nothing could have kept the divers out of the water now that they finally had full tanks. After a quick breakfast of muddy coffee and soggy, left-over fried fish we headed for the wreck site. I assigned different working areas to each boatload of divers, but within minutes after we dropped anchor, the reef looked like Grand Central Station at rush hour. Divers were climbing all over each other, knocking masks off and fighting for crowbars, which were in short supply, in their eagerness to hack out goodies. After his harrowing experience the year before, Clay decided against using a hookah again, and Wally, the expedition's photographer, required unrestricted maneuverability so that he could roam freely around the entire wreck site, so I asked Al Arnold, the best of the Mexican divers, if he would like to use the other hookah unit.

Al and I worked side by side that day, spending six of our eight hours underwater hacking three cannons and two anchors loose from their coral beds. Pablo had asked us to raise them in order to supply some good action photos that the more than thirty members of the press on Cozumel were hounding him for. The other two hours we spent in a very tedious, delicate operation: one of the cannons, we discovered,was resting partially on four intact green wine bottles (how this had happened is still a mystery), which we had to extract without letting the cannon, which weighed nearly a ton, roll over and crush both us and the bottles. There must be some affinity between iron cannons and glass, for under another one we discovered a huge pile of colored plate glass, probably destined for some cathedral windows, but this glass was very brittle and we were unable to recover any entire sheets.

This first day of real diving separated the sheep from the goats. A lot of nonsense was written in the press about Mexican–American rivalry during the expedition, but none of it was true. If there was any split into factions, it was between the workers and nonworkers. Wally, whom I had asked to keep an eye on everyone as he cruised around the reef taking photographs that day, reported that almost everyone had lost interest after one hour of diving, preferring to sun themselves on deck. That left for the rest of the day—and the rest of the expedition—a small group of lunatics, who somehow enjoyed spending eight hours a day being tossed around on a reef and hacking away at cement-hard coral (anyone paid to do it would have gone on strike after five minutes): Al and Reggie Arnold, Pete García, and Ramón Zapata—even though all of his efforts were in searching for his blasted bronze plaque—from the Mexican contingent; and Wally, Clay, Bob Allen, John Frizzle, and myself from the American contingent. Wally probably worked harder than anyone. He had to be everywhere at once, photographing, keeping tabs on the divers, especially the hookah divers, Al and me, whom he saved from drowning on several occasions, as well as doing a lot of digging.

Then there was our young Texan friend, Momo, who was in seventh heaven, even though everyone else looked upon his job as the equivalent of an assignment in the Siberian salt mines. I put him in charge of a digging party on the beach to continue searching for that rumored buried treasure. Working in temperatures of over 100 degrees and covered with just about every known insect of the tropics, he and his team proceeded to re-excavate the beach at Punta Matancero, sifting every shovel-full of sand and even smashing the heavy rocks. Aside from the usual items found there already—nails and buttons and potsherds—they found two badly rusted muskets and a sword handle with stones that looked like rubies, but no chests of gold coins. Momo soon picked up a smattering of Spanish words most frequently used in the camp, and often the men in the boats offshore would break out laughing, when through the roar of the surf they would hear Momo cussing out his diggers, and swearing he would feed them to the sharks if they did not work harder.

The main problem the small Mexican-American group of workers had was the nonworkers, who continually got in the way and seemed to develop enormous appetites from sitting around and doing nothing at all. Some evenings we would get back to Acumal hungry enough to eat half a steer each, only to find that there was nothing left but a small amount of fish someone had speared. Even when the *Pinch-Hitter* was able to get through with supplies, it always seemed that the nondivers managed to get in the chow line first.

Around the middle of the expedition's first week, the *Pinch-Hitter* arrived with forty more "camp-followers," none of them divers of course, and each time it returned it brought more and more of these worthless additions to the expedition. Finally I was forced to have a showdown with Pablo over the matter. I explained about the food crisis and warned him that most of the divers who were working were threatening to call a strike if something wasn't done to make their camp life a bit more pleasant. Finally agreeing that the "open house" policy had to go, he carried back over three-fourths of the people then in camp and promised to keep others from arriving. That was the turning point. We still had many visitors after that, but they came for brief, half-day trips and didn't really get in the way. So that by the end of the first week there were less than fifteen persons in camp.

Even before that, most of the expeditioners, except the real hard-core divers—Al, Reggie, Pete, Ramón, Clay, Wally, Bob Allen, John Frizzle, and myself—had stopped bothering to go to Punta Matancero even for the ride, and we were able to get along well with only my *Aguilucho* as diving tender. The remaining days of the first week were spent mostly in raising the three cannons and two anchors for the "action shots" the press were demanding from Pablo. Captain Argüelles lent his large schooner *Cozumel* for this operation, a long and arduous job, since each piece had to be hauled up slowly by hand. We had no chains, only hemp line, which snapped on two occasions, sending a cannon crashing down to the reef again, although luckily none of the divers was in the way.

On the first day of our second diving week we awoke to find the sea flat calm, and we were able to get in a record day of digging, averaging more than ten sacks of goody-laden coral for each diver. Some areas were more lucrative to dig in than others, but it was almost impossible to find anywhere on the reef that didn't have something buried under the coral. Al and I tried to establish exactly how deep under the coral the goodies extended, and dug down six feet in some places without reaching the bottom of the mother lode. As soon as we reached camp each evening, everyone set to work on the beach, breaking apart the day's haul of coral chunks. Metal items were cleaned further in a mild muriatic acid solution, while organic materials, such as wood, leather, rope, bone, and horn, were coated with paraffin to await preservation. After making a full inventory, I placed all the things in a large chest guarded by Pablo Bush's personal bodyguard, who had been left at the camp for that purpose; then either the *Pinch-Hitter* or the helicopter would arrive to take them back to Cozumel, where Pablo had set up a storeroom and a makeshift preservation lab.

Even though it was unusually flat calm all that second week, there were the inevitable mishaps that always seem to accompany diving expeditions. Al and I were the most accident-prone, or rather the hookah units we used were; they were kept running from eight to ten hours daily, often covered with salt-water spray, and periodically went on strike. The usual problem was the fan belts, which would fly off into the water, and the diver's air supply would stop until someone from the boat dove in, recovered the belt, and got the compressor working again. During this interval, whoever was without air would rush over to the other hookah user and share his, passing the mouthpiece back and forth. This was such a frequent occurrence that if an hour went by without either my air cutting off or Al's, we would begin to worry. However on four occasions that week, twice for each of us, when our air stopped we could not find the other hookah diver and had to rush over to the *Aguilucho* at breakneck speed and climb up the anchor line to the surface until the compressor was running again. Al and I each blacked out once from lack of oxygen, unable to reach the anchor line quickly enough, but each time Wally was on the spot to pull us out of the water.

No one really spent much time worrying about the hazards or the aching muscles. Each day the pile of goodies recovered was larger than the last. The supply of spoons, buckles, holy medals, and crucifixes seemed inexhaustible. These were the standard items, so familiar that we would simply toss them on the pile without comment, and our excitement was reserved for the unusual discoveries: one day it was paper needle packages with the manufacturer's name (a Johanes Esser von Ach from Aschen, Germany) still legible; another, it was pewter plates with English hallmarks; and still another, it was the lead seal of a French merchant. Our original theory about the identity of the wreck, that it was a Spanish ship, had been influenced by the vast quantity of crucifixes and holy medals, but after we started to find so many English items, we began to wonder if it could have been an English ship smuggling in a cargo to Spain's colonies or maybe a French ship carrying English products. Each day we renewed the search, hoping for the scrap of evidence that would point conclusively to the identity of the ship.

Al even found some of the Punta Matancero "treasure": about midway through the second week he surfaced with a bunch of gold leaf, weighing in total six pounds, which probably had been destined for gilding a church altar. A chest full of gold *escudos* could not have created more problems. In fact a rumor started shortly after we shipped the find off to Cozumel that we had recovered 300 kilos (660 pounds) of gold leaf. This rumor in turn set off another rumor (also unknown to us at first) that a group of Castroite raiders working out of a secret base in the Quintana Roo jungle was planning to attack our camp and steal the half-million dollars' worth of gold to help finance Castro's guerrilla war against Batista.

When this rumor reached Pablo Bush in Cozumel he immediately called for military protection from the Mexican government, and you have to hand it to Pablo, he always gets results: two days later we had two Mexican Navy corvettes cruising off Acumal, several helicopters for air reconnaissance, and fifty marines landed ashore to guard the camp. The Castroite raiders never appeared, but two of our divers were almost killed when they made nocturnal visits into the bush to answer a call of nature, and the marines, thinking they were raiders, opened fire on them. It is a miracle there were no fatal accidents, since all the expeditioners were issued loaded pistols as an added safeguard, and they were constantly competing for the fastest draw.

The third week of diving began with rough weather again. But in spite of the bad diving conditions we made excellent finds the first day: Wally found the only silver fork and serving platter of the whole expedition; Reggie came up with three Spanish silver coins and part of a human skull with hair still on it; Al found a gold chain with several quartz gems attached and five Spanish coins, two gold and three silver; and I found three silver spoons and a small, inch-high gold crucifix.

Al and I had a running bet (loser to stand winner to a good healthy drunk) over which one would make the best find of the expedition. So far he was way ahead with his six pounds of gold leaf, but the next morning I announced that this was the day I would beat Al. Within the first hour I had recovered two small gold bells, but Al was keeping pace, finding two silver plates and another gold coin within the same period. Even my boatmen, Elías, got into the act that day; Wally taught him how to use an aqualung and he was on the bottom hacking away at the coral with the rest of us.

After I had been working for about six hours, I began to feel dizzy, but I could not go topside because I had seen a small glint of gold sticking out of the coral and was engaged in the delicate job of extracting it. It was gold, a perfectly preserved gold pocket watch, and when we opened it later we found the name of the maker, "William Webster Exchange Alley London," engraved inside. Also inside were several pieces of English newspaper, cut to fit neatly between the watch and the watch case, which were still dry and perfectly legible. Back in Cozumel Al declared that I had won the bet. I argued that his six pounds of gold leaf was the better find, and in the end we called it a draw and got drunk together.

All in all, that was the most productive diving day of the expedition, but unfortunately it was also to be the last. As soon as I had extracted the gold watch and jubilantly shown it to Al, I climbed aboard the *Aguilucho,* so dizzy I could hardly get up the anchor line, and when I reached the deck I began to retch violently. Clay summoned everyone else on board, and we rushed back to Acumal, where they carried me, half delirious, to a cot in the hut. Someone radioed the expedition's doctor at

Cozumel, and within half an hour a helicopter arrived with the doctor to take me back to Cozumel. Everyone at the camp thought I had the bends, but the doctor ruled this out, since the maximum depth I had been working in—thirty feet—was too shallow, and diagnosed malaria instead. Later other doctors claimed it was plain exhaustion; I was already weakened by amoebic dysentery, and the eight to ten hours of hard labor each day had finished the job. Whatever it was, I felt like hell.

Al and some of the other divers had put in almost as many hours underwater as I. They did not have dysentery, but the daily menu at Acumal was enough to weaken anyone without any outside help, and the doctor was convinced that the others were in danger of collapsing also. The weather had been getting rougher by the day, anyway, so that Pablo decided to call the expedition to an end, and the following day the Navy corvettes brought back the rest of the men.

After a few days the doctor reluctantly let me get out of bed, figuring that I was not getting much rest anyway: I had had a constant stream of visitors, which even included a four-piece band Al and Reggie brought to cheer me up—that is, until the doctor arrived and threw them out. I went to the storehouse-laboratory Pablo Bush had set up and found Wally and Clay busy cataloging and photographing all the goodies. I could hardly believe my eyes when I saw exactly how much we had recovered. In total there were about 50,000 items, excluding pins, needles, and the thousands of beads and paste emeralds and diamonds. Wherever the ship had been heading, there must have been an insatiable market for trinkets. We had recovered over 5,000 crucifixes; 6,000 belt and shoe buckles; 4,000 buttons; 2,000 knife handles; and several thousand pieces of costume jewelry such as earrings, rings, necklaces, cufflinks, and bracelets; besides the bottles, glasses, plates, spoons, forks, and other goodies mentioned earlier. Added to these were several thousand musketballs, cannon balls, thimbles, flints, keys, tools, hinges, mirrors, two pairs of gold-rimmed eyeglasses, and countless other items. A few weeks later, Mendel Peterson, Curator of Armed Forces History at the Smithsonian Institution, flew down to Mexico City, where the goodies were on display, and after examining them, declared that our wreck was "the richest merchant ship and most important marine archaeological discovery yet made in the Western Hemisphere." Yet, even though the CEDAM expedition had produced at least fifty times more goodies than all my previous dives there, I knew the reef was far from being cleaned out. The ship must have been stuffed to the gunwales with cargo—no wonder they couldn't pull her off when she ran aground.

We had found no real treasure other than the gold leaf, the watch, the bells, and a few coins, but the haul was far from valueless. I estimated that the goodies, if sold to antique shops and museums, would bring in between $100,000 and $200,000 and I already had big plans for what I would do with my share. I would build a boat specially designed for underwater exploration and salvage to cruise the Caribbean in search of old shipwrecks, and when I told Clay and Wally of my plans they both said that instead of my giving them a part of my half of the goodies, they preferred to go into partnership in my salvage company.

Clay convinced me that I should go up to Washington, while I waited for my share of the loot, and help him in the research to identify our wreck. Two weeks after he, Wally, and all the other expedition members had gone, I sadly said goodbye to Cozumel, which had been my home for three wonderful years. Half the islanders went to the airport to see me off, and when Cappy, Elías, Blackfish, and all my other crew members stood around with tears in their eyes, giving me farewell *abrazos,* I had a hard time holding back the tears myself. But I had big plans.

In less than a week my big plans for a special salvage boat went suddenly down the drain. Pablo Bush came up to Washington also, with Mendel Peterson, and on the last day of his stay, while we were driving him to the airport, he announced that the Mexican government had just notified him that all the artifacts recovered had been declared of "intrinsic archaeological value." In plain words, I was not to get more than the one solitary crucifix that every expedition member had been given as a souvenir.

I was willing to concede that some of the items, like the gold watch, were unique, and that the Mexican government would naturally want to keep them for permanent display (I also thought it would be nice if I were paid half the value of at least the unique items I had found personally, but that was something else again). What I failed to see was how all the crucifixes, for example, exactly identical except for a few dozen, could be declared of intrinsic archaeological value. Were they planning to display all five thousand of them? Pablo swore that he would fight to see that I got my share or at least a part of it, but that was one fight that Pablo did not win. I never did receive any of the goodies, except a few crucifixes and buckles that I later bought in an antique shop in New York. How they got there is anyone's guess.

There was still one last item of business to clear up with the Punta Matancero wreck: its identity. I still had an idea it was Spanish, mainly because of the large number of Roman Catholic artifacts it had carried. But Mendel Peterson insisted it was English, since most of the other artifacts seemed to be of English manufacture. The English merchants, he argued, even though Protestant, would have thought nothing of trading in Catholic religious articles, as long as they brought them a fat profit.

Peterson may have been correct about the trading habits of English merchants, but he was wrong about the identity of the ship. I started off with the only available evidence, the goodies recovered, and spent weeks in the Library of Congress trying to trace their origin. Some, like the watch and hallmarked pewter plates were definitely English, but others, as it turned out, were not: they came from a variety of European countries, mainly Spain. This still did not prove anything one way or another, although we were able to narrow down the date of the wreck to the period 1720–1750. Then one day I finally hit pay dirt. I was working in the library of the Franciscan Institute of Latin American Studies under the supervision of Father Lino Gómez Canedo, a Spanish member of the order, who suggested that I read every issue of the Mexican newspaper, *La Gaceta de Mexico*, from 1720–1750, in which the shipwreck might have been published. I thought I was dreaming when on the front page of the February 17, 1736, issue I read a brief notice reporting that a Spanish ship was due to return to Spain in the next convoy, and the name of the vessel was *El Matancero*. In another issue, of 1737, the same vessel was mentioned as being in Havana, and in 1738 it was reported returning to Spain again. Then *El Matancero* disappeared from the *Gaceta*. There was no report of its loss, even though I covered all the issues up to 1770, but I knew it was our wreck. Punta Matancero had not been named because of a slaughter or massacre after all, and the ship itself, I found out later, was named after the place where it had been built, Matanzas, Cuba.

Father Lino suggested I continue my research in the Archives of the Indies in Seville, Spain, where over fifteen million original documents are stored relating to Spain's former colonies in America. Instead, Clay was able to persuade the *Saturday Evening Post* to send him over, and although he was unable to read Spanish (let alone decipher old Spanish documents), he directed the work of professional researchers there and came up with the full story of *El Matancero*. He returned to the United States with microfilm copies of the account of the wreck and subsequent salvage attempts, of courts-martial held to try the ship's officers for negligence, and finally all the cargo manifests, which corresponded exactly to what we had found on the site, except for a few items unaccounted for, which were probably contraband.

El Matancero, or *Nuestra Señora de los Milagros* ("Our Lady of the Miracles"—all Spanish ships had a formal religious

name or saint's name, plus a nickname) was a Spanish merchant
vessel of 270 tons. She was pretty far off course, on her voyage
from Cadiz, Spain, to Veracruz, when shortly before dawn on
February 22, 1741, she ran aground off the deserted coast of
what is now Quintana Roo. Navigation in those days was not a
very precise science, and the pilots had probably miscalculated
the ship's position, and on a dark night with heavy seas running,
only a line of white breakers marks that low-lying coast. All but
three of the sixty-nine passengers, officers, and crew reached the
shore safely. A small group set out for help, but when two
salvage vessels returned several weeks later all the rest of the
survivors had set out overland; some of them turned up in
Campeche (on the other side of the peninsula) during the next
few months, but the rest were probably killed by Indians.

We also found that we were not the first to attempt
salvaging *El Matancero:* many unauthorized salvagers, as well as
the official vessels, sent out from Campeche, picked over the
wreck before she finally broke apart completely in the surf. Then
the waves scattered the rest of the cargo all over the reef, which
eventually swallowed it up in a coral grave, while the sea teredos
went to work on the broken hull, until all that remained visible
were the large heavy cannon and anchors, which probably settled
not far from where the ship had run aground.

Was there any treasure on *El Matancero?* Not according to
the documents Clay brought back from Seville. But sometime in
1962, while I was searching for data on other shipwrecks in the
Archives of the Indies, I accidentally came across a new one
pertaining to *El Matancero* (a very frequent occurrence in that
maze of uncatalogued manuscripts). It was the testimony of one
of the survivors, who arrived at Campeche three full months
after the salvaged vessels had returned, having trekked alone all
the way across the peninsula. He declared that among the many
things washed ashore from the ship were two chests, one full of
gold and silver coins and the other full of gold chalices and other
religious objects. Their owner, a Spanish merchant, had stayed

behind with the declarant after the remaining survivors had set off overland, unwilling to leave his treasure behind. Finally the declarant had decided no help was coming and had left also. No trace of either the treasure or its owner had been found by the returning rescuers, and the survivor was certain that the merchant had dragged the heavy chests into the bush behind the shore and buried them there. But this was never proved, since the merchant never appeared in Campeche or anywhere else.

So perhaps Captain Argüelles's tale of the Indians and the treasure chest of Punta Matancero was true, after all!

Chapter
Six
•
Ghost
Wrecks
of the
Caribbean
◆

Clay had returned from his fruitful trip to Seville with "document fever," which he tried to communicate to me: "Man, there are millions of documents on shipwrecks in those archives. You'd go out of your mind."

I still had plans for salvaging wrecks in the Caribbean—although on a much smaller scale, since the expected proceeds from the *Matancero* expedition had evaporated—but I had to veto Clay's suggestion to start off with a stint of research in Seville. I was used to a very active life and was already stir crazy after more than two months sitting and reading all day long in Washington libraries; just the thought of doing the same for another six months or a year was dreadful. I already had over 24,000 entries in my wreck file, and even though 99 per cent of them had been obtained from books and charts on sunken treasure (very untrustworthy sources), I felt that some of them must be worth investigation. We finally arrived at a compromise: I would spend a year checking out a hundred different wreck sites, which we painstakingly selected from my list of 24,000, and if at the end of the year I had not scored a big hit, then I would go to Spain and compile a new wreck file from original documents.

The wreck sites were scattered all over the Caribbean and the Bahamas, and for fourteen months—from December 1959 to February 1961—I roamed the area from the Gulf of Honduras to the San Blas Islands off Panama, and from Trinidad to Grand Bahama, visiting every island, reef, and rock in between. Some are low-flying coral humps with nothing more than a few coconut palms to break the glare of the blinding white sand; others are the tips of submerged mountains whose high slopes, able to catch the rain clouds, are covered with thick vegetation. One of these, the Dutch island of Saba in the Leeward Island group, is really an extinct volcano with sheer cliffs rising straight out of the sea for almost three thousand feet (its main village lies in a crater eight hundred feet up). But whatever the size or shape of the island, they all had a few things in common: cheap booze (either native rum or, in the many that were free ports, the best Scotch whiskey or French cognac for $1.50 a bottle), plenty of beautiful girls, good food, and warm clear water.

What about my hundred wreck sites? Well, in the end I had to go to Spain after all. I located only two of the wrecks on my list, and they were duds. This is not surprising, as I was to find out later during my several years of research in Spanish and other European archives. Out of the hundred wrecks, seventy-four never existed at all, but were merely the creation of some imaginative authors of treasure-hunting books. Of those that did exist, eighteen had in fact sunk with treasure on board, but on the high seas (with little chance of recovery) and not in the shallow water close to land where these same authors had conveniently placed them; four others did sink in shallow water, but hundreds of miles from the sites given in these fictional sources; the remaining four existed, and the locations given were accurate (two of them were the ones I found), but they had not carried an ounce of the several million dollars' worth of bullion the treasure books claimed. And these one hundred had been chosen as the most promising—that is, with the most precise locations, and the most lucrative as far as treasure was concerned!

I would have been better off searching the Caribbean without having read one phony book or seen one phony chart. In fact, I located nearly two hundred *authentic* old wrecks that were not even on my master list of 24,000 wrecks, simply by talking to the local fishermen on the numerous islands I visited. As soon as I hit each island or a port on the mainland, I would go down to the nearest wharf and start asking if anyone had seen any cannons or big anchors—I soon learned not to ask about "wrecks," because a "wreck" to the local fishermen was invariably some modern cargo boat or yacht that had sunk within the last fifty years at the most. It never failed. Someone, or his father, or his grandfather, was bound to have snagged a fishing net or a trap on some "old guns," and even without an accident like this, the Caribbean fishermen, who often spear fish and always use glass-bottomed buckets, know the local sea bottom like their back yards.

Not that the local fishermen were always helpful. My first wreck site to check out was off the island of Barbareta, one of the Bay Islands off the coast of Honduras. According to a number of sources a Spanish galleon ("loaded with gold," of course) had sunk off Barbareta in the late seventeenth century. It seemed one of the most promising; in fact I had about eight different treasure charts, which differed only on the amount of gold aboard the wreck, ranging from two to ten million dollars' worth, and I decided to start out my year's reconnaissance with a bang, figuring I could probably forget about the other ninety-nine wrecks on my list. I invited some friends down from the States, and we rented a ketch in Belize, British Honduras, equipped with all the latest diving equipment.

We cleared from Belize one sunny morning in December 1959, and twelve hours later dropped anchor off the lush little island of Barbareta. The islanders were exceptionally friendly, greeting us in their strange West Indian dialect with its strong flavor of Elizabethan English (the Bay Islands were first settled by English logwood cutters, pirates, and their African slaves in the early seventeenth century). We showed them our charts. No, there were no cannons in that place, they said, but there were some on a reef around the other side of the island. They would be glad to take us there tomorrow, but first they would hold a party to celebrate our arrival, since they had so few visitors. Within an hour a five-piece steel band was playing calypso, rum was flowing freely from two casks, and a pit was built to roast two small pigs.

The party was a great success, especially for the islanders. Staggering aboard the anchored ketch about sunup the next morning, we found it as bare as Old Mother Hubbard's cupboard. Everything from the steering wheel to the stove was gone—sails, rigging, auxiliary engine, even the toilet seat and the plumbing fixtures. We estimated it must have taken at least six men working the entire night to strip our vessel so thoroughly. The only thing they failed to get was our money, since the wall safe was badly battered but still locked.

Ashore, everyone, of course, was astonished by the news and swore that some boat from another island must have slipped in during the night. I would be willing to lay a heavy bet that everyone on Barbareta was involved in this venture, living up to the tradition of their pirate forefathers, and I wonder who is wearing my good cowboy boots right now. There probably was an old wreck with a pile of cannons on the reef, just as the islanders had said, and perhaps it was even a treasure-laden galleon, but since all our diving equipment had been taken also, there was nothing to do but arrange for the bare hull of the ketch to be towed back to Belize. I'm not sure, but I think this expedition must hold the record for the shortest-lived treasure hunt ever undertaken.

I did gain something from this first leg of my reconnaissance tour, however, and it was to prove very valuable in future treasure hunts: a new view on shark behavior. Back in Belize, while waiting for a flight to my next port of call, Omoa, Honduras, I ran into a friend of mine from my Cozumel days, Jimmy McIver. Jimmy could easily step into the leading role in some pirate movie without one ounce of makeup. Massive in size, he has a big red beard and a mass of red hair, always flying in the wind, that surrounded a face only a paler shade of red, with two wicked little eyes that can send icy shivers up the back of anyone he happens to stare at. Now Jimmy was known to be a heavy drinker, but rarely did he begin his drinking until late in the afternoon, so I thought it quite strange to find him completely drunk at seven in the morning. I invited him for a chat and over another pint of pink gin he told me his troubles.

Jimmy had been in the smuggling business for years, but not one to go about things stealthily (he even had a business card noting his profession as smuggler with the motto: "I carry anything anyplace, if the price is right"), he had been caught twice the past year, once in Mexico and again in Honduras. Both times his vessels had been confiscated along with their contraband cargo, besides his having to pay huge fines. Having lost his life's savings in these two misadventures, he had sworn off smuggling, borrowed some money, and gone into the lobster business. He became very prosperous, exporting the frozen lobster tails to the States, and was about to invest in building a tourist hotel when the bubble burst.

About six months before, one of the fifty local skin divers he employed had mysteriously disappeared while spearing lobster. Three months later another diver was climbing back aboard the lobster boat, and while he was standing on the boarding ladder, a large, white-tipped shark bit off his left foot. He had nearly bled to death before they could get him back to Belize, and half the divers quit. Then only a week before I ran into Jimmy, still another diver disappeared without a trace on the same reef. This time everyone was sure a shark had gotten him, for the day he disappeared the same white-tipped shark, which one of the boatmen had harpooned after he had bitten off the diver's foot, was seen cruising around with the harpoon head still imbedded in his back. This latest tragedy left Jimmy with only three brave (or foolhardy) divers and no business at all.

I, of course, knew that sharks were really harmless. The two missing divers had probably blacked out and drowned from holding their breath too long underwater, and the one that had lost his foot—well, that was a freak accident. "Cheer up, you old pirate," I said. "I'll kill that shark for you. We'll show your divers that sharks are easy to handle and I bet they'll all come back to work for you."

Jimmy was so happy over my offer that he gave me a rib-crushing bear hug and ordered another pint of gin to celebrate.

The next morning, with about forty of his divers and many other curious people crowded aboard his boat, appropriately named *Jolly Roger,* we headed for the reef where the accident occurred, which was in the Turneffe Island group, a four- or five-hour run from Belize. It was quite rough, and Jimmy had to anchor about 150 yards off the reef, which skirted one of the smaller islands. Worse still, he had neglected to bring along a skiff, so that I would be diving without any cover. I had only a small two-rubber gun, but on the spearpoint I had a specially designed powerhead with a 12-gauge shotgun shell, which on other occasions had exploded a big hole in a shark's head and killed it instantly.

For nearly two hours I swam up and down the reef, without sighting the white-tipped shark or any others. Having spent most of the previous night drinking and swapping tales with Jimmy, I had a big hangover and decided to call it quits. Soon after starting back toward the *Jolly Roger,* I sighted a good-sized grouper, which I dove down to shoot, after removing the power-head from the spear, but even before I reached the surface again, the white-tipped shark, still with the harpoon head in its back, appeared out of nowhere and snatched the fifty-pound grouper in one bite, snapping the 3/8-inch spear shaft in half at the same time. I was still staring in disbelief at the broken half of my spear, when the shark spun around and came for me. Its huge mouth gaped with what seemed like a third of the animal's twelve-foot length, showing row upon row of sharp teeth. Taking both ends of the speargun, I held it out in front of me to ward off the shark. But the shark wasn't fussy about his menu; it snapped the gun in two, swallowing one half, while the other half dropped to the bottom. I carried no knife that day. Not that it would have done any good, since a shark's hide is so thick that even on land it is difficult to penetrate, and in the water, which cuts down one's thrust, a knife is little more use than a toothpick. I did have the explosive powerhead stuck in my belt, but without the spear, whose sharp point acts as the firing pin, it was useless.

There was nothing to do but run for it. I set out for the *Jolly Roger,* breaking Olympic swimming records, I am sure. The only trouble was that sharks had been clocked at speeds up to fifty miles an hour. I had not traveled fifty feet when the shark was back again, and the only things I had to defend myself with were two trembling hands. I grabbed the shark's snout with one hand, getting pushed through the water like a torpedo in reverse, and pounded with the other on its snout, which I knew is the most vulnerable part of a shark's body, and all the while its jaws were gaping only an arm's length from my stomach.

The same scene was repeated at least a dozen times, with the added hazard of bullets from Jimmy's rifle dancing around me (fortunately I wasn't hit, but neither was the shark), and each time I was sure it would be the end. While Jimmy was firing, others cut the anchor line and tried to reach me, but the vessel drew too much water to enable them to bring it any closer than fifty yards. Then, while the shark was making one of its slow, sweeping circles in preparation for a new charge, I was lifted by a large wave, carried right over the barrier reef, and dropped into the placid lagoon waters on the other side. I was so exhausted I just floated on my back trying to catch my breath (my face mask and snorkel had been knocked off sometime during the battle). I was sure the shark would not come into the shallow water after me, but the first warning that I was wrong was the splash of rifle bullets nearby. Before I could look around, I felt a tingling sensation in the toes of my right foot, and looking down, I found that half of my right fin was gone down to the toes, and a small part of the other fin. Then I had an even greater shock when I was suddenly yanked out of the water by a pair of brown arms and dragged aboard a *piragua* which had come out from the cay to help me. The shark completed his circle and came right for the canoe, but took off after one of the Indians hit it a few times on the snout with a paddle, and that was the last we saw of it.

So sharks do bite! And in case I needed any more proof, two incidents within the next six months provided it. Once, while diving in the murky waters of Port-of-Spain in Trinidad, a huge shark, I would guess over fifteen feet in length, grabbed my aqualung tank in its jaws, jerking me violently through the water until it gave up trying to penetrate the steel tank, dropped me, and took off. The second incident occurred barely a month later. I was spearfishing in the Grenadines (a long chain of small islands and cays, located between Grenada and St. Vincent, in the Windward Islands group). One of the other divers I was with had just speared a red snapper and was holding it by the eye sockets, as most spearfishermen do, when a small, five-foot lemon shark grabbed both the fish and the man's hand and swam away before any of the rest of us, who were watching the horrible scene, could aim a spear at it. Blood swirled out of the severed stump of the man's wrist, but we were able to apply a tourniquet and keep him from bleeding to death while we rushed him to a hospital on the island of Grenada.

As for that white-tipped shark off Belize, its diet of lobster divers was cut off. After the story of my bout with it had gotten all over British Honduras—in a matter of a few days—Jimmy could not get divers to go anywhere near the water. He was eventually forced to return to smuggling, but he got caught again, this time by British customs agents, and the last time I heard he was serving two years.

Belize is only one of the many bases around the Caribbean from which enterprising traders like my friend Jimmy supply foreign luxury goods to the hungry markets of Latin America without benefit of import duties. The Dutch island of Curaçao off the coast of Venezuela is another. However, I was unaware of this when I arrived there a few months after leaving Jimmy to resume his old trade. I was interested in some seventeenth-century smuggler-pirates (the dividing line in those days was not very clear) who, according to my wreck list, had lost a richly laden prize off the island in 1629. And then, having found no trace of this or any other promising wrecks, my main interest was getting from Curaçao to my next port of call, the Venezuelan island of Margarita—no simple matter, since there was no boat or plane service directly there from Curaçao.

I was having a cold beer in a dockside tavern in Curaçao's main port, grumbling to myself about the lousy transportation in that part of the world, when a shoddily dressed Dutchman came up to me, wanting to know if I was the American who had been asking about transportation to Isla Margarita, and did I know anything about boats. I said yes, and he went on, "Good. It so happens that I am leaving on a fishing trip tonight and my first mate is sick. If you could lend me a hand at the wheel, I would be glad to drop you off at Margarita." It seemed such unbelievably good luck that I accepted on the spot.

That evening Captain Jan, as he called himself, led me to a

secluded inlet on the island's eastern end, where his boat was tied up. On board already were two other men who muttered low greetings in Spanish. Their accents I took to be Venzuelan, but they did not look like fishermen, and when Captain Jan started up the two powerful motors and blasted off at thirty-five knots, I knew it was no ordinary fishing boat either. He said he would take the wheel first, and finding it too wet topside because of the flying spray, I grabbed my suitcase and climbed down into the cabin, which was crammed with cases and crates. They had not even bothered to paint over the labels: Johnny Walker, Dewar's White Label, Bols, Courvoisier, Omega, Tissot, Rolex, Leica, Canon, and some Japanese brand of what I think was transistor radios.

Now there was no doubt about the nature of this fishing trip, but what puzzled me was why I had been roped into the deal. The mystery was cleared up when I returned on deck and demanded to know what the hell was going on. Captain Jan, adjusting a pistol I had not noticed before to a more comfortable position in his belt, said, "Nothing that concerns you. All you have to do is remember that you are the skipper of this American yacht bound for Trinidad." Then, turning the wheel over to me, he went below and came back with an American flag, which he raised in place of the Dutch one, and a piece of plywood with the words, "Mary Jane II," and below that, "Miami," which he nailed to the stern over the boat's original name and home port. An old smuggler's trick from way back—a quick change of nationality.

No further explanation was offered, and I asked no more questions. At sunrise our speed was dropped to a less suspicious ten knots, and Captain Jan said, "Now remember, if any vessels approach, tell them this is an American yacht, and if anyone tries to board or make trouble, my friends and I will take over." But no vessels did approach, and those were about the only words spoken all day. Both Venezuelans lay seasick in the cabin, and Captain Jan either sat silently playing solitaire or relieved me at the wheel. Late in the afternoon I sighted an island off our starboard bow. Jan looked up, grunted, "Tortuga," and went back to his card game.

As soon as it was dark and we had crept past Tortuga Island, our speed was increased to thirty-five knots again, and the boat went leaping from one wave peak to the next, drenching the deck with spray. A few hours later we were within five miles of the western tip of Margarita, our speed was reduced to less than five knots, and all lights, including the binnacle light, were put out. Jan's two friends, also with pistols protruding from their belts, appeared on deck. All three went to the bow, and directed me to steer for a small indentation in the coastline, where a red light was flashing on and off.

Captain Jan came back to me when we were fairly close to shore, handed me an envelope with $300 in cash in it, and said, "Guess you'll be leaving me here. You could get yourself into as much trouble as me, but this ought to help you forget my face."

We were about one hundred yards off the shore. By then I could see the entrance to a small cove, which Captain Jan motioned me to head for. Suddenly I was blinded by the glare of a huge spotlight coming from the direction of the cove, soon followed by the rattle of machine-gun fire. The same second that the first pieces of glass and splinters went flying past my head, I pulled the throttle to stop and dove over the side. From the water I could see a large boat, obviously a Venezuelan *guardacosta,* speeding out of the cove and bearing down on us. I swam for shore, closely followed by Jan and his two friends, who had also jumped overboard after firing off a few futile rounds. Just as I reached the beach I heard a crash and looked out to see the boat being rammed by the cutter, with all my gear on board.

Meanwhile Jan and one of the two Venezuelans came ashore, dragging the other, who was bleeding badly from a large hole in his shoulder. We barely had time to bind up the wound, before a troop of soldiers and policemen came running up to hustle us into a couple of waiting jeeps. We were taken to a jail in what I imagined was the island's main town and grilled separately. I claimed I knew no Spanish, but an interpreter was brought in and for several hours I told my story over and over. Naturally they refused to believe it, and I had to admit to myself that it sounded pretty fishy, but finally several other policemen walked in and told my interrogators that Jan and both Venezuelans claimed I was innocent too. Then a big debate took place, which they thought I could not understand. The ones who had been questioning me were skeptical and wanted to use a little "persuasion" to make me confess that I was involved; while the other police officers said no, it was pretty obvious that I was innocent, and it was foolish to make trouble for Americans, since they have so much money and power that in the end they get out of it anyway. They finally decided that I was still guilty of entering the country illegally.

I was thrown into a cell with two bunks, one of which was occupied by a guy who snored so loudly that I finally shoved him and told him to shut up. He jumped out of the bunk and at first I thought he wanted to fight, but then I heard: "Marx, you old s.o.b., what the hell are you doing here?" It was none other than my old friend Goggin, who only two years before had gotten me out of jail in Mérida, Yucatan.

After telling him my crazy story, which sent him into such a fit of laughter that a guard banged on the door for us to be quiet, he told me his, which was equally crazy. He had come to the island on a project authorized by the Venezuelan government to excavate several sixteenth-century Spanish sites, and only that afternoon had discovered two three-foot-high jars full of pearls that had been stashed away centuries before (Isla Margarita was the main pearl-producing area in the New World all during the Spanish colonial period). They were all badly deteriorated, almost to the point of turning into dust, but before Goggin had a chance to treat them, he was arrested without any warning or explanation and carted off to jail a few hours before we made our spectacular arrival.

I wish I could say that I got Goggin out of jail, but I didn't. About nine the next morning he was released, without any help from me, but with many apologies for the inconvenience he had been caused. He never knew exactly why he had been put in jail. It just seems to be a conditioned reflex with Latin-American policemen: whenever anything resembling a treasure is found, someone, anyone, has to be arrested. After spending a few minutes telling them off soundly, Goggin once again set off on the task of getting me out of jail. He wired the U.S. Embassy in Caracas, but before he even received an answer, I was released the same day around noon.

I don't know what ever happened to Captain Jan and his two friends, but after that dirty trick they had pulled on me I did not waste much sympathy on them. While waiting for a new passport and copies of my precious treasure charts—everything had been lost when the "Mary Jane II" sank—I helped Goggin in his dig and explored the local waters. In the end the pearls Goggin had found were sent to the University in Caracas, but Goggin was given the two clay jars, and this made him happy since he was much more interested in pottery and ceramics—his life's work—than pearls.

I had gone to Isla Margarita mainly to see the pearl divers in action. The Indians had been recovering pearls there long before Columbus discovered the island on his fourth voyage to America, and for centuries afterward the Margarita divers were famous all over the world for their stamina and endurance. What a letdown to find that they now use aqualungs, if they go down at all, and that the pearl oysters are mainly harvested with drag nets!

There was another Caribbean diving legend I came across during my island-hopping jaunt: Big Anthony of Buccoo Point, Tobago. But Big Anthony was not a myth, although I would pass the following story off as pure fiction if I had not experienced it myself.

There is nothing I enjoy more than testing skin divers' tall tales. I can't say how many people I have run across who boasted of being able to stay underwater on their own breath for five minutes, only to come gasping to the surface after a minute or two; or how many who bragged about free diving to one hundred feet or more, but could barely reach forty. A good diver after years of practice can stay underwater as long as three minutes, but he would have to remain completely motionless in order not to consume oxygen, and the average length of each dive during a day's spearfishing is usually about thirty seconds. As for depths, an experienced diver can dive to seventy feet or more, but unless he is tired of living, he usually limits himself to thirty or forty feet, because if he runs out of breath at much deeper depths, he stands a good chance of blacking out and drowning before he reaches the surface. An example of foolhardy diving was a world spearfishing championship held in Europe several years ago, when four expert divers blacked out and drowned while making deep free dives. I have yet to find anyone to whom these basic rules of diving physiology do not apply—except "Big Anthony."

After checking into a hotel on Tobago, I asked the manager if he knew where I could find a local diver named Big Anthony, about whom I had been hearing all sorts of fantastic tales in Trinidad, and he directed me to a nearby beach where the fishermen bring their catches ashore every evening. Now there are not many people that I feel like a dwarf next to, but Big Anthony is a sight to behold. I would say he is closer to seven feet tall than six feet, weighs at least three hundred pounds, all solid muscle, and has hands the size of an average man's chest. What is even more startling is that, despite his size, he moves as gracefully as a ballerina whether in or out of the water.

Big Anthony is a man of very few words, but he hums or sings continuously in a soft bass voice, as he did while we sped along the next day toward a reef he had agreed to take me to. After we anchored, I began to put on my diving gear and noticed that he wore no fins or snorkel, only a face mask. But then I looked down at his sixteen-inch feet and realized why he didn't wear fins: he didn't need them.

Another reason Big Anthony doesn't use fins, I decided, was that he doesn't actually dive, or at least not like anyone else I've ever seen. Grabbing a battered old speargun, he simply stepped over the side feet first and, instead of kicking to get down head first, sank like a stone to land erect on the sharp coral bottom twenty feet below. Once on the bottom he glanced around, and not seeing any good-sized fish in the immediate vicinity, he started walking around as if he were on dry land, humming all the while. Soon a group of red snappers approached. Maybe the humming had hypnotized them (Big Anthony has a good voice). They just stayed there swimming in close circles, while he shot four of them, extracting the fish from the spear each time and reloading, all without surfacing. It seemed as if he was down there for an eternity and then, with a fish under each arm and one in each hand, he sort of drifted up to the surface. I swear his feet weren't moving and I can't say what propelled him up.

I was so fascinated that I threw my gun back in the boat and continued snorkeling above him. Each of his dives was the same, except that sometimes he would walk over to a cave and start grabbing lobsters with his bare hands, instead of shooting fish. Twice he pulled small octopi out of caves, bit off their heads and stuck them on his chest—the suction in the oval discs lining their arms remains even after death—where they stayed until he surfaced and pulled them off. All this time I was wearing my underwater watch and timing each dive he made, or, more accurately, his underwater strolls. Every one of them was around four minutes and one lasted almost five, yet the only thing that seemed to limit them was the amount of fish or lobster he could carry. Within an hour the skiff was almost sinking from the six hundred pounds of fish and nearly forty lobsters he had caught, and we had to head back to shore. Big Anthony sang all the way back, looking as fresh and rested as when we had started.

The following day he agreed to take me to Man o' War Bay, the site of a British frigate that had sunk around 1750. This was one of the few wrecks on my list that really existed, but I didn't need the list, since Big Anthony knew exactly where it was. After making a few quick glances at the shore he dropped the anchor, claiming it would be right on top of the wreck (and it was, as I found out when I reached the bottom). I had rented several aqualungs, since the wreck lay in 120 feet of water. I donned one set, jumped in, and stopped for a moment about twenty feet down to clear my ears, when Big Anthony came past—feet first, of course—sinking rapidly because he held a large rock in his hands. He wore no gear but his usual face mask, and I thought he must be insane to try to reach that depth on his own breath. Swimming after him as fast as I could, I reached the bottom to find him already busy pulling a piece of the ship's timber off the huge pile of ballast from the wreck. Then he began to throw ballast stones to one side, and after making a hole right in the middle of the pile, he reached down and extracted a pewter mug and a small silver porringer. He showed them to me, grinning at my wide-eyed stare of disbelief, then pushed the bowl into the top of his swim suit, gripped the stem of the mug between his teeth, and started up the anchor line hand over hand. Minutes later he was down again working beside me. He made at least a dozen of these dives, as if the water were twenty feet deep, instead of 120, and some of the dives lasted nearly five minutes. We spent several hours at the wreck site and recovered two muskets, one sword, two cutlasses, two pewter mugs, one silver porringer, six cannon balls and one empty Coca Cola bottle.

Expecting that Big Anthony would appreciate a good feed after the day's dive, I invited him to have dinner with me at my hotel that evening. He looked even bigger in shirt and tie—

especially since the tie reached only about one third of the way down his massive chest. I was hoping to pry from him the secret of his fantastic diving feats, but when I started the conversation telling him he was the greatest diver I had ever met or heard of, he simply laughed and said, "Mon, you should have known me in my younger days." He was, he admitted proudly, nearly sixty! He couldn't give me any other reason for his extraordinary strength and endurance except that he had begun diving almost as soon as he could walk, but he did say that he ate fish three meals a day and had never smoked nor touched a drop of booze in his life.

Many who read this will probably think I was suffering from "raptures of the deep" when I was diving with Big Anthony, but any skeptic who doubts me can go and see for himself. However, anyone who fancies himself a good diver and doesn't want his ego deflated had better not dive with Big Anthony of Buccoo Point, Tobago.

From Tobago I worked my way north along the chain of Windward and Leeward Islands—Grenada, the Grenadines, St. Vincent, St. Lucia, Barbados, Martinique, Dominica, Guadeloupe, and others. Not all of them were included on my wreck list, but by that time I was beginning to realize I was better off relying solely on the local fishermen. I also had great faith in the old sea captains whose sturdy trading schooners are still the only form of communication the smaller, less developed islands have with the outside world. One ancient retired captain I met on the Dutch island of Bonaire near Curaçao claimed that his forefathers had been sailing in the Caribbean since the seventeenth century (he and his brothers, he said, were the ninth generation of seafarers), and when I asked if there were any tales of sunken treasure in his family, he said no, but he did have an original map of a buried treasure on St. Kitts that had been handed down to him. Of course I ended up buying the map, which he probably ran off by the hundreds on some backroom printing press, but it looked authentic, with faded ink and the edges slightly browned and curling. He claimed to have used the map himself, but was unable to locate the treasure. Before reaching St. Kitts, I had a friend send down a metal detector, which I planned to use in the search. For all I know, the map may have been genuine, but before I even had time to clear the metal detector through customs, I became convinced that the climate on St. Kitts was not very healthy, at least not for me.

After checking into my hotel, I headed straight for the bar to grab a cold beer, as I always did when arriving at a new place, since bartenders always seem to be a gold mine of information and always help me get started on the right track. I had barely swallowed my first thirsty gulp when a well-dressed Englishman tapped me on the shoulder and said, "My good man, I would be most grateful if you would join me for a drink." After I motioned for him to sit down, I noticed that the bartender moved his glass-polishing operation very close to us, but I didn't think much of it at the time. The Englishman ordered a drink and after spending a few minutes in idle talk about the "delightful weather" and other irrelevant matters, he came to the point.

"Am I correct in assuming that you are a skin diver? I saw you enter the hotel carrying your harpoon and other underwater paraphernalia." I nodded. "I represent a London insurance brokerage," he continued, handing me one of his business cards, "and I am in need of the services of a diver. I am prepared to pay well, say even to the sum of three hundred pounds sterling, which is about eight hundred dollars in Yank money." My ears opened at this, and I asked him just what services he had in mind. "Oh, quite simple," he answered. "There is a wreck in the harbor—you can easily see its masts above the water if you look from the pier—and all I need is someone to dive down and tell me whether or not the sea cocks are open."

After the episode with Captain Jan in Curaçao, I was a little suspicious of generous strangers who offered something for almost nothing. I couldn't believe that he was willing to pay so much for so simple a job and also wondered why he had not hired any of the local people (on almost every West Indian island there are scores of excellent divers). I told him to hold the check he was writing out until I could think it over, and he walked away after I declined an invitation to lunch.

Then the bartender, whom I had barely spoken to, leaned over and whispered, "Boss, that man is bad music and I beg you to forget what he says." I spent an hour trying to pump more out of him, but he refused to say more on the subject. I ate a few sandwiches at the bar and went up to my room for a siesta.

Soon after dozing off, I was awakened by four men who barged in without knocking and stood around the bed, as their spokesman said, "Mister, you had better heed our advice or your next sleep might be a very long one." He explained that he and his three brothers were the owners of the sunken vessel in the harbor. They would give me fifty pounds sterling to be off the island within twenty-four hours and under no circumstances was I to go near the wreck in the meantime. I told him I would have to be crazy to pass up a job paying £300 that would only take me minutes to do. "You would have to be more crazy if you did the job. We are prepared to go to any lengths to keep you or anyone else from snooping around that wreck."

I told them that I would think it over and let them know that evening. Minutes after they left, the Englishman came running in, demanding to know what the owners had wanted from me. I told him the whole story, but before I was finished he was writing out a check for £750, which he handed to me, saying, "I am sure that this will allay any qualms you might have about the job." Again I refused, telling him that I would think it over and give him my decision that evening.

In no mood to continue my siesta, I dressed and started strolling around the town, finally stopping for a drink in one of the small bars near the docks. The owner was very friendly, and talkative, and I soon found out that the job would not be worth doing for even £7,500. Apparently I was the only person on the island who did not know that the four brothers had deliberately scuttled their vessel for the insurance money. About a month before, the insurance man, a claims inspector, had arrived with a diver from England who, despite a number of warnings, had inspected the wreck and seen that the sea cocks were open. He was to have made a sworn statement in front of a justice of the peace the following day, but that same night he met with an accident: a day or so later his body was found floating in the bay with his brains spilling out of a large hole in his head—the work of thieves, according to the newspapers. The insurance inspector flew out in a hurry, and the islanders thought that that was the last of him, but a week later he was back with a skin diver from Barbados, who left on a boat that same afternoon after learning what had happened to the other diver. "Now I hear that the insurance inspector has some other white man going to dive for him on that wreck," the bar owner continued, "and I really feel sorry for that white man."

Without even finishing my drink, I left the man a big tip and returned to the hotel to find out when the first boat was leaving for the island of Nevis, my next stop. The desk clerk said there would be a boat leaving at midnight, then added: "But Sir, I thought you were going to Antigua. There is a plane ticket here for you that leaves in about an hour. You have plenty of time to make it. You are already checked out, your bill is paid, and your luggage and other things are here behind the counter. Also some gentleman left this for you." Opening the sealed envelope he handed me, I found £50 in cash. No note, but the message was pretty clear without one.

I did have plenty of time to catch the flight, but I had already been to Antigua and decided to wait for the midnight boat to Nevis. Grabbing my bags and spearguns (they might come in handy, I figured), I headed for a nearby movie house and sat through the feature, a horror movie, three times, making a total of four, since I had already seen it before on another island. Then around 11:00 P.M. they played "God Save the Queen," and the theater emptied. The six or seven bags of greasy popcorn had not stopped the grumbling noises in my stomach, so I made for the nearest restaurant, but had barely begun to read the menu when in walked one of the four brothers. Looking very pleased with life, he sat down at my table. "I knew you looked like a sensible lad and would see things our way."

"Maybe the next diver won't see things your way," I said. "Maybe he'll manage to stay alive until he makes his declaration about those open sea cocks."

"Oh, the sea cocks," he replied breezily. "Don't worry about them. We had some local boys close them for us soon after that English diver met with his unfortunate accident."

My face got red: "Then why in hell are you trying to keep me from diving and making a fat bundle of loot? It wouldn't hurt you any."

"Ah lad, there you are wrong. You see, besides the vessel, we also had a very valuable cargo insured. How that English diver didn't notice there wasn't any cargo is a mystery. He didn't even notice that the vessel had been stripped completely before she went down, but a more perceptive person like yourself might."

I still could not see how these thieves were going to get away with it, since everyone on the island seemed to know the story, and I asked him how he was going to keep everyone quiet. Someone might sell out to the insurance firm and get away before the brothers knew what was happening.

"Lad," he said, "perhaps you aren't as bright as I first thought you were. Everything has been taken care of. We have many friends on the governing council, and only this afternoon the council voted unanimously that the wreck, which is a serious hazard to navigation, must be blown up immediately. There is nothing we islanders dislike more than people coming out from Mother England to pry into our business."

Just then the boat whistle blew. I bolted down the rest of my food, paid my tab, and said goodby to my entertaining supper companion, but he grabbed one of my bags and insisted upon coming along to the boat. I noticed the insurance investigator lurking behind some bales on the dock, waiting for an opportune moment to speak to me, but my companion stayed right with me until the lines were cast off. Then he jumped ashore, shouted a friendly farewell, and walked jauntily down the dock. As the boat pulled away, I got my last look at the insurance investigator: he was sitting down on the filthy dock, knees up, and staring glumly out into the harbor at the masts of the wreck sticking above the surface of the water.

Three weeks later I stopped briefly back at St. Kitts and learned from the same informative bar owner that the brothers had been awarded the full amount of their insurance claim. The wreck was gone without a trace, except for some small pieces of debris on the bottom. Its demolition had been very thorough—you see, one of the brothers had been awarded the contract for dynamiting the wreck.

I had not planned to make another stop at St. Kitts, but then nothing on that particular leg of my island-hopping jaunt went according to plan. I had spent a few lucrative weeks at Nevis diving on the sunken city of Georgetown (once the island's main port which went down in a combination earthquake and tidal wave in 1698), and then headed for the island of Montserrat. This place was a perfect drag; there were no wrecks, sunken cities, or reefs in the water, and no ruins or interesting dames on land, so I decided to leave on the first boat that arrived. This happened to be an eighteen-foot, motor-powered boat belonging to two Frenchmen from Guadeloupe who were on their way to the island of St. Martin to hunt for turtle. They had stopped at Montserrat because their engine was acting up and burning oil at a great rate. Taking me aboard, plus several gallons of oil, they headed north for St. Martin, but late that afternoon we had to stop at St. Kitts to pick up more oil—and rum, which both men were consuming as fast as the engine burned oil. My knowledge of French was not the greatest, but we managed to communicate a little. There were, as far as I could make out, only two main topics of interest: Jean-Pierre had seventeen daughters (twenty-four children altogether) and faced the almost impossible task, according to him, of finding husbands for them; and Jacques talked on and on for hours about his life's dream, which was to set up a rum distillery (he would have been his own best customer). When they weren't talking, they were singing. It looked like an interesting boat ride.

Around midnight, when we were between St. Kitts and the Dutch island of St. Eustatius, the engine exploded, sending scalding water and oil flying all over the small engine room. I ran forward and threw over the anchor so that we wouldn't drift. Jean-Pierre and Jacques broke into fits of laughter: even though we were fairly close to land, we were in water over a mile deep and naturally the anchor line couldn't reach the bottom. Feeling like a bloody fool, I hauled the anchor back on board and went to see what damage had been done. The engine block was cracked in several places and all we could do was drift, since the boat had a mast but no sails. But we were close to land and the sea was calm, so that there did not seem to be any great cause for alarm. In fact, Jacques and Jean-Pierre continued their drinking and singing as if nothing had happened at all. They both assured me that we would be picked up in a matter of hours and towed into some port, since hundreds of boats frequented those waters, so I returned to my perch on deck and fell asleep again.

Sunrise brought a few surprises: no vessels were in sight and we had drifted about twenty miles to the south, although St. Kitts still seemed fairly close. I climbed the mast to hang a white rag, hoping that someone would see it and take it as an emergency signal. Jean-Pierre and Jacques thought this was almost as funny as the anchor episode the night before. Their rum was finished, so I shared my bag of mangoes and bananas with them for breakfast. For lunch each of them slit open one of the twenty or so small tuna they had caught that morning and ate the raw flesh, but I refused to join them, even though my belly was already growling and no boats were in sight. In fact, we never saw a vessel that whole day.

Even before the sun went down, the horizon to the north had become very black, and an hour after sunset we were hit with heavy rains and gale-force winds. The boat tossed about wildly until Jean-Pierre threw out a sea anchor, which brought our bow around into the wind. We were riding it out very well but the lightning flying all around drove the three of us below in the forward hold, which was very comfortable, but stank to high heaven, because they normally carried dry fish in it.

We should have tried to catch some rain water for drinking, but no one thought of it until the following morning when Jean-Pierre went aft to the engine room to get the twenty-liter jug of water and found that it had broken during the storm. (Judging from the way everything on that boat was run, I'm sure it had been improperly stowed.) After extracting three slivers of glass from Pierre's foot—the engine room deck was covered with broken glass in addition to water and oil—we had a breakfast of raw sugar, which only made me thirstier. The wind was still from the north, blowing between thirty and forty knots, and although the rain had stopped, it was so overcast I could not make out land anywhere. The two Frenchmen, as usual, seemed completely unconcerned, eating raw fish whenever the spirit moved them and handfuls of raw sugar. I subsisted on sugar and an occasional gulp of sea water, which they assured me would send me into convulsions.

Not one boat was seen that day, although we did hear the engine of one passing fairly close. Then, around midnight, we saw the light of a large vessel nearby, and I used up our entire supply of matches lighting a tar torch I had made for signaling, but the wind was so strong the torch would not burn right, and the vessel finally disappeared into the dark again.

It rained for about ten minutes around dawn and I was able to catch half a cupful of water which we shared. But these few drops did me little good: when my two friends began vigorously attacking their smelly raw tuna, I found that my mouth was so dry the sugar I ate would not even dissolve.

I was beginning to think that both of them were insane. They acted as if we were out on a picnic, never once stopping their singing and joke-telling. I finally did tell them I thought they were nuts and found out that they were old hands at drifting around on the sea. This was the first time that year, but the previous year it had happened four times. Twice they had run out of gasoline, but they were picked up the same day by passing vessels; the third time their rudder had fallen off (they were great seamen, these two), and they drifted three days before being rescued, but it was no hardship since they had plenty of rum; and the fourth time the engine had broken down and they had drifted for twenty-two days before finally wrecking on the coast of Venezuela. This had been a little more serious because the supply of rum had run out early. They had been put in a hospital for a few weeks, but went right back home to Guadeloupe and quickly built another boat—the one we were now on.

During the afternoon I finally decided to eat some of their raw and already rancid tuna, but it stank so badly that I could not even get it into my mouth. I tried to catch some fresh fish but had no luck. Then, after I had given up and was lying topside in a light drizzle trying to catch rain water, with my mouth open and all available containers scattered around the deck, a six-inch flying fish leaped aboard and landed right on top of me. But I could not get even the thinnest sliver of the fish down my swollen throat. I finally remembered something I had learned in a Marine Corps survival course, and when a twenty-pound bonito got hooked on one of my lines, I put all the fish guts and liver in a T-shirt: by twisting and twisting the mess over a pot I managed to extract nearly a pint and a half of oily but drinkable liquid. Both Frenchmen refused to share any, but it did the trick for me. My thirst was quenched temporarily and I was able to get down a substantial amount of raw fish coated with sugar.

That night four ships passed within a mile of us, but they either did not see us—it was very dark and still rough—or didn't realize we were in trouble. We had a small crisis during the middle of the night. The line holding the sea anchor, which was probably rotten, parted, and our boat turned beam ends to the heavy seas, shipping a lot of water before we could rig up another sea anchor and head her bow back into the wind.

More raw fish for breakfast, this time without sugar, which we had finished off the night before. The sun came out for brief intervals between dark, low-lying clouds, but neither land nor vessels were in sight. I knew we were drifting south-southeast, but I had no accurate way to measure our rate of drift. Well, Jean-Pierre and Jacques had the right idea. What did our position matter, anyway? The Venezuelan coast, which was the nearest land in that direction, was still at least ten days off.

Another monotonous day passed, listening to Jean-Pierre and Jacques singing away like two loony birds. I had heard their songs so many times already I could have joined in, but my throat felt like sandpaper.

Jacques was on watch that night around eleven when he woke us excitedly with the news that there was a light due south of us. At first we thought it was a boat, but after awhile I decided it had to be a lighthouse because of the regularly spaced flashes, although both Frenchmen insisted there was no land out where we were. Finally, after much arguing, we decided that no matter what the light was we should try to reach it. We pulled in our makeshift sea anchor—by now the wind had fallen below twenty knots, and the sea was calmer—and using several planks we ripped off the hatch covers, we made for the light, with two men paddling and one at the wheel.

We made good progress, helped by the favorable current and wind. The light kept getting brighter and brighter, although it was so dark we could see nothing else, and finally when it seemed that the light was almost above us, we were suddenly lifted by a big sea and thrown onto a reef. The next wave washed us over the reef, capsizing the boat, and we hung onto the overturned hull until our dragging feet touched bottom. We pushed the boat in closer until it grounded and then crawled ashore on a smooth sandy beach. A quick survey revealed that we had landed on a small cay—no more than a quarter of a mile in diameter—that was completely deserted except for some birds, land crabs, and an unattended light beacon.

We lay on the beach until the sun came up, exhausted from our five hours of paddling. Our first task was to right the capsized boat and pull it up as far as we could on the beach. Then, while the two Frenchmen went off to see what they could find in the form of food on the island, I made an inventory of what we had salvaged from the boat. There wasn't much: besides my two bags of soggy clothes and books and ruined photographic gear, a set of snorkeling equipment and two spear-guns, we had assorted tools, a can of gasoline, several pots and other metal containers, rope, and some empty burlap sacks. I laid everything out to dry and was starting off to join my shipwreck companions, when I saw them heading back, singing as usual.

They were each carrying several booby birds and their shirts were full of birds' eggs. We ate the eggs raw but let the birds go since we had no matches to build a fire. We made a good lean-to out of pieces of driftwood and planks ripped off the boat and spent all day in it, sheltered from the blinding glare of the sun reflected off the cay's pure white sand. By midday, the sun beat down so fiercely that we could see steam rising for several feet off the damp sand.

Toward evening, when we could venture out without being blinded, we decided to explore the cay carefully. In several places we found turtle tracks leading up from the water's edge to the higher parts of the cay, where we discovered hundreds of turtle eggs that had recently been laid. Turtle eggs are delicious even when raw, and we gobbled them down almost as fast as we dug them up. After digging numerous holes all over the cay in search of water, Jean-Pierre discovered a supply of rather brackish but drinkable water only a few feet under the surface, very near the beach.

The following morning I went spearfishing, and when I returned with several fish and lobsters, we unanimously agreed that we were going to get a fire started somehow. Striking two pieces of metal together didn't produce enough sparks, so we tried the old trick of rubbing together two pieces of wood, but this went on for hours with no results until I finally remembered that the two pieces must be of different varieties of wood. Substituting a piece of pine for one of the two pieces of oak we had been using, we soon had smoke and then sparks. But Jean-Pierre nearly got roasted instead of the fish. Seeing the first sparks, Jacques quickly emptied the can of gasoline over the wood, spilling quite a lot on Jean-Pierre in the process. He was instantly on fire too. Both of us jumped on him, smothering the flames, but all of his hair and many patches of skin were burnt off. Jacques ran to the boat, and after opening some part of the worthless engine, returned with two handfuls of grease which he smeared all over poor Jean-Pierre's blistered hide. We had to begin all over again, but we got another fire started and decided to keep it going as long as possible, both as a signal to passing ships and for cooking purposes.

That evening we had a sumptuous meal of roasted fish and lobster and fried booby bird and then boiled turtle eggs for dessert. Except for the crabs that crawled all over us, we slept comfortably, taking turns to watch for passing ships and to add driftwood to the fire we kept going constantly.

The five days and nights that followed were completely uneventful. I would spear fish and lobsters, while the Frenchmen caught booby birds and dug up turtle eggs, and then we would take turns cooking. We had plenty to eat and drink, and when I think of some of the treks I survived in the Quintana Roo jungle, the sojourn on this deserted cay was little more than a lark. I could not have had more jovial companions—even the painful blisters that covered Jean-Pierre didn't dampen his good spirits. When they weren't singing or having a friendly argument about something, Jacques and Jean-Pierre would teach me some of their French patois, and I would teach them English, which they were both eager to learn so that they could haggle over prices for provisions and fuel when they stopped at the English islands, such as St. Kitts or Montserrat. Our only real headache was finding enough wood to feed our hungry fire, and after using all the driftwood lying on the beach and stripping the boat almost down to the ribs and keel, we had to resort to digging for other driftwood buried under the sand.

Late in the afternoon on our seventh day, we sighted a boat that seemed to be heading for the cay. I quickly soaked some dried seaweed in water and fed the fire with it. Smoke billowed up, but I could have saved myself the trouble, since the boat was coming to the cay anyway to fish and catch turtles. After it anchored we swam out and climbed aboard to find that it was a Dutch fishing boat from the island of Saba. The captain spoke English, and my first question was: "Where the hell are we?" He said we were on Aves ("Bird") Island. He pulled out a chart and pointed to a little speck about 130 miles due west of the northern tip of Dominica Island and about 120 miles southwest from the channel that separates St. Kitts from St. Eustatius, which is where we had started our leisurely drift (exact position: 15° 35′ north latitude, 63° 45′ west longitude). It is not surprising that neither the Frenchmen nor I had never heard of the place, since I have later checked on many maps and charts and found that it is hardly ever shown except on very enlarged ones.

I was content to drink plenty of fresh water, but Jacques and Jean-Pierre never drank water if there was rum around. The Dutch captain broke out a bottle on request and watched in amazement as they emptied it in minutes. But it had only been half full, and I told the captain that in a six-hour stretch, between Montserrat and St. Kitts, I had seen them down four fifths of rum without any effect, except singing a little more off-key than usual. The Dutch captain also attended to Jean-Pierre's burns, most of which were healing already.

The boat stayed around the cay for a week, fishing and turtling, and all three of us helped out—Jean-Pierre and Jacques with hand lines and fish traps, and I with my speargun. The captain and seven-man crew were exceptionally generous, sharing everything they had, including their supply of rum which the Frenchmen polished off during the first three days. (They could easily have done it in one, but I could see they were trying to be polite.) Then, instead of heading straight to Saba, the kind Dutchmen went out of their way and carried us right to the port of Pointe-à-Pitre on Guadeloupe, where Jacques and Jean-Pierre lived. And to top it all, they refused any remuneration for their help.

Landing at Pointe-à-Pitre, we found that no one had even thought we were lost, since both Frenchmen often went off fishing and turtling for months at a time, without even contacting their families. I spent a few weeks there helping them start on another boat and consuming great quantities of delicious creole food, but I was finally driven away by my desire to stay single—Jean-Pierre was set on marrying me to one of his daughters, six of whom were over twenty and still unmarried—and after exchanging sad goodbyes at the airport (I had had enough of boats for awhile) with my two crazy friends and their families, I caught a plane and headed for the Virgin Islands.

By the time I reached the Bahamas, the last leg on my island-hopping jaunt, I had already spent a complete year hunting wrecks and had made a complete circle of the Caribbean from my starting place in Miami. I had saved the Bahamas for last on purpose. It was to be my ace in the hole, for if there is anyplace in the West Indies associated with sunken treasure it is the Bahamas. First, this group of islands is a natural wreck ground with thousands of low-lying cays and twice that many treacherous reefs scattered over an immense area, a real night-mare to any ship's pilot, especially on a sailing ship at the mercy of winds and currents. And second, the Bahamas lie right along what was for three centuries the traditional route of the homeward-bound Spanish treasure fleets.

As I had expected, there was no lack of wrecks in the Bahamas. In only two months of diving I found, or was led to, over seventy sites scattered from Bimini—only fifty miles west of Miami—down to Grand Turk Island—about one hundred miles north of Haiti. But it was the same story as the rest of my search: no treasure.

It was getting very close to the time when I would have to abandon my island-hopping and either head for Spain, as agreed upon earlier with Clay Blair if I had not found a great treasure, or welch on my deal and do something else, since my finances were finally wearing thin. After fourteen months, in which over two hundred wreck sites had been explored, I had found all sorts of interesting goodies, but in the line of gold (Clay and I had agreed that nothing else could count as treasure), I had a paltry two gold coins to show for my efforts. I wanted to give it one last try, but had exhausted all my one hundred wreck sites, as well as my contacts with fishermen throughout the Caribbean and Bahamas, or I thought I had exhausted all my contacts.

I was sitting in a wharf-side bar in Nassau, feeling very dejected at the prospect of burying myself in some musty old archives for a year, when an old fisherman, whom I had spoken to many times before about wrecks, came in. I called him over to have a beer and listen to my troubles. Talk naturally got around to the topic of treasure, and the old fellow started telling me about a friend of his who had supposedly discovered a sunken horde of gold coins, which he had been selling one by one over the past fifteen or twenty years.

The story smacked of pure fiction, although he did mention the man's name—King—and where he lived—an island in the Grand Cay chain up in the northwest corner of the Bahama

Bank. And when all of the many friends I asked in Nassau, which is as treasure-conscious a place as any on the face of the earth, had never heard of this man King or his sunken treasure, I concluded that the old man had been spinning a yarn. I decided then and there to admit defeat and leave the next day. I was wandering around town in search of a present for the Blair children (I generally stayed with the Blairs when I was in the States), when I noticed several gold coins in the window of an antique shop and asked to see them. They were dated 1695, minted in Mexico, and did not look or feel like the many counterfeits that were circulating at the time. The store-owner refused to say where he had obtained them, which made me suspicious, and I wondered if there might be some tie-in with the story that old fisherman had told me. Starting at one end of town, I visited every antique or curio shop in Nassau; in three of them, identical gold coins were for sale, and all three shopowners displayed the same reluctance to say where they had come from. I canceled my plane reservation, determined to stay until I had found out the source of those gold coins.

Figuring, from personal experience, that alcohol is the best tongue-loosener, I invited the most promising shopowner, who simply happened to be a luscious blonde, for a drink, on the pretext that I wanted to sell her many of the goodies I had found on wrecks. I soon had the answer, and it was what I had expected. The gold coins had come from King. For years he had been selling them to the shops and also to tourists he met casually on the street, but until recently he had never sold more than a few at a time (to avoid detection, since the Crown was legally entitled to half of any treasure trove). Now he needed the money because his eldest son had killed a man in a drunken brawl and seemed sure to face the gallows, unless some sharp lawyer could get him off on a charge of manslaughter. Over the past few weeks alone, she had bought nearly one hundred coins from King, selling most of them in England and the United States, in order not to bring any suspicion on herself. When my blonde friend told me the miserly price she had been paying him and the great profit she had made, I became thoroughly disgusted and walked out on her. Hell, gold is more interesting than dames any day, or at least I think so.

Two days later, I caught a ride with a lobster boat heading in the direction of the Grand Cays, and for a few bottles of rum they went a bit out of their way to drop me off on the small cay where King lived. Finding him was easy—there were no more than ten or fifteen families on the cay. King's little cottage looked about the same as the others from the outside, but inside it had very fancy furniture, even a television set and a hi-fi record player, which were purely for show since there was no electricity on the cay. But getting information out of him was something else again. I couldn't blame him for being suspicious, especially after he told me that other white men had come around pestering him, some even threatening to kill him, in order to find out where his treasure was hidden. Not that King wouldn't talk; he talked incessantly. But he said nothing, and all I knew at the end of two hours was that the coins had definitely come from an old wreck. I also had an idea that the wreck could not be too far off, but that was because I had noticed that the only boats on the island were small dugout canoes.

Failing to convince King that he needed a diving partner to help him bring up the rest of the treasure, I left him, wondering what to do next. It looked like a few nights of sleeping out on the beach until the next boat came along, since I couldn't expect much hospitality from King or his neighbors. Just then I saw a fast speedboat racing toward the cay from another one about half a mile off. It ran right up into the shallow water near where I was sitting, and a man jumped out, calling in good Americanese, "Man, you look like you need a pad." He introduced himself— let's call him Roger Stillman—and said he owned a large house on the other cay, where he and his wife lived part of the year to escape the Boston winters.

I accepted his invitation to stay with them until the next

boat arrived. Of course there was a catch. During lunch, I learned that Stillman had the treasure bug even worse than I did. In fact, he had bought that cay and built his house there mainly so that he could be near King and either buy his hoard or find it himself—not that he really needed it, from the looks of his house. He had a crow's nest built on top of his house from which he followed King's every movement with powerful binoculars. But Stillman swore that King either must go out at night to pick up his coins or he had them buried right on the cay near his cottage, since he never saw him go out in his canoe, yet he knew that in the past month or so King had made three different trips to Nassau to sell gold coins.

Where did Stillman get his information about King's gold-selling trips to Nassau? From that same blonde shopowner who had told me and who had also radioed Stillman that I was coming up. Stillman didn't like competition and had invited me to stay with him, hoping that we could make a deal. I don't know who disgusted me more, this greedy millionaire or his blonde spy, but two can play at this game, I thought, and I agreed to work with him.

After listening to his sad tale of how he had spent more than three years, off and on, without finding King's treasure, I saw that the main reason for his failure was complete stupidity. Although he watched King like a hawk, it had never occurred to him to watch King's two sons, who I learned went out fishing nearly every day. Stillman's explanation was that King had sworn to him that only he, King, knew where the treasure was.

"Hell," I said, "what do you expect from a man you are trying to rob, the truth?"

For the next week I went out every day, hoping to follow King's sons to the wreck, but instead of going together as they had always done before, they now went out in two separate canoes. King was no fool, for he gave instructions that whichever one I followed was to act as a decoy and lead me away from the wreck, because King feared that I might accidentally stumble upon it by diving. This I didn't know at the time, but by the end of the week I knew the old man would outsmart us, as he had so many others, unless I tried another tactic.

I finally decided that I would search for the wreck myself, with Stillman's help, of course, since I was using his boat. We found quite a number of wrecks, but not the right one, and as we came in one afternoon toward the end of the second week, King himself, looking very upset, was waiting on the beach near the Stillmans' house. It seemed that his son Philip had gone out after conch early that morning and still had not returned. His other son had gone out to look for him and now both were lost. He asked Stillman if he would look for them in his speedboat, since it would soon be dark, but Stillman refused—stupid and selfish. Here he had a chance to make points with King—aside from any humanitarian reasons—and he was too tired! I offered to go and search in the area where King thought they might be.

A few miles out I located the second son, who said he had searched everywhere and was now returning home because he didn't like being out in his small dugout at night. I left him and, clipping along at twenty knots, I covered a great amount of water but found no signs of Philip at all. Then I noticed something sticking out of the water on a reef, which looked a bit peculiar, not like coral at all. It was Philip, and not in very good shape either, since he had been hanging on to the reef for nearly ten hours by then. He had been diving for conch that morning when somehow his canoe got away from him, drifting faster than he could swim, and after a long chase he had finally climbed up exhausted on this coral head. Twice, he said, his brother had passed within half a mile of him but hadn't heard his shouts. He had almost given up hope when he heard the noise of the speedboat and waved his arms to attract my attention.

King was overjoyed to see his son alive, hugging and patting him while he scolded him for losing his canoe. I left to head back to the Stillman's, but King came running out after me, gave me a warm handshake, and handed me six gold coins. Both Stillmans were so impressed by the coins, the first they had seen (except for those they had bought from their blonde friend in Nassau) after three winters of effort, that I gave each of them one.

The following day I decided to try my luck once more with King. This time he was very friendly, inviting me to take a walk down the beach for a chat. For hours we talked, or I should say he listened while I told my sad story of the many times I was on the point of finding a great treasure, only to have it slip away in the end. After listening to my sort of scientific approach to treasure-hunting, he laughed softly and said, "What good are your fancy books, charts and equipment? The Lord helps the poor man like me. I went for sponge one day with a long pole. I had no mind to search for gold. But I see some pretty, shiny things on the bottom and I go down to grab them. I don't even know what they are until I go down to Nassau and take my wife to the doctor and ask if I can pay him with them."

He went on to tell me how he wished he had never found that gold, since it had caused him so many troubles already. He blamed the gold for his son's having killed that man in the brawl. His son would never have been drunk, or even been in Nassau, for that matter, if it weren't for some cursed gold coins which he had stolen from King and run away with to Nassau to have a good time.

Finally, King said, "Master Bob, you seem like an honest man to me. Maybe you can help me." I said I would willingly, and he took me back to his cottage, where, after chasing out his wife and several children, he reached down into a barrel of flour and pulled out two bars, one silver and the other gold. After dusting off the flour he handed both to me for inspection. The silver bar was badly corroded on the outside, so that I could not read any of the markings on it, but the gold bar was like new. The assayer's mark, the marks of the King's treasury officials, and the date—1693—looked as clear as the day they were stamped. I couldn't believe I was holding so great a fortune in my hands—a smaller (King's gold bar weighed about twenty pounds) but similar bar found on a wreck in Bermuda had brought the discoverer $25,000. King said that he had been selling bars like this one over the years to some people in Florida for $50 each, but a few weeks ago another American over on Walker Cay had offered him $100 apiece. He didn't want to offend any of them, but he needed money badly now because of his son and thought the bars might be worth even more than $100 and wanted my opinion.

It needed no genius at mental arithmetic to figure that the bar, if pure gold (and the assayer's mark seemed genuine) was worth at least $10,000 for the gold alone.

"Mister King," I said, "you've been had. If you go halves with me I could get you at least $5000 apiece." At first he simply stared goggle-eyed at me as if I were crazy; then he saw that I was serious and realized he had been swindled royally.

"Master Bob, I don't know what to do," he said glumly. "You see, I need big money now, so I promised those people in Florida I would sell them fifty bars."

"Fifty!" Now my eyes were popping out. "How many do you have left on that wreck?"

"Many, many more," he replied, "that I can tell you."

"No, man," I argued. "You'd be cheating yourself if you go ahead dealing with those crooks." Of course, at that moment I could not have bought one bar, let alone fifty, but I was sure I could raise the money for a couple of them for a start, and by selling them off gradually to collectors, King and I could become millionaires. What a prospect!

Not that the old man cared a hoot about becoming a millionaire—all he cared about was saving his son from the gallows—but nobody likes being cheated, and I had pretty well convinced him to hold off those Florida people, at least long enough for me to get back to the States and raise some cash, when his son Philip came pounding on the door to announce that the monthly mail boat from Nassau was arriving. King quickly threw both bars back into the flour barrel and we walked nonchalantly down to the pier to watch the boat unload.

I lay awake the whole night figuring where I could raise the money for the first few bars and how I could get the best price—but mostly how I was going to spend the million or so I would make on the deal. I heard an engine during the night but didn't think anything of it at the time, since many boats pass close to those cays.

By morning I had decided I would leave that very day on the mail boat and rushed over to King's place before breakfast to put the finishing handshake on our deal, only to find that he was gone. "Gone where?" I demanded. His wife, looking very upset, said she didn't know where, or with whom, or anything, only that he had taken a trip. He must have left in a hurry; flour was spilled all over the floor, and sticking my arm down to the bottom of the flour barrel, while King's wife stared in amazement, I found that both bars were gone.

I walked back to the beach, puzzling over King's mysterious trip. Then I suddenly remembered his having mentioned this other American over on Walker Cay who had offered him $100 apiece for his gold bars. Since I couldn't think of any place else King might have gone, I jumped into the speedboat and blasted off at full throttle to Walker Cay. I was within a mile of the cay's landing dock, when a seaplane came taxiing right past me and took off before I could even see who was aboard. The passenger, I learned to my great surprise from Bill Griffiths, who runs a fishing camp on the cay (another American—the Bahamas is crawling with them), was none other than a very close friend of mine from New York—let's call him Pete Castelli.

"Pete Castelli! What in hell is he doing here?" I asked, and was even more astonished to find out that Pete was the mysterious American who had been trying to buy King's gold bars. He had been at Walker Cay for some time and apparently had no idea I was staying only ten miles away on Grand Cay.

When I asked where he had gone, Griffiths replied, "I'm not sure, but I have a good idea, and if he isn't careful he's going to get into real trouble, maybe even get himself killed." Pete, it seems, was one step ahead of me. Only a few hours before, he had learned that King had gone off before dawn in a big fancy yacht—local informants didn't know its name but claimed the home port painted on the stern was Palm Beach, Florida, and also claimed that besides King it was carrying a load of gold bars when it left. Pete decided to cut himself in on the deal, whatever it was, and radioed for a chartered seaplane to pick him up. By the time Pete took off in pursuit, the yacht had had a headstart of more than seven hours, and Griffiths was fairly certain that Pete had headed straight for Palm Beach. It seemed that Pete, the practical down-to-earth type who was forever razzing me about crazy treasure hunters, now had the bug worse than anyone. Well, it was his first case.

I decided to hang around and wait for King to return, hoping we could still make some kind of a deal; but after ten days and no King, I finally decided to admit defeat and return to the States. Then, as I was passing through Nassau, something in the paper made me think that King was in Nassau, too: a famous trial lawyer had been engaged to defend King's son on the manslaughter charge. I rushed to the lawyer's office, but all he could tell me was that he had received a large retainer by mail from New York.

New York—that was strange. Then I remembered that Pete lived in New York and decided he must have cut himself into the deal after all. I caught the next flight and five hours after my initial brain-wave I was pounding on Pete's door, even though it was after midnight.

Now it was Pete's turn to be astonished, when I greeted

him with, "Christ, Pete, you ought to be more careful. You nearly swamped me off Walker Cay with that damn seaplane." I told him my connection with King, and soon as he recovered from the shock, he told me what he had been up to. He had flown to Palm Beach, where he had tracked down the outfit that had bought this and other smaller loads from King, but when he tried to contact the man he was sure was the mastermind behind the deal, he found that this man had packed up his business in West Palm Beach and disappeared only a few days before. He had no idea where King was or what had happened to him, and other leads he had followed had been a dead end also.

"But what about the gold itself?" I asked. "It's not that easy to keep a thousand pounds of gold under cover or even dispose of it, which is what it would be if King really sold fifty twenty-pound bars as he had promised." That was one lead Pete hadn't thought of. We both spent the next week trying to learn if any large amounts of gold had been deposited or sold to any of the Federal Reserve Banks, but those treasury people are more close-mouthed than dead men.

In desperation, mainly because I was flat broke and Clay Blair wouldn't turn over any of the funds I had set aside for Spain before beginning my Caribbean jaunt (I have to admit now that he did me a big favor), I called it quits. But not Pete. He returned to the Grand Cays and spent months haunting King, who eventually returned home. But even though this time Pete tried to make a really honest deal, instead of the measly $100 a bar, King refused to speak to him or anyone else about the treasure, nor did any more gold coins appear for sale in Nassau. As for my host on Grand Cay, Roger Stillman, I think he's still sitting up in his crow's nest with his binoculars trained on King. Many mysteries remain unraveled in this tale. Had King been forced to sell to the Florida people against his will? How had the gold been disposed of? What had King done with the rest of the gold bars? I can make a good guess about some of them, but if I knew all the answers I probably wouldn't be writing this book: I would be writing checks against a bank deposit of a million or two.

The frustrating gold chase in the Bahamas was a real climax to my Caribbean treasure quest, and it left me only more determined to find a great fortune in sunken gold. Although I had not found any treasure myself (discounting my two paltry gold coins), I knew there was plenty to be found—King's little hoard was proof enough of that if I had needed any convincing —and no doubt there was plenty on some of the wrecks I had dived on, but the big problem was, which ones? The chances of having a lucky break like King's and just happening to find some "pretty shiny things" lying on the bottom one day are pretty slim. No more messing around for me. I wanted to know for sure which wrecks had treasure on them and which were duds. And the answers lay buried in the archives in Spain.

Chapter Seven

•

Following Columbus

•

I arrived in Seville at the beginning of Holy Week, 1961, to find the Archives of the Indies—and everything else, except the cafés and churches—closed for business. For seven days and nights the entire population jammed the narrow streets to watch the processions of penitents, each headed by a jewel-bedecked Madonna. The sight was impressive, especially at night when the Madonnas seemed to float along on a wave of candles, but I was itching to see what was waiting for me among the several million documents housed in the archives.

Several hours after the heavy, brass-studded archives doors swung back on the Monday after Easter, I had a case of document fever that made my previous bouts of treasure fever seem like the sniffles. There was everything I had dreamed of and more. I do not know how the Spaniards found time to colonize an empire, because from the look of things they must have spent every waking minute scribbling documents. Port officials did not just record the departure of a treasure fleet from Cartagena or Veracruz; they listed every nail that had been driven into every ship that cleared port. A governor did not just write back that a ship had run aground on the coast of, say, Florida; he gave the exact location whenever possible, eye-witness accounts of the disaster by the survivors, and detailed reports on the salvage attempts.

There was so much material that I was soon forced to hire several research assistants, and within a few months I had to find a larger apartment, squeezed out of the first one by all the crates and sea chests of notes I was accumulating. For I was gathering data not only on shipwrecks, but also on the whole system of *flotas,* or Spanish treasure fleets that sailed annually from Spain to the New World and back for several centuries. During my months of library work trying to identify the wreck *El Matan-cero,* I had become as disillusioned with the published sources on Spanish maritime history as I was with the popular books on sunken treasure. It was not so much that the information was false as that there simply was none, or at least nothing solid and detailed, based on original documents. So Clay Blair and I had decided to fill the gap ourselves by writing a two- or three-volume work on the treasure fleets.

After working only a few months in the archives, I realized that something essential was missing in the material I was gathering—the human element. If we were going to write a really interesting history of the *flotas,* I reasoned, we ought to include what life aboard the galleons was like. I found countless ship's logs and even voyage relations written by passengers, but they rarely mentioned the things that we thought readers would want to know: how the crews and passengers felt during the long, tedious ocean crossings; what they did to while away the time during calms; what their reactions were to the violent storms that came up without warning; how it felt to eat weevilly biscuit and drink the putrid green water—these and many other things were lacking from the documents.

How I eventually solved this problem is a long story, and the best place to start is on a hot August day in Seville. I was sitting in the hushed reading room of the archives, sweating blue blazes in a jacket and tie (that was shortly before I led a strike for less formal working attire for researchers), when a familiar voice boomed out: "My God, look who's turned scholar. Pirate Marx himself." The pince-nez perched on the nose of the wizened little old man in front of me fell to the glass-topped table with a clatter at this infringement of the reading room rules. I looked up. Standing at the entrance to the room with a broad grin on his face was—who else?—John Goggin.

Goggin and I just could not seem to shake each other. He had come to Spain, I found out after we adjourned quickly to the nearest sidewalk café, to do some original research on Spanish ceramics and pottery. I had told him that I was going to Seville, but he had not taken me seriously and was just as surprised to see me as I was to see him. We spent about a month touring southern Spain from Seville to Gibraltar, photographing every old jar and pot we could find and looking for private collections of documents that might have material for my *flota* book. We even photographed a large clay jar (and its contents) dug up from the crypt of an old Carthusian monastery outside Seville that probably contained the bones of Christopher Columbus. Columbus had in fact been buried in that monastery, and although many people claim that his bones were moved to Santo Domingo, there is no documentary evidence to prove it. But my roll of film, unfortunately, was confiscated, and Goggin was refused permission to carry back a small sliver of bone for spectroanalysis: there is a big Columbus monument in the cathedral of Seville, supposedly containing the bones of the "Admiral of the Oceans" (there are also similar "tombs" in the cathedrals of Santo Domingo and Havana), and there are a lot of people who would look awfully silly if that lowly clay jar turned out to contain the real thing.

I believe those were the bones of Columbus, and I shall tell you how the old Admiral came to repay me for accidentally stepping on one of his thigh bones after Goggin had laid out the contents of the clay jar for me to photograph. Goggin was as responsible as anyone else for the episode that follows: I was telling him one day about my problem with the history of the Spanish treasure fleets—the missing human element in all the material I was finding—and he replied, "Of course, you can't really know what a toothache is like unless you've had one."

"Who's talking about toothache? I'm talking about seventeenth-century Spanish galleons."

"So am I," Goggin replied. "What I mean is that you can't know how those people lived aboard the old galleons unless you've sailed on one yourself. Why don't you build a replica?"

Now that was exactly the kind of advice I wanted to hear from somebody. After being ashore so long, I was restless for some action, and here was Goggin suggesting something I had often dreamed about but thought was too crazy to attempt. I would build a replica of a seventeenth-century galleon, sail it to the West Indies, and then back again to Spain. I kept Goggin up half the night, spilling out ideas about the voyage: how it would have to be absolutely authentic, with no modern navigational aids, radios, or survival gear; everything from the food and cooking equipment to the sails would have to be the kind carried on an old galleon. Goggin agreed. The only thing he would not agree to was to come along for the ride. Digging and diving were his lines, he said, not teetering around on a yardarm fifty feet above some deck.

I wrote Clay about the idea immediately. He thought it was great and, besides signing up for the voyage himself, convinced the editors of *The Saturday Evening Post* to help back the venture in return for exclusive magazine rights. Clay's only suggestion was that I finish out my year of research before taking off, and I agreed, since it would take at least that long to make all the preparations, the main one being the construction of the ship. So, in addition to my regular research, I set about gathering all the information I could for the voyage, especially material on early navigational methods and the rigging and handling of old square-sailed ships. I checked out suitable shipyards and per-suaded a good friend of mine, a naval historian in Madrid, to draw up the plans for the two-hundred-ton galleon I would build.

What I did not know was that someone else had a plan very similar to mine. News of my project eventually spread all over Spain, and one day in June 1962, when I was up in Madrid doing some research in the Naval Museum, I received a phone call from a Spanish naval lieutenant from Pamplona named Carlos Etayo Elizondo, who said that he was building a replica of the caravel *Niña,* the smallest of the three vessels Columbus used on his voyage of discovery, and asked if I would be inter-ested in joining him. My galleon was still only on paper, he said, but his caravel was in the water. He had a point there, and we arranged to meet several days later in Madrid.

Carlos was not the rough-and-ready sea-dog type with a rolling gait I had expected. Shy and slight, he confessed that the only sailing experience he had had was a brief cruise twelve years before on a four-masted Spanish navy training schooner. But what he did have was a contagious determination to sail his vessel to America. He had been working secretly on the project for almost ten years, but only six months before, after receiving a modest inheritance, had he been able to start building his caravel. By the time of our meeting, the bare hull had been launched, and the shipwrights were then working on her masts and rigging.

Carlos offered me the job of pilot-navigator, and I ac-cepted—as he had said, my galleon was still only on paper. But there was one hitch. There would be no point in making the voyage, as far as I was concerned, unless we duplicated the same conditions under which Columbus and his crew had sailed—fifteenth-century victuals, clothes, navigational instruments, charts and equipment—otherwise one might as well sail across in a modern yacht. Carlos balked at the idea, claiming that it was all very well for us to endure those rugged conditions for the love of history, but we would never find any seamen willing to sail without a radio, life rafts, and other safeguards. I argued for hours, saying that he underestimated his countrymen's love for adventure and stressing the contribution we would be making to naval history. Finally, after I made it clear that I could not participate otherwise and would go ahead with my own plans to sail a galleon, Carlos agreed to duplicate fifteenth-century conditions, and the bargain was sealed.

The following day, I canceled all work on my galleon and started to help Carlos prepare for the voyage of the *Niña II*. A theatrical costuming firm was contracted to design and make fifteenth-century clothes for us and the crew; the Madrid Naval Museum agreed to make replicas of the charts and navigational instruments used in Columbus's time; and the Artillery Museum set to work making replicas of fifteenth-century cannons, swords, and other period arms. I spent several weeks combing *El Rastro* (the Madrid flea market) and antique shops for original fifteenth-century items, such as bowls and cutlery, flints for making fires, candlesticks, and sand-filled hourglasses, and whenever originals were not for sale, I had reproductions made.

As soon as all these preparations were completed, I drove up to the north of Spain to meet Carlos, who had been busy supervising the work on the *Niña II* at Pasajes, a small port on the Bay of Biscay close to the French border.

My first glimpse of the *Niña II* was a shock. No pictures or models of any of Columbus's three ships have been preserved, but a lot of clues about their size and design have been uncovered from other sources, and none of these clues tallied with what I saw lying at anchor in the Pasajes shipyard. The common opinion of naval historians is that the original *Niña* was between seventy-five and one hundred feet in length with a capacity of about sixty tons. There may be room for slight disagreement, but the *Niña* Carlos had built was barely forty-two feet long, with a capacity of about fifteen tons (an estimate given later by several naval architects, although Carlos claimed that his ship was thirty tons burthen). But she was not even a pint-size version of the original; there was nothing in the *Niña II's* squat shape and deep draft (eight feet) to suggest the graceful lines of a fifteenth-century caravel, a vessel noted for its speed—up to eighteen knots—and ability to sail close to the wind.

I had spent weeks fretting over the authenticity of the cooking implements we would use and other minor details, without even thinking about the most important item—the ship. I had assumed that Carlos had followed the commonly accepted opinions of naval historians, among whom some of the foremost are his own fellow Spaniards, but he had done his own research, and he countered my criticisms with the claim that the experts were wrong. Even Columbus was wrong: he had stated clearly in his log that the original *Niña* carried three masts, but the *Niña II* was fitted with only two, the mainmast and the mizzenmast. I had a momentary urge to make quick tracks back to Madrid and take up where I left off on my galleon project, but by then I felt as deeply committed to the Columbus voyage as Carlos. I consoled myself with the thought that at least we would be sailing under the same conditions as Columbus and his men, even if the vessel was *somewhat* modified in design. Closer inspection of the *Niña II* brought an added consolation: if nothing else, she was solid, built by hand from the keel up with the same careful workmanship (and even the same type of tools) that had gone into the original *Niña*.

There was still plenty of work ahead to prepare for the voyage. One of the main tasks was to select a crew. Carlos and I had both been swamped by hundreds of applications from adventure-seeking men (and women, too), most of whom had never been to sea before. Instead, Carlos signed on three Basque seamen from the Pasajes area. The first was José Valencia Salsamendi, who had spent most of his thirty-eight years at sea and turned out to be the best seaman on the voyage. The next was Nicolás Bedoya Castillo, a white-haired man of sixty-nine years who had seen nearly fifty years of service in the Spanish navy (however, all but two of them, I was to learn later, had been spent ashore tending lighthouses). And the third to sign on was a powerfully built fisherman, Antonio Aguirre Oroñoz, forty-two years of age, who had formerly been a professional boxer. Antonio was a good cook and an excellent harmonica player in the bargain.

Carlos and I stayed in Pasajes trying to rush the finishing touches on our *Niña*—rigging, sails, anchors, hatch covers, caulking, ballast, and a million odds and ends. The tasks seemed endless, especially with the almost daily fiestas (all attended by our crew, sailmakers, and ships' carpenters) and the throng of curious spectators who came over from the big summer resorts in San Sebastián to have a look at both this odd craft and the lunatics who were planning to cross the ocean in her. Finally, on July 28, she was ready for her first sea trial. Under the skeptical gaze of hundreds of onlookers, we cast off our moorings and started to row out of the sheltered habor, only to discover that our long oars, called "sweeps," were not long enough and barely reached the water. Yet they were so unwieldy that we could not maintain a steady beat and did little more than bang them together and curse each other for being so inept. Meanwhile, a strong incoming tide began to carry us toward a mudbank. We managed to keep off the mudbank, but that was our only triumph of the day. When after three hours of rowing we found we had covered only three hundred yards, with a thousand more to go before clearing the entrance to the harbor, Carlos decided to call it quits. We rowed back to the dock, smarting under the jeers and catcalls of the laughing spectators. José summed up my feelings perfectly when he asked, "How are we going to sail this crate across the Atlantic when we can't even get her out of port?"

Three days later, this time with longer sweeps and several more men hired to help us, we made another attempt. We had about the same success as on the first try, until I convinced Carlos to try a new method of moving the *Niña*—by warping, or being towed by a skiff. There was nothing ignominious about this, since it is the way sailing ships were brought in and out of port in the old days whenever the winds were not favorable. Once outside the harbor we hoisted sail, and the unbelievable happened. The *Niña* could not sail, at least not in a straight line: she staggered and reeled like a drunk on his way home after closing hours. Then to top it off, our mizzenmast, improperly stepped in the quarter-deck instead of the keel, came crashing down on the deck, and with the loss of our mizzen, the most important sail to help steer, the wind and current started to carry us toward shore. We manned the sweeps again but the wind was too strong, and only the timely arrival of a fishing boat, which took us in tow, saved our *Niña* from a premature end on the rocky coast.

The fishing boat took us to the small port of Guetaria, east of Bilbao, where we quickly set about making essential repairs and alterations. Having a new mizzenmast constructed and stepped in the keel was only the beginning. We had to find a way to make the *Niña* sail. The rudder was enlarged and lengthened and ballast moved aft to bring the bow higher out of the water. These and other minor alterations did the trick. When we took her out for new sea trials on August 12, we found that the *Niña* could now actually sail, not very fast, but at least in a straight line. She would not sail at all with the triangular lateen sail Columbus had first used on the original *Niña* (the mainmast was too far aft), but the large square mainsail he had replaced it with in the Canary Islands for the main part of his voyage did work, and at this point we were not prepared to be fussy over details.

We were very pressed for time, since we had hoped to duplicate Columbus's voyage exactly, leaving the port of Palos in southern Spain on the same date he had, August 3. It was already too late to do that, but Columbus had spent nearly a month in the Canary Islands before setting off on the last leg of his voyage across the Atlantic on September 6, and we figured that we could catch up with him there. This meant that we had to get down to Palos, and then on to the Canaries with a minimum of delay.

There was the expected last-minute panic. The official permission to sail that we needed from the Spanish government had not come through yet, and I shuttled back and forth between Guetaria and Madrid to hound every influential contact I had. Carpenters had to be urged on to complete repairs, and supplies had to be rounded up and loaded on board. Even on this preliminary leg of the voyage down to Palos, we would carry exactly the same kind of food stores as Columbus: vinegar, olive oil, biscuit, lard, chick peas, rice, beans, almonds, raisins, sugar, salt, garlic, onions, sardines, wine, brandy, and water. Since tobacco was not known in Europe at the time of Columbus's voyage, we tried to talk the crew, who were all heavy smokers, into giving up cigarettes until we reached America (no problem for either Carlos or me, since we don't smoke anyway), but they protested that this was carrying the authenticity bit just a little too far.

In Guetaria we signed on two more crew members. The first was a twenty-nine-year-old Frenchman, Michel Vialars, a trained veterinarian who had recently completed an army hitch in Algeria. He had no sailing experience, but he did very well in the *Niña's* second sea trials and was signed on as ship's doctor and apprentice seaman. Since no Spanish ship would be complete without a chaplain, the Reverend Antonio Sagaseta, a forty-six-year-old Catholic priest from Carlos's home town of Pamplona, was signed on next. Father Sagaseta, or "Padre," as we called him, had served as a gunnery officer during the Spanish Civil War before being ordained, and he was also put in charge of the *Niña's* four artillery pieces. Padre brought along a decrepit, one-eyed cat, which I named "Circe," as ship's mascot. But Circe, with that strong sense of self-preservation possessed by all animals except man, took one look around the *Niña* and jumped ashore. We fetched her back, but after the tenth escape we had to keep her tied up to the mast until we got to sea; that cat obviously had more brains than the rest of us put together.

Finally, on the morning of August 23, everything was ready—everything, that is, but the weather. Shortly before we were to leave port, a strong northwest wind, exactly the opposite of what we needed, began to blow and was predicted to last ten days. Carlos and I decided to swallow our pride and arrange for a tow that would take us around Cape Finisterre, the northwest tip of Spain, to where we could pick up more favorable winds and make the rest of the 950-mile trip to Palos under sail.

The towship arrived the next evening, August 24, and by 1900 we were underway. The three hours that followed were a nightmare, for the *Niña* wallowed on her towing cable in the huge seas like a seasick whale. A few times we swung so far to one side of the towship that the *Niña* was pulled sideways through the water and almost capsized. Two, sometimes as many as four, men had to man the tiller. One minute fighting the helm was like an hour on a bucking bronco, and all of us were covered with bruises before the night was over.

The tow continued for two more days and nights. Carlos and I averaged about three hours of sleep each a day, and everyone was so exhausted from the work at the helm that no one even attempted to cook a hot meal. When the towship finally left us, we had passed Cape Finisterre and were only a few miles north of the port of Vigo near the Portuguese border. It would be smooth sailing south to Palos, we thought. It was smooth all right: about the same instant we cast off the towing cable the wind disappeared, and for the next fifteen days we literally drifted to Palos, a trip we had estimated would take no more than three days. Only on two occasions was there enough wind to use the sails. Most of the time we were lost in fogs so thick that we could barely see a hundred feet, even in the middle of the day. We were in constant danger of collision with passing fishing boats and freighters, and one of us had to keep watch on the bow constantly, beating on a metal pan with a spoon to warn off approaching vessels.

We finally reached Palos on September 11, looking as if we had been at sea for years—bearded, covered with fleas (thanks to Circe), and badly in need of a bath and change of clothes. This unofficial leg of our voyage had been nearly disastrous. All our drinking water had spoiled after a few days out and we had had to stop several boats to get fresh supplies. Then the ship's biscuit (a type of hard bread), which had been specially baked according to an old fifteenth-century recipe and was guaranteed to keep for a year, soon turned so moldy that it looked like a solid mass of penicillin. To me the greatest problem had been the lack of discipline on board. Everyone did as he pleased, working and following orders if he felt like it, and not, if he didn't, which meant that the burden of work fell on a few. Little did I suspect that all the calamities and problems that arose then were to set a pattern for our long voyage across the Atlantic.

At Palos we found quite a welcome waiting for us, even though the newspapers had claimed for the past week that the *Niña* had sunk with all hands lost. For eight full days we were wined and dined in a continuous round of fiestas, with hardly a free moment to attend to the work needed on the *Niña*'s sails, which we had found were improperly made, to clean the rotten barrels that had caused our water to go bad, and to do the countless other essential tasks. We met many of the descendants of Columbus's original crewmen from the Palos area and, just as Columbus had done, we stayed at the thirteenth-century Franciscan monastery of La Rábida. We even had our new supply of ship's biscuit baked in a massive old brick bakehouse that many claim Columbus's biscuit had been baked in almost five centuries before.

At Palos we took on two more crewmen, who brought the ship's complement up to nine. The first was Manuel ("Manolo") Darnaude Rojas-Marcos, the thirty-three-year-old scion of a prominent Andalusian family, a keen amateur sailor and the holder of a navigator's degree from a Spanish merchant marine academy. Realizing that all of us, except perhaps José, had hardly any experience handling sailing vessels, with little likelihood of becoming experts overnight, I had persuaded Carlos that Manolo's skills would be very useful. The ninth addition to our crew was made purely by accident. We had found a comical little guy named Pepe Robles (aged thirty-nine) hanging around the dock at Palos and hired him to guard the *Niña* while we were all ashore living it up. Soon after leaving Palos, I went below to consult a chart and, instead of one of the crewmen holding the tiller, I found Pepe. When I asked what in the hell he was doing there, he said that we had not paid him, so he had decided to stay on board until we did. Carlos wanted to hail a passing boat and send Pepe back to Palos, but I persuaded him that we could use Pepe. As it turned out, he was one of the best seamen we had, even though his normal occupation ashore was goatherd. Maybe scrambling around the rocks after his charges is what had made him so agile, but nobody could scurry up the mast like Pepe; in fact, few of us dared try it at all.

At sunrise on September 19, we started down the river leading from Palos to the open sea, to the accompaniment of Gregorian chants sung by the Franciscan friars in the cliff-top La Rábida monastery. As we crossed over the bar at the mouth of the river, dozens of Spanish air force planes buzzed us, and we waved our final goodbyes to all our friends aboard the scores of yachts and fishing boats that had escorted us out to sea. Padre was eager to fire a parting salute, and Carlos gave permission to fire the falconet, one of the four small cannons the Artillery Museum had made for us. But there is a big difference between a fifteenth-century falconet and the modern artillery Padre was used to. He used too much powder, and in the explosion part of the charge backfired through the fuse hole right at José, who had lit the fuse. For the duration of the voyage, José was busy digging tiny scraps of metal and powder from his face, chest, and arms.

This accident was a fitting curtain-raiser for a voyage that was plagued with bad luck from beginning to end. For three straight days the wind blew strong from the west, nearly carrying us through the Straits of Gibraltar into the Mediterranean. Then the unfavorable wind died down and was followed by a period of calms, although fortunately the current was running in the direction of the Canaries. On the sixth day out, while we sat eating our noon meal of rice and beans and watching a school of porpoises play around our drifting hull, the dead calm was broken by a gust of hot wind straight from the African desert that felt like someone had opened a furnace door. Bowls, cups, pots, and people smashed against the lee gunwale as the *Niña* heeled over a a 65-degree angle, the tips of her mast almost touching the sea, and within seconds the wind had risen to sixty knots. The sky became dark, and huge seas curled over the *Niña's* tilted decks, to which we were all clinging for dear life. All the sails had been set during the calm, in order to catch any chance puff of wind, and we all realized that unless they were lowered or cut away the *Niña* would soon capsize. José saved the day. Grabbing a knife, he scrambled out on the almost horizontal mainmast over the churning seas and started to slash the lines holding the mainsail in place. Manolo and I then followed suit with the smaller mizzen, and when both sails had been loosened, releasing the tremendous pressure of air trapped in them, the *Niña* righted herself. But our problems were far from over. For thirty miserable hours the gale raged on, and the storm sail we rigged could not persuade the *Niña* to ride the huge seas stern to the wind. She preferred to face them broadside on and received such a terrific pounding that we all marveled that she did not fall to pieces. She did leak a great deal, however, and during the entire thirty-hour period one of the two hand pumps had to be manned constantly. Our small cabin was a shambles, with mattresses, clothes, and gear sloshing around in the water that covered the deck. A ten-gallon jug of olive oil had broken loose and smashed, making it impossible to move around the cabin at all except on all fours.

When the gale finally abated we went below to inspect the provisions and were met by a disheartening sight. It looked as if a tornado had passed through the hold: nearly all the clay jars containing water, wine, vinegar, honey, and brandy were broken, as well as many of the barrels and crates containing our other stores. While several of the men repaired our tattered sails, others tackled the sticky, slimy mess in the hold and cabin.

Carlos and I had agreed that I would navigate with only the fifteenth-century instruments, such as the astrolabe and quadrant (both work on the same principle of measuring the angle of the sun's zenith at midday to determine latitude), that the Naval Museum had reproduced for us. But during the voyage he insisted upon double-checking my calculations with a modern sextant he had brought along as a precaution when we left Palos. After the storm had ended on the seventh day out from Palos, both of us took sun fixes and placed our position at about two hundred miles west of the nearest point on the North African coast. Later that night we spotted the blinking light from a lighthouse; this meant that we could be no further than thirty miles from shore and that Carlos and I were both unbelievably bad navigators. Manolo, who had no navigational instruments, nor had he even consulted the charts, had told us earlier in the day that our estimated position was at least 150 miles off, and now he was proven correct, much to our embarrassment.

As we gradually moved south into lower latitudes, the temperature naturally grew warmer. In a way this made life more comfortable, but it also intensified a problem that had been with us from the start—hygiene. My biggest headache during this phase of the voyage, aside from trying to master the science of navigation, fifteenth-century style, was the sanitary conditions on board the *Niña*. Few of the crew saw anything wrong with discarding cigarette butts, leftover food, and any other trash on the decks and in the cabin, and only Michel and Manolo shared my views on the subject of bathing, taking daily sea dips with me. Nicolás swore that bathing caused rheumatism, Antonio claimed that it led to scurvy, and the others had similar excuses. At times, especially during calms, when no dissipating breeze entered the cramped cabin, the stench inside was so unbearable that I would resort to throwing buckets of sea water over the deck and dousing the walls with sweet-smelling brandy, of which we had an abundant supply.

One would have thought that, after the experience we had on the voyage from Guetaria, extra-special precautions would have been taken with water and victuals in Palos. They were not. Instead of replacing the acidy barrels that had caused the water to spoil, Carlos had decided to use some chemical to keep it drinkable. Not only was the chemical an unauthentic, twentieth-century innovation, but also we forgot to put it in the barrels until we were a week out of Palos, by which time all the water had spoiled again and we had to depend exclusively on wine. This meant nothing to José, since he never drank water anyway, even when we were in port. I can attest to the fact that during the six months I lived in close contact with the man, he never touched one drop of water, even using wine to brush his teeth. All the rest of the crew, although not as exaggerated as José, had been brought up on wine since early childhood, but I never got used to it as a substitute for water and always found that it only increased my thirst.

Like the water, our specially baked biscuit once again went bad only a few days out. I do not know what secret the old-time sailors had to keep it fresh, but I suspect that their biscuit was much dryer and less like regular bread and was also stored better than ours, which was kept in the damp, unventilated hold. As a substitute, I began to make a kind of Mexican tortilla out of moldy flour, olive oil, and sea water. They looked like mud pies but tasted very good, or at least my customers said so, and I never seemed to be able to keep up with the demand.

On October 3, we reached the Canaries, although we missed our intended landfall by seventy miles. We were supposed to put it at the island of Gomera, as Columbus had done, where about fifty members of the press were waiting for us, but Carlos decided to put into Las Palmas on the main island of Grand Canary instead. We were welcomed by thousands of cheering islanders and tourists, and after a series of speeches from local officials and clergy, we were bustled off to a fantastic banquet at one of the main restaurants. Hours later, with bulging stomachs and swaying heads—I lost count of the toasts proposed to us and by us after about twenty-five—we were deposited in palatial rooms at the Hotel Metropole. Several of the crew, especially Pepe, who had known little more than the harsh life of a goatherd, and José, who had endured the even more rugged life of a Spanish cod fisherman on the Newfoundland Banks, were dumfounded at the sight of such luxury. But all of us (including Manolo, whom I later found out was Spain's answer to Beau Brummel) looked like nine ragpickers among the elegant clientele of the hotel's dining room that evening.

There is nothing to beat Spanish hospitality (except, perhaps, Mexican): our whole stay in Las Palmas was a duplication of the week-long fiesta in Palos. One fiesta ran into another, and there was not a moment's attention given to the *Niña's* sails and rigging, which were both badly in need of repair. Here, too, was an opportunity to replace our rotten water barrels and a few hundred other tasks, but I had finally met someone who beat me at trusting to luck and endurance rather than careful preparations.

Sometime between banquets and cocktail parties I managed to find time to draw up a list of provisions, which the local authorities had offered to supply gratis. During the voyage from Palos, the *Niña's* top speed under the most favorable conditions had been four to five knots. I had no reason to believe she would be transformed into a contender for the America's Cup on the crossing from Las Palmas to San Salvador in the Bahamas, and I calculated our provisions on the basis of a forty-day voyage with a reserve supply for another thirty days. Carlos was more optimistic. Columbus had made it in thirty-three days, he said, and he cut down my list by more than half. Columbus had sailed across on three ships, not drifted on an oversized barrel, I argued. Carlos finally agreed that we would take on more provisions at Gomera, but even so, I made some silent prayers for favorable winds on the crossing.

Praying was very big on the agenda in Las Palmas. Almost every church in the area claimed the distinction of being the scene of Columbus's last Mass before he set out on his voyage of discovery, and in order to keep peace, we too attended Mass at all of them in between fiestas.

We had long before given up the pretense of duplicating Columbus's sailing date. As it was, we barely got away from Las Palmas before the date on which Columbus *arrived* in America —October 12. On the morning of the tenth, we staggered down to the dock, all nursing bad hangovers, and began to load on provisions and water. Our plan was to leave at noon, but after everything was aboard, Manolo noticed that we had neglected to obtain any firewood for cooking, and most of the crew took off in taxis to scour the island for wood. I took off on my own, having remembered that the *Niña* had no mascot (Circe had finally jumped ship in Palos; she leaped overboard the minute we dropped anchor and swam ashore, never to be seen again). I returned with a fluffy, flealess little kitten which Antonio promptly named "Linda," meaning "pretty" in Spanish. Linda soon made friends with "Pinzona," the other new addition to the *Niña*, a nanny goat Michel named after a girl he had met in Palos.

Accompanied by the fanfare of a brass band and the cheers of thousands of spectators crowding the docks, we cast off late that afternoon and started to row for the open sea against a strong wind. By the time we had almost smashed into several anchored vessels, we shamefacedly accepted a tow. Once we were out of the harbor and our tow lines had been cast off, we hoisted sail. The wind promptly died down, but we were all relieved to be at sea again after the hectic round of fiestas ashore, and we drifted lazily for the rest of the day, grateful for the much-needed rest. That night a good breeze sprang up and we headed in the direction of Gomera, 150 miles to the west. We were supposed to make a brief stop there for additional stores and also to appease the irate islanders and members of the press who had been waiting there for weeks. For all I know they are still waiting. We overshot the island, and Carlos, reluctant to waste time beating back to windward, ordered me to set a direct course for the island of San Salvador, 3,360 miles away. I thought he had to be joking: the *Niña* was already leaking badly and her rigging was in sorry shape; our food and water supplies had been inadequate in any case, and two of the nine water barrels had leaked dry since we left Las Palmas. But he was serious, and even though the rest of the crew were against this plan also, I did not fancy myself in the role of Christian Fletcher. San Salvador it would be.

Our original plan after leaving Gomera was to sail nearly due west with the northeasterly trades, as Columbus had done, since San Salvador is almost in the same latitude as the Canaries. But even the steady, dependable trade winds played fickle with the luckless *Niña*. For fourteen straight days we either drifted or were forced to sail due south (a square-rigged vessel cannot sail very close to the wind, even less so when her crew is as inept as we were). We moved further and further away from San Salvador each day, and at one point we approached so close to the Cape Verde Islands that several of the crew claimed they could sight the high mountain peaks from the top of the mainmast.

From the start our main worry was the dwindling supply of food and water. By the end of the first week we found that over 40 per cent of our water had leaked out of the faulty barrels; the fresh fruit, stored in the hot, damp hold, not surprisingly went bad, and the same happened to the fresh supply of biscuit (our third batch, also guaranteed to last for years) that had been baked in Las Palmas. The whole food situation was beginning to seem like a recurrent nightmare. Carlos ordered immediate rationing of water, but discipline on board the *Niña* was not the strictest, and water continued to dwindle at an alarming rate. I tried drinking small amounts of sea water, soon joined by Michel and Carlos, and by the end of the voyage the three of us were downing about a quart of sea water daily, usually mixed with a small amount of wine. We never noticed any ill effects, even though it is a common belief of sailors that drinking sea water will drive one mad, but then we had to be half crazy to have started on this venture in the first place.

Fishing, which the sailors of Columbus's day (and before and since) depended on heavily to supplement their shipboard fare, was for us a pitiful farce. Between Guetaria and Palos, we caught only one small shark, even though fishing lines were out and tended around the clock. The catch during the Palos–Canaries run was even less impressive: one small amberjack, caught as we entered Las Palmas harbor. After Carlos's decision not to stop at Gomera, we doubled the number of fishing lines trailing from the *Niña*'s stern, using a different kind of bait on each one. But for some mysterious reason we caught nothing, although the ship was constantly surrounded by hundreds of fish, including porpoises, sharks, and even whales.

Finally, on our ninth day out, Antonio hooked four small amberjacks, which we ate for supper along with two undigested squid in the stomach of one of them. Then, three nights later, the Padre, who had never fished in his life, hooked a ten-foot tiger shark. It was full of fight, and chaos ensued when several of the others tried to help him pull it aboard. The powerful shark thrashed around the deck, as Nicolás tried to tie its tail to the mainmast, while Antonio stabbed it with a large harpoon, and Carlos chopped away at its head with an axe. Carlos, the deck, and everything else was drenched with blood. Pinzona bleated in terror, and Linda scampered up to the very top of the mainmast, refusing all efforts to coax her down again for hours. Still the shark fought on, and soon all nine of us joined in the battle, adding sledgehammers, a speargun, and clubs to the axe and harpoon. Even so, it took us nearly an hour to finish off the shark, and just when it seemed we could all get back to sleep (except the two men on watch), Manolo hooked another shark, probably attracted by the first one's blood, which was draining out through the scuppers. This one was only an eight-footer, but the same mad scene was repeated and, after polishing off the second shark, we were all too keyed up to sleep. Antonio broke out his harmonica, and we spent the rest of the night celebrating our good luck over a bottle of brandy.

This fresh meat came none too soon. The next morning we discovered that our remaining supply of salted meat was full of worms and all of it had to be flung overboard (a hasty decision we were to regret later; worm-ridden food is better than no food). The cheese and dried fruit were in the same condition, but we wisely decided against chucking them overboard with the meat and eventually we ate them, worms and all.

Even though we plowed along at an unbelievably slow pace, this was no leisurely cruise with time to loaf around. The sails needed constant attention, unless we hit an absolutely flat calm. Any time the breeze stiffened, the bonnet on the big mainsail had to be taken in, only to be let out again when the wind decreased. This operation, which was repeated at least several times a day, required the whole crew, since the heavy yard and sail had to be lowered partway and raised again: the sheets, as well as the smaller mizzen and jury-rigged spritsail, could generally be handled by one or two men. Even in a flat calm two men had to be on watch, one at the tiller and one as a lookout on the quarter-deck, although, strange as it seems, we sailed for over two months before we sighted the first passing vessel. The helmsman's job was never easy—in the low cabin, less than five feet high, he had to stand bent over for hours at a time—but in strong winds it was hell, and sometimes as many as four or five men were needed to hold on to the bucking tiller to keep the *Niña's* stern into the wind.

There was always some task to be done for those not on

watch: pumping out the bilges, calking the leaks below deck, tending the fishing lines, and airing out the already putrid provisions, to name a few. Repairs were unending, especially on the rotten rigging and sails. (We had brought no spare set, but the useless lateen sail was steadily cannibalized until there was nothing left at all.) Nicolás was excused from watches, being too nearsighted either to serve as lookout or keep a steady compass course, but he was a wizard at splicing lines and patching sails. Some of the rest of us had special chores also: Pepe, our ex-goatherd, was delegated to milk and tend Pinzona; Antonio did most of the cooking, except for my mouth-watering tortillas; and I had the self-appointed job, assisted by Linda, of keeping down the fly population that had accompanied us all the way from Palos. But they seemed to breed faster than we could kill them (my record was 203 in one hour), and by the end of the voyage there were more flies than when we started.

I had brought along a chess board and a set of dice, which I knew sailors in Columbus's time had used to while away off-duty hours, but only once during the whole voyage did our crew have time to use them and that was when I staged a chess game in order to shoot some photographs. I suppose we could have played in the evening—we had candles and later, when they ran out, rags dipped in olive oil—but the men preferred to relax by singing, accompanied by Antonio's harmonica, or in the favored pastime of Spaniards—arguing, about politics, religion, women, the relative merits of *tabaco negro* and *tabaco rubio* (dark versus light tobacco), anything. Most of the men slept in the cramped, foul-smelling cabin, but there was room for only six at a time, and some of us preferred to stretch out on the open quarterdeck in all but the foulest weather.

For the first two weeks everything went fairly smoothly, even though we were sailing south, further from our destination each day. Then, around sunset on our sixteenth day out, a bad gale struck, again without any warning. Seasoned mariners might possibly have sensed it coming. I don't know; all I know is that a sudden gust of wind struck the large mainsail with such force that the mainmast cracked in several places and was wrenched loose from its step, or socket, on the keelson. Again the *Niña* heeled way over, taking on large seas and threatening to capsize any minute.

I was at the helm at the time, and because all the other hands were needed to lower the torn and flapping sail and to man the pumps, I had to continue holding the tiller alone. It was a tug of war between a man already weak from malnutrition and the powerful seas that crashed against the ship with increasing violence. The *Niña*, as usual, was bent on self-destruction; sometimes only by lying almost prone across the tiller and bracing my feet against the bulkhead could I keep her from turning broadside to the waves. After about an hour I collapsed from exhaustion, but luckily Manolo was nearby and quickly ran to grab the tiller.

The gale died down the following morning, but worse was to come. Pepe went below to fill the wineskin and reported that the hold already had four feet of water and was filling rapidly. Both hand pumps were broken by then, so we quickly formed a bucket brigade to keep the vessel from sinking. For two full days we bailed continually, stopping only long enough to grab an occasional piece of dried shark meat and a swig of wine, and all this time we simply drifted at the mercy of the wind and current with no time to repair the tattered sails and rigging. Finally, realizing that we were fighting a losing battle—Nicolás, Padre, and Carlos had already dropped out of the chain from sheer exhaustion and the rest of us were not far behind—I decided to try one last ace in the hole. Although it was not authentic, I had brought along my set of snorkeling gear for use in the Bahamas. I went over the side secured by a lifeline and searched the submerged hull for the source of the leak, which none of us had been able to find from the inside. After nearly an hour I located a hole, only about an inch in diameter, where a wooden peg (called a "treenail") joining a plank to one of the ribs had

worked loose. While Antonio and Nicolás were busy shaping a
wooden plug for me to insert, I remembered the story of the
Dutch boy and the hole in the dike, and like an idiot I put my
thumb in the hole as a temporary plug. Each time the ship rolled
and my head came above water I got a quick gulp of air. Then
suddenly the *Niña* caught a particularly heavy sea and I was
pulled way under as the vessel heeled over on top of me. I held
my breath, waiting for her to roll back, but she did not—the vast
amount of water in the hold prevented her from righting herself—and when I tried to pull my thumb out I found that it was
stuck. I reached for my knife and was just ready to cut my
thumb off (it was either that or go down) when the vessel rolled
back enough for me to gulp a precious mouthful of air. I quickly
enlarged the hole with my knife and extracted my swollen
thumb, and a few minutes later the plug was ready. Three hours
later we had bailed the hold dry.

The gale had pushed us even further south, and by the
evening of the eighteenth day we were wallowing along within
insect range of Africa. By this time Columbus was better than
half way across the Atlantic, while we were actually seven hundred miles further away from San Salvador than when we first
left the Canaries. We had two choices ahead of us: continue on
to San Salvador with the risk of running completely out of food
and water before we reached there, or to head east for Africa and
safety.

That night I called a meeting of the whole crew. Carlos was
opposed to the idea at first, but I argued that everyone had the
right to help make a decision on which all of our lives might
depend. Michel reported on the woefully small supply of ver-
minous food and putrid water, Manolo did the same on the state
of our leaking vessel, and Carlos and I admitted that we did not
know our exact position, but were fairly sure we were now some
four thousand miles away from San Salvador. The voting was to
be secret. Each man was given a sliver of wood: if he wanted to
head for Africa, he was to place the sliver in Pinzona's empty

water dish, and if he wanted to keep on for San Salvador, he was to throw the sliver overboard. It was very dark. One by one the men filed out, cast their vote and returned to sit wordlessly on the cabin deck. I was the last to vote and found the water dish as I had expected—completely empty. It would be San Salvador or bust!

Whether it was our vote of confidence or just plain luck, the next morning we finally hit the long awaited southeast trades, and for the first time since leaving the Canaries we were able to sail toward, instead of away from, San Salvador. That first day the *Niña* fairly clipped along, covering 117 miles, which for her was amazing. The winds became lighter the next day and we only averaged fifty miles in each twenty-four-hour run—a snail's pace, but at least it was in the right direction. The favorable wind really worked wonders with everyone's morale. Nicolás, who had sworn that both of the hand pumps were beyond repair, got one of them working; Michel helped me improvise plankton nets so that we could supplement our diet; and Manolo and José made hand spears for spearing fish. I was even able to bring all the crew around to my ideas on shipboard sanitation. We scrubbed out the cabin with vinegar, and for the first time on the whole voyage everyone—except Nicolás—took a sea bath.

Food was still our principal concern, since rations were now down to starvation level. We had devoured the raw, dried-out shark meat much faster than anticipated and were back to a daily diet of one hot meal of rice and beans plus several of my tortillas, a few cloves of garlic, a quarter of an onion, and about an ounce of worm-ridden cheese per man.

We tried every method of fishing possible, but with little success. Even though we knew that the porpoise is a sailor's best friend and should never be killed under any circumstances, this rule meant little to starving men, and each of us took turns at the bow throughout the daylight hours, trying to harpoon one of the many porpoises that constantly played around the vessel. But these creatures are so intelligent that the moment anyone would lift an arm to throw the harpoon, they would sense it and scoot out of range until the arm was lowered again.

Manolo and I had both bought spearguns in the Canaries, but neither one saw much use. One night Michel shot a large dolphin from the deck with my gun, but the line broke, and the fish got away with the spear. Several days later I grabbed Manolo's gun when a school of yellowtail appeared around the *Niña*, but, unknown to me, the line supposedly connecting the spear to the gun was untied. I fired and actually hit a fish, only to see it swim away with the spear through its middle: so much for these two unauthentic items. We then made several hand spears from our Columbus swords, and whenever it was fairly calm both Manolo and I would dive under the hull and try to spear some of the hundreds of fish that lurked in the shade, feeding on the heavy marine growth that covered the bottom. This was the most frustrating method of fishing ever devised. We had no file aboard to make barbs on the ends of the spears, so that, for every hundred fish we speared, ninety-nine managed to wriggle free before we could grab them with our hands.

About the only really happy creature aboard the *Niña* was our little kitten Linda, who received constant affection from everyone, including the few men who had claimed they hated cats. Linda had grown plump and frisky on her diet of fresh milk, courtesy of Pinzona, but then Pinzona, as undernourished as the rest of us, ceased to give milk, and Linda began to grow thin, too, until she developed a taste for raw shark meat. Pinzona had even more versatile tastes: after her supply of alfalfa ran out, she started to nibble on her wooden water bowl; in fact, she ate everything within reach, including parts of the canvas mainsail, the anchor cable, and the deck planking. As our own food supply ran lower and lower, our hungry stares increasingly fixed on Pinzona; we had grown fond of her, but we knew there would come a day when hunger would override any feelings of sentiment.

The prospect of a slow death by starvation was always with us, but on November 1, our twenty-third day out, all thoughts of hunger were pushed into the background by a much more immediate danger. What we had thought were bad storms before were little summer squalls in comparison to the one that hit us that day. This time we had sufficient warning: menacing dark patches on the horizon became steadily larger until by nightfall the sky was totally black; then lightning flashed all around us, as the seas rose to immense size in a matter of minutes and violent gusts of wind filled the sails to the bursting point.

The only sensible thing to do was to lower the sails immediately (actually we should have taken in canvas long before) and either set a storm sail or put out a sea anchor. But we were not sensible men; we were madmen obsessed with the idea of reaching America before our food ran out completely, and the powerful wind coming from the east was pushing us toward our destination at a speed we never thought possible on the *Niña*. Whereas her top speed had been four, possibly five knots, we were soon doing ten, and the *Niña*'s bow crashed through the seas like a half-submerged torpedo. But the feeling of exhilaration was short-lived. The wind steadily increased in force, and as I watched our two quivering masts bend forward like archer's bows under the strain, threatening to snap in two, I was sure the end was coming. For the first time in my life I felt real fear. It was too late to lower the sails properly; instead, we slashed them with harpoons and hand spears to release some of the tremendous wind pressure, then pulled down the spars and gathered in the tattered, billowing canvas. Sailing under bare poles, the *Niña* was now almost impossible to steer. We threw out a hastily improvised sea anchor, but even several men hanging onto the tiller could not hold her steady. The waves seemed to come from every direction, twirling the ship like a cork or engulfing us in tons of water as they crashed right over her decks. If I had had time to think about it then I would have been grateful that the

Niña, ungraceful in design or not, had been built like a water-tight barrel filled with air, for I am sure that this is the only thing that kept us from going under.

The night seemed endless, but the next day was even worse. It was so dark that only my watch told me that it was daytime. If anything, the storm increased in fury, the wind reaching at least seventy knots. We all huddled like zombies in the cabin, which protected us from being washed overboard but nothing else. The strain on the masts before the sails were cut down had loosened the deck planking overhead, and sea water and rain poured down on us through the many openings. Inside it felt as if the whole vessel was being tossed like a basketball and pounded with battering rams all at the same time. No one even thought of eating. Antonio lapsed into a feverish coma that was to last for six days, Nicolás crouched in one corner of the cabin, not talking or even moving for two full days, and the rest of us sat almost as silent, wondering how long the *Niña* could stay in one piece.

During this second day of the storm, I was on tiller watch when suddenly the tiller shaft broke off the rudder head, whipping my left wrist against the bulkhead. Luckily it was not broken, only painfully sprained, but now we were in serious trouble. Both sea anchors had been carried away and without any means of steering the ship to keep her bow headed into the heavy seas, the danger of capsizing was added to that of being pounded to splinters. At times the *Niña* would be turned over a full 90 degrees, with her keel above water and the tips of her masts awash. Fortunately the crates and barrels of provisions below had been securely stowed, for with the slightest shift of the cargo in her hold, she would have turned turtle.

The next morning, the third day of the storm, we decided we had to do something about the rudder. There seemed no end to the storm, and we knew that our vessel could not stand much more pounding before one of her sides was stove in. We ripped out one of her rowing benches, cut it in two, and made a sling on which Carlos and Manolo lowered me down the stern, so that I could assess the extent of the damage. I found it even worse than we had expected: not only had the tiller broken off from the rudderpost, but also the rudder itself had split in two and was barely hanging onto the ship, so that the next heavy sea crashing against the stern could easily have wrung it loose.

The first task was to mend the rudder. It was far too heavy—more than a quarter of a ton—to lift onto the deck, and the only solution was to mend it in place. This turned out to be the most desperate and frustrating piece of underwater work I have ever attempted. One moment a fifteen-foot wave would lift the stern high and dry, and the next most of the vessel, and me along with it, would be underwater. I was continually smashed against the barnacle-covered hull, and the blood flowing from the numerous scrapes and cuts inevitably attracted several sharks. Manolo and Michel stationed themselves on the fantail with harpoons, ready to strike if any came after me, but fortunately they kept their distance. Just to drive the first nail into the hard oak rudder planks took over an hour. Both the rudder and my slingseat heaved up and down in the water, but never in unison, and all I could get was passing swipes at the nail; sometimes not in thirty swings did I hit the nail once, although I averaged much better on my own fingers. It took nearly six hours to drive in the eight nails necessary to hold the broken rudder together. We still had the problem of the rudderpost and tiller, but I was too exhausted to tackle that chore, and it had to wait for the following day.

It took two full days more to repair the rudderpost and tiller, but since this involved less underwater work, Carlos, José, and Michel were able to take turns relieving me on the wildly pitching slingseat. By this time the storm, which we later learned was a full hurricane, had died down, although the seas were still heavy. But everyone was so feeble that another full day was spent mending the rigging and sails before we could get underway again. Then, only a few days later, just as it seemed we had everything squared away, we were hit by another gale, but it was less severe and this time we were prepared for it. We had several sets of storm sails Nicolás had worked steadily to finish and four well-constructed sea anchors. Twelve days after riding out this storm, still another storm struck us, but by then we were such old hands at weathering gales that the damage, both to morale and the vessel, was minimal.

After recovering from this last gale, we found our hunger so great—aggravated by not being able to cook our daily hot meals of rice and beans during foul weather—that the end finally came for our goat, Pinzona. She was already half-starved and would have died soon anyway, so that we looked upon it as a mercy killing. Michel, the veterinarian, had the job of slitting her throat after José had stunned her with a sledgehammer. She was so skinny that she yielded only six pounds of meat, but nothing was wasted: the intestines made a good soup, and the blood was fried with onions. For days afterward Linda moped around sadly, probably thinking that she would eventually meet the same fate.

After weeks of dragging the plankton net, we finally caught a substantial amount. Michel, José, and I scooped out spoonfuls of the gelatinous mess from the net and began to eat it, claiming that it tasted like caviar. The rest of the crew were not convinced, and their skepticism was justified. José suddenly dove for a *bota* of wine, yelling that his mouth and throat were on fire. Then Michel and I felt it too, and within minutes the three of us were hanging over the gunwales retching violently. As soon as we recovered we examined the net closely and found that the glop we thought was plankton was actually hundreds of tiny stinging jellyfish.

We gave up on plankton after that, but we had better luck with sargasso, a type of seaweed that floats on the surface of the sea and is so thick in a certain area of the mid-Atlantic that it gives it the name of the Sargasso Sea. It tasted like iodine, but it was very filling, and I was later told that the sargasso was probably what saved us from any serious cases of scurvy, since our fresh fruit had gone bad only days out of Las Palmas. Manolo and I also began to collect barnacles and other marine growth from the *Niña's* hull which, together with rice, beans, and seaweed, made a passable soup. The worst problem for everyone, except José, was thirst. We had almost unlimited supplies of wine, which curiously enough never leaked or spoiled like the water, but wine is not a real thirst-quencher, and because of our meager rations of food, most of us found that even small amounts of wine made us as drunk as a quart of brandy would under normal circumstances.

On our forty-eighth day out, a violent squall struck us. It was over in less than two hours, but its sudden appearance and violence made up for its short duration. Once again our sails were torn and the splits in the mainmast opened more, wide enough in some places for us to stick a knife straight through the middle of the mast.

Even worse than the gales and squalls, though, were the long periods of calms that followed. During the crisis of a storm, we were usually so intent on the immediate problem of saving the ship that we had no time to brood about food and water, but morale sank to its lowest point in these deadly calms. Days would pass without a breath of wind to move us closer to our destination. Everyone lay on the blistering deck getting thirstier, more pessimistic, and more quarrelsome by the hour. It was almost a blessing that we were all so weak from hunger, for senseless arguments broke out constantly, but rarely did the men have enough strength to do more than trade insults. Not all of us scrapped and argued. The Padre kept pretty much to himself, and Carlos and Nicolás brooded in their own private purgatories, sometimes going for days without speaking a word to anyone. Nicolás was not too bad as long as we could keep him busy calking the deck and the skiff, splicing lines, or repairing the sails, but Carlos had nothing to do during the calms but stare at the chart, as if by doing so he could move us closer to our destination. The only consolation, if one could call it that, was that these mid-Atlantic calms, or doldrums, were a common curse of old sailing ships whenever they passed through the area called the Sargasso Sea, and it meant at least that we had covered more than half the distance to America.

On the morning of November 30, the fifth day of calm, a heavy swell started; there were light, erratic puffs of air that changed direction every minute or so, and a long line of storm clouds darkened the horizon. It seemed certain that another hurricane was brewing, and we prepared for the worst, doubting that the *Niña* could survive another battering like the last one. The heat was even more oppressive than usual, and by mid-afternoon we all lay sweltering on the deck or in the cabin, almost looking forward to the storm—anything seemed preferable to that terrible heat. Nicolás, who had spoken hardly a word to anyone in the last two weeks and who usually could not even see our makeshift bowsprit if he was standing on the fantail, suddenly shouted that he had sighted a plane and that it was heading straight for us.

We had mixed reactions at the sight of the plane, a U.S. Navy P2V hurricane hunter. Manolo and I knew it was a hurricane hunter and thought it had come to warn us of the hurricane we were expecting; Carlos and Michel thought that the plane's appearance was accidental and that the crew had no idea who we were; the rest figured that it had come to help us, and as it turned out, they were right. Unknown to us, the *Niña* had supposedly gone down somewhere in the middle of the Atlantic: we were long overdue and had not been sighted by any passing vessels since leaving the Canaries, so that the world press had reported us lost at sea. Clay Blair had then contacted some friends high up in the Navy and convinced them that an air search should be mounted. The British, Spanish, Portuguese, and French air forces had joined in the search, which began on November 24, and for six days planes scoured the Atlantic for thousands of square miles, but all to the north of us, since we had originally planned to follow the exact route taken by Columbus. On the last day of the search, one U.S. Navy P2V, piloted by Commander Vernon F. Anderson, ventured further south and, after searching for six hours, was heading back to its base on Puerto Rico when the radar operator reported a contact: the contact turned out to be the *Niña II.*

After making several terrifyingly low passes over us, the plane dropped three bundles. None of the parachutes opened, but José and I jumped in the leaking skiff we were towing behind and retrieved them. One package contained a rubber life raft, but the bottle of compressed air had been triggered off on impact, blowing the raft, which was tied in a bundle, to shreds. The next package contained a Gibson Girl emergency radio that had been smashed into an accordion shape on hitting the water. But the third package, with emergency rations and survival gear, was intact and very welcome, especially the two cartons of cigarettes it contained. Our supply had run out weeks before, and the men had resorted to smoking the dried-corn-husk stuffing of our sleeping mats.

The Navy plane next dropped a one-way sonobuoy which enabled me to speak to them, and they answered by wagging the plane's wings or dropping notes in sealed tins. We were relieved to learn that the storm we had been preparing for was not headed our way, but the next item of information was shattering: our true position was latitude 19 degrees, 41 minutes north and longitude 51 degrees, 20 minutes west, more than four hundred miles to the east of our estimated position. Without a chronometer, which had been invented long after Columbus's time, or even a good watch on board (mine had been smashed when the tiller broke), we could not have expected to measure our longitude with any great accuracy, but even so it was a shock to discover that we were so much farther from our destination than we had thought.

Nevertheless, this brief contact with the outside world after so many weeks was the high point of the voyage, perhaps even more of a relief than our final landfall at San Salvador. That night we celebrated accordingly. Michel broke out several bottles of warm champagne he had been saving for a special occasion, and we sang and joked late into the night.

Three days later two more Navy "Bluebirds," as I had baptized them, arrived and dropped another sonobuoy along with a list of questions they wanted me to answer. The main one was whether we planned to head for the nearest land, which was Puerto Rico, about six hundred miles due west, or would still try to reach San Salvador, fifteen hundred miles to the northwest. We made a quick vote and the answer was San Salvador: we had already struggled along for fifty-five days and 2,750 miles and we were not going to give up now. Fresh fruit, canned goods, more cigarettes, and a bunch of magazines and newspapers were parachuted down to us and quickly retrieved in the, by now, half-submerged skiff. We pounced on the newspapers and magazines, eager to learn what had been happening while we were cut off from the world, and were surprised to read that the sighting of the *Niña* was big news—we had not considered ourselves lost, merely delayed. Most of the magazines, mainly copies of *Playboy*, had a short life. Padre found the photographs "scandalous" and, against all our protests, dumped them overboard.

This same day, the steady easterly trade wind started up again and, instead of drifting toward our destination, we began to sail at a fairly good clip—good for the *Niña*, that is, for if she had been built and rigged like a proper caravel we would have been averaging 160 miles a day instead of only 60. We were still faced with the problem of water, since even with an emergency reserve of 160 quarts we had somehow overlooked and found again, we still had barely one quart per day to last us the thirty days we calculated as the minimum time it would take us to reach San Salvador. But it was no longer a question of reaching our destination or dying of thirst; in a dire emergency we could always signal for water from either the U.S. Navy and Coast Guard planes that came to check on us nearly daily or the passing vessels that for the first time in the whole voyage we began to sight. Now our main concern was to preserve the authenticity of the crossing, and reach San Salvador as we had planned, without any modern aids.

Then tragedy struck the *Niña*. One morning we awoke to find Linda missing. All of us searched frantically in every conceivable place she could have been sleeping, although she usually spent the night in the cabin nestled against one of the crew. There was no sign of her, and we finally had to assume that she had fallen overboard sometime during the night, since she was quite a daredevil, forever climbing up the masts, out on the spars, and along the handrail. We had all grown so fond of her during the long voyage that her disappearance sent us into a glum state again.

A few days later we had another mascot, but it failed to replace Linda in our affections. It was a thirty-foot whale which we decided thought the *Niña* was another whale of the opposite sex and had fallen in love with her. Whatever the reason for the attachment, the whale stayed with us constantly. During the day it cruised around the vessel, and Manolo and I both swam with it a few times, holding on to its fins and even touching one of its huge eyes. At night it would lay right under the ship, snuggling against the keel and keeping us in constant fear of the *Niña's* thin hull being crushed. The animal's heartbeat was so strong that the whole vessel throbbed, and it was like trying to sleep right on top of an African tom-tom. Then, on the third afternoon, José flung one of our harpoons at our mascot. Whether he actually thought we could catch and eat the animal, I don't know, but that was the end of the *Niña's* short love affair with a whale. The startled beast swam off, easily snapping the harpoon line, and we never saw it again.

Even though we were making fairly good progress toward San Salvador, it seemed that our tempers grew worse every day. Finally Carlos had to order that no one bring up matters of religion, politics, or food, which seemed to be the three most explosive topics, always resulting in a bitter argument and occasionally even a fist fight. One time when I was speaking into a sonobuoy microphone to one of the Navy planes, José and Pepe got into a loud and violent discussion right next to me—over what, I don't know. I tried to shut them up so that I could speak into the mike, and when that failed, I gave them both a shove to separate them. Pepe instantly went berserk, but instead of attacking me, he started to pound his head against the mainmast, opening a large gash before the others could restrain him. On another occasion, Antonio and José went for each other with knives out on the deck, and only the quick action of several of us prevented bloodshed. The fact that tempers flared up more and more as we came closer to the end of the voyage is not so surprising, as I look back. Up to then we had been engrossed in the business of just keeping alive. Arguments stopped short of physical violence, when you reasoned that a storm might hit the next day and your opponent might be the only one near a life line if you were washed overboard. But now that these dangers seemed past, we turned on each other.

Several minor storms struck us, but the trade winds remained faithful and so did the planes. They appeared nearly every day to drop badly needed fresh water, small supplies of food, and notes giving our positions, which were invariably different from the ones we estimated. We were getting closer and closer to San Salvador, and, on December 23, we established a round-the-clock lookout from the mainmast, fearful of missing our landfall. We had a dozen false alarms, and nobody paid much attention when, at around 1500 hours on Christmas Eve, José announced that he saw something on the horizon. But within an hour even those of us on deck below could make out the low, dark shape on the horizon—San Salvador, our first sight of land since we had left the Canaries seventy-six days before. We all broke into cheers and then joined Padre in singing the *Salve Regina* and reciting prayers of thanksgiving.

By sundown we were off the southern end of San Salvador,

but found ourselves at a loss what to do since in our desire for authenticity we had declined to take any charts of sailing directions for the island. Manolo and I were for anchoring until morning, but everyone else sided with Carlos, who favored heading round to the western side of the island for the town of Cockburn, which is supposedly the site of Columbus's landing. By midnight we had gotten within half a mile of the town's pier but, unable to beat to windward against the strong easterly trade wind, we got no closer. We lit a lantern and waved it frantically, but we had made such good progress in the past two days that we had arrived a full day before we were expected, and no one was on watch for us. We lowered the sails, set out the sea anchor, and settled down to a sad Christmas Eve within full sight of the town lights ashore.

A few hours later Manolo shook me awake to report that a very strong current was pulling us away from the island. We roused the others, raised the sails again, and tried to beat back to windward toward the island. It was fruitless. By dawn we were fifteen miles from San Salvador and being blown steadily west toward the dangerous reefs surrounding Cat Island. At noon I signaled a passing Bahamas Airways plane with a flare from the survival kit the Navy had dropped; in about an hour a U.S. Coast Guard plane appeared, circling overhead, and several hours later a small Navy boat came out from San Salvador and took us in tow.

It was a humiliating end to our seventy-seven-day voyage. After covering the 4,250 miles from Las Palmas on our own, we had to do the last fifteen miles behind a towline, but at that point pride was the furthest thing from our minds. For weeks we had been set on reaching San Salvador by Christmas and we did, although just barely: when we finally staggered ashore, it was a few minutes before midnight on December 25. A large welcoming party was there to greet us with a calypso band and a feast that lasted for hours. Manolo has since told me, and everyone else he meets, that he is not sure which was the most amazing moment of the whole venture: when I calmly attacked my third platter heaped with spaghetti or, on finishing that, when I started on a half-gallon serving of ice cream without a pause.

Was it really worth it? Up until that point it was, for I gained what I had sought from the voyage. Not that I learned very much about how the old sailing ships were handled; I am sure that Columbus and the other skilled mariners that followed up his voyages of discovery would have had a good laugh at our fumbling attempts to imitate them. But I had learned how it feels to cross an immense body of water, completely at the mercy of wind and current; to face the constant threat of violent storms; to be so hungry and thirsty that you will eat maggot-infested meat and drink water that smells like a cesspool without turning a hair. There were the moments of joy, too: when the sails filled with a stiff breeze after days of calm and, most of all, that first sight of land after months of nothing but ocean.

If I have any misgivings about the voyage, they concern only its aftermath, a disgraceful squabble over money and pride that received almost more coverage in the Spanish press than the voyage itself. I ought to know, for I was cast as the villain of the piece. The hero? Who else but Carlos?

Some of the allegations were laughable. I had a good chuckle over one article in which I was said to be such a bad photographer that none of my photos of the voyage came out and which, of course, was illustrated with a few of the over eight thousand photos that had come out. Others were not so funny. The reports that I had made a fantastic fortune from the *Niña* voyage (figures went as high as $150,000), all of which I kept for myself, are easily disproved by a few little scraps of paper: receipts signed by Carlos for his 65 per cent share of all proceeds from my articles, my movie of the voyage, and my radio and television appearances, plus the 20 per cent of my share that was to go to the crew. But it is unpleasant to think that the other men, except Manolo, with whom I have stayed in close contact, believe I cheated them.

The other main issue—my accounts of the voyage—is less easy to resolve, since it involves personal opinion. My statement that we were all frightened during the worst hurricane that struck us is a case in point. I believe the others were frightened; I *know* I was, and I'm convinced that anyone who failed to feel some fear under those circumstances would have to be either insane or a fool. Maybe I was wrong, but all I could do was write what I saw, thought, and recorded in my daily log. There is nothing to keep anyone else from writing his own version, even if no one else bothered to keep a log. In fact, several of the crew members have written their own accounts. Nicolás claimed in his book, for example, that I talked incessantly about women during the whole voyage. I don't think I did; I was usually too hungry to think about much besides food, and the main day-dreams I recall involved huge plates of spaghetti. But if he remembers it that way, that is his prerogative.

The ludicrous hubbub over the aftermath of the *Niña* voyage eventually died down, after raging on for more than a year alongside news of world-shaking international events. It is a shame, though, that a basically idealistic venture which could have been remembered with pride by those who participated in it should have been turned into such a sordid mess.

Chapter
Eight
•
Westward
Ho
•

Ever since I had first stumbled across those Maya ruins in the middle of the Yucatan jungle, with frescoes depicting men with European features standing in galley-like vessels, I was convinced that Columbus was not the first Old World mariner to reach America. The theory of pre-Columbian voyages to America was not an invention of mine. For a long time scholars have used it to explain some of the puzzles in the history of the Maya, the Toltecs, the Incas, and the other ancient civilizations of America. One of the most intriguing puzzles is the legend about a bearded, fair-skinned god known in Mexico as Quetzalcóatl and in Yucatan as Kukul-cán, who came from the east long before the Spaniards. He brought with him many cultural and technical advances which he taught to the inhabitants, and then he left, promising to return again. This ancient legend was an immense help to Cortés in his conquest of Mexico, since the Aztecs at first believed that the Spaniards were messengers from Quetzalcóatl, announcing the Fair God's return from the east.

Who was this Quetzalcóatl? Who were the bearded men in

those galley frescoes, and the many other bearded figures depicted in paintings and sculpture? Some people would say that they never existed in fact, but only in the imagination of the Maya and other pre-Columbian peoples. However, there is another explanation: they were ancient mariners from the Old World who accidentally discovered America many centuries before Columbus. Take the Phoenicians, for example, probably the greatest seafarers in the ancient world. It is an accepted fact that the Phoenicians ventured well beyond the Pillars of Hercules, or Straits of Gibraltar, and established trading posts halfway down the west coast of Africa. Even a landlubber looking at a chart of the Atlantic Ocean could see that the outward journey on these voyages of exploration and trade would have been a fairly simple matter, since the prevailing winds and currents, which are from the northeast, would easily take any vessel from the Straits of Gibraltar southwest along the coast of Africa. But getting back home was something else again.

The Phoenician vessels were of shallow draft, either completely deckless or only partially decked, and had only one large square sail for propulsion (the ancient Mediterranean seafarers depended on oar power only for battles and for short voyages). Thus they were almost completely at the mercy of prevailing winds and currents, since they could not beat to windward. The only possible way they could have reached home again from the western tip of Africa was by heading out into the mid-Atlantic and working their way up to higher latitudes, where the prevailing westerly winds would carry them back to the European continent. Not only the Phoenicians, but also the seafarers who came after them, such as the Carthaginians, the Greeks, the Romans, and the Vikings, were faced with the same problem, until vessels like the caravel and the pinnace were developed that could sail fairly close to the wind.

I find it hard to believe that many of these vessels, when trying to beat their way back home, were not hit by heavy storms. If they were, they had no choice but to run before the wind or their undecked vessels would have been swamped, and some of them could have been carried right across the Atlantic to the shores of America. A well-known example is Pedro Cabral's accidental discovery of Brazil in 1500, while trying to work his way down the west coast of Africa round the Cape of Good Hope. He was caught in heavy weather and, even in a newly invented caravel, a better sailor than any other ship in Europe at the time and certainly far superior to a Phoenician vessel, he was forced all the way across the Atlantic. As recently as the nineteenth century there are many references to sailing vessels operating off the African coast and the outlying Canary and Cape Verde Islands that were caught in the same straits as Cabral and were blown to America.

After reading everything possible relating to the subject of pre-Columbian voyages to the New World, I started to correspond with different authorities in Europe and America and soon found that I had stumbled upon a real hornet's nest of controversy in the academic world. There were a small number of geographers and historians who took the theory seriously, but they were arrayed against a whole battalion of highly skeptical colleagues. Although most accepted the idea that the Vikings could have reached North America via Iceland and Greenland, the idea that any mariners before Columbus could have sailed across the southern Atlantic was considered completely ridiculous.

There are three main objections to the theory of pre-Columbian voyages. One is that there is no documentary evidence. If Phoenicians or Greeks reached America, it is argued, why is there no recorded mention of the fact? That is simple: in the first place, the ancient discoverers did not necessarily return home (which would also explain why there were no attempts to colonize the new lands); and in the second place, if they did go home, the records might not have survived or perhaps not even have been made at all. The Phoenicians, for example, were noted for their secrecy; they never publicized any of their voyages and even invented stories about sea monsters and other hazards to keep their trading competitors away. The second objection is that the galley-like vessels used by the early mariners, built for the Mediterranean, were too frail to survive in the rougher waters of the Atlantic and would have either broken apart or been swamped. Yet the facts remain that the Phoenicians did sail out into the much rougher waters around the British Isles to carry on their tin trade with Cornwall, and that similarly built Viking vessels withstood the really foul sailing conditions in the North Sea and over to Greenland and Newfoundland. The third objection—that the early mariners never ventured far out of sight of land for fear of losing their way—is nothing but an old wives' tale. It is true that they had no compass, sextant, or other modern navigational aid, but they were very skillful in navigating by the sun and stars, and they did venture far from land. The Greeks, for example, sailed back and forth between India and East Africa, not by hugging the coast of the Arabian peninsula, but by striking out straight across the Indian Ocean.

However, it would take a lot more than arguments to convince the skeptics. One step would be to prove that pre-Columbian voyages to America were at least possible, and the only way to do that would be to reproduce such a voyage: to sail a replica of an ancient Mediterranean vessel from the Straits of Gibraltar to Yucatan, depending entirely on the sun and stars for navigation. I cannot remember exactly when the idea for such a venture occurred to me—probably during one of my ill-fated expeditions into the Yucatan jungle, when my mind was not functioning along very sane lines anyway—but it was already at the back of my mind as a vague project when I left for Spain to do research on shipwrecks and the Spanish treasure fleets, and by the time I set out on the *Niña II* to get my first taste of transatlantic drifting (you could hardly call it sailing), I was already making serious plans for a voyage that would help prove that Columbus was a latecomer to America.

A number of things happened while I was in Spain to keep my interest in pre-Columbian voyages from dissipating. A few months after I started to dig for material on wrecks and *flotas,* while searching for one document I found another, which happens often in the largely uncatalogued Spanish archives. It was a letter from an early Spanish missionary in Yucatan to the superior of his religious order in Spain. He told of locating a large group of old ruins near what is today Mérida, the capital of Yucatan, which were very different from all the other buildings in Yucatan because they had been constructed with iron reinforcing rods in the roofs (the Maya used wooden beams to support their roofs and, like the rest of the pre-Columbian peoples, did not know iron at all). Even more unusual was that on all the inside walls were paintings of Christian saints, the most frequently depicted being Saint Catherine of the Wheel. When asked who had built these ruins, the Indians had replied, "White men who came in boats very long ago." The missionary said that he believed these white men were Carthaginians but gave no reason for this belief. In another letter dated eighteen months later he told the superior how he had been unable to prevent the new governor from destroying these ruins and carting away the stones to build the city of Mérida.

The missionary's mention of Carthaginians puzzled me until I realized that he was referring not to the ancient Carthaginians whose city was destroyed by the Romans in 146 B.C., but to later inhabitants of the third or fourth century A.D. He must have known, as I learned, that Saint Catherine of the Wheel had lived in Carthage in the third century A.D. and was also the patron saint of most early Christian seafarers. I wonder if he also knew another interesting fact I discovered: that the people of Carthage were the first, and actually one of the few until modern times, to use iron rods for reinforcing the flat roofs of their houses!

A number of other documents concerning mysterious traces of Old World culture in America turned up during my research, not only in Spain, but also in Rome, Paris, and Vienna. Then there was the encouragement I received from the noted Portuguese geographer, Dr. Armando Cortesão. Dr. Cortesão had seemed the most knowledgeable and helpful of all the scholars I had been corresponding with about pre-Columbian voyages. He has dedicated his life to the study of this subject and in 1954 made a cartographic discovery that rocked the skeptics back on their heels. Hidden away in an obscure Portuguese library he found an old sea chart, dated 1424, showing many islands in the area today known as the Caribbean; these islands are now called the Antilles, and on the 1424 chart they were marked "Antilia"! The publication of the chart caused a great deal of excitement and also many charges that it was a fake, but it was put to every available test and declared authentic, substantiating the many legends that Portuguese seamen reached America in the fourteenth or early fifteenth century.

However, Dr. Cortesão is among the small group of scholars who believe that the Portuguese were only the most recent in a series of pre-Columbian voyagers that goes back at least to the Phoenicians, and when I wrote him of my idea to reproduce an ancient Atlantic crossing he invited me to visit him at the University of Coimbra to talk over my plans. He was very enthusiastic about the idea, claiming that such a feat would be very valuable in helping to gain acceptance of our theory. But he pointed out a snag, one that had been bothering me for some time, too: very little is known about the construction of early Mediterranean vessels; there are a few drawings and seals showing their over-all design and most important features but no plans or scale models to show exactly how they were put together. I might find that I would have to give up the idea of a Phoenician vessel altogether, he warned, and build a later type, say a Greek ship, about which more is known. Otherwise, all my efforts would be in vain, for the skeptics could claim that my vessel was unauthentic and my voyage proved nothing except that I could navigate like the ancients. He promised to keep me informed of any new material on ancient shipbuilding that he might come across, but I knew that it would require a great deal of research on my part, as well as luck, if I were going to build a replica that had any claims to authenticity—that is, unless one of the many divers poking around the sea floor of the Mediterranean would do me the favor of finding a Phoenician shipwreck.

The pre-Columbian voyage plan was put on the shelf for over a year while I worked on the more urgent plans for a galleon voyage, scrapped them in favor of joining Carlos Etayo on his *Niña II,* and more or less followed Columbus's route (with a small detour of about one thousand miles) across the Atlantic. During the *Niña II* voyage I had plenty of opportunity to navigate by the sun and stars and to assure myself that I could make a more accurate crossing that way than we were making on the *Niña* using a compass that I was sure was way off. (I later learned that the compass deviation was nearly fifteen degrees.) I also had plenty of time at night while topside on the deserted quarter-deck to think about the problem of an authentic replica for my pre-Columbian voyage. Naturally I had a brainstorm.

While digging up material on early vessels I had noticed how little the design had changed over the centuries, how similar the drawings of ancient Mediterranean ships were to the Viking ships of the Middle Ages: shallow draft, little or no decks, steerboards instead of stern rudders, the single large square sail, and the high-swept bow and sternposts. Now the details of construction of Phoenician and Greek ships may still be debatable points, but not those of Viking ships, for a tenth-century Viking vessel, called the "Gokstad Ship," has been excavated in Norway in a remarkable state of preservation and is now on display in an Oslo museum. Why not build a replica of a Viking ship instead? I had always included the Vikings among the possible accidental voyagers from the Mediterranean to Central America, blown across during one of their southern raiding trips—perhaps the bearded Fair God Quetzalcóatl was a

Viking. At any rate, a Viking voyage would prove that this type of ship could make it under the same conditions (the Vikings also depended upon the sun and stars for navigation), and then, if anyone in the meantime had come up with the remains of a Phoenician ship, I might even make a Phoenician voyage afterward—I was so voyage-happy by then that two more crossings seemed like an even better idea than one.

Anyone would think that the *Niña* crossing would have put me off even rowboats for the rest of my life. In fact, most of my friends, who suspected I was slightly nuts anyway, decided I definitely ought to be locked up when I told them of my plans for a Viking voyage barely a few weeks after I stumbled ashore on San Salvador. Before this next adventure, or misadventure, was over, I was beginning to think they might be right.

In May 1963 I was able to start work on the main item, the ship. I flew over to Denmark, Norway, and Sweden to consult with the different experts on Viking ships and to look for a good shipyard that could make me a precise replica of the original Gokstad Ship, using the same type of wood, fittings, and techniques. I finally located one in Bergen, Norway, that agreed to do the job for an estimated $10,000, at the most. Three weeks later, when I returned to New York from my European trip, I found a letter from the owner of the shipyard informing me that they had miscalculated the costs, which were now estimated at $35,000. I blasted off a sharp reply, saying I would try to raise that amount but was not sure I could, and instead of assuring me that this estimate would not be exceeded, they sent another letter raising it to $50,000. I canceled the contract and went on a week's drunk.

That seemed the end of my Viking voyage, but a month later I ran into an old friend who was then working in the publicity department of Columbia Pictures, and when I told him about my bad luck with the Viking vessel, he said: "Marx, you lucky dog, you can call me Santa Claus, because I'm going to *give* you a Viking ship."

I thought at first that he had had too many martinis, but he explained that Columbia Pictures was making a Viking movie in Yugoslavia called *The Long Ships,* for which they had had three Viking ships built. My friend said that they would probably be destroyed after the movie was finished anyway, and he was sure that Columbia would sell, loan, or maybe even give me one of them. But I was skeptical. These ships were movie props, I protested, probably just pieces of junk, and certainly not seaworthy enough to make an Atlantic crossing. He said he would check into it and let me know in a week or so.

I could not wait that long. After two sleepless nights I decided to go and check for myself. I obtained a visa for Yugoslavia in the record time of two hours (it normally takes two weeks) and that same day was on a plane heading for Belgrade. Arriving at Budva, a village halfway down the Adriatic Coast of Yugoslavia, where the movie was being made, I was pleasantly surprised to see what looked like three faithful replicas of the Gokstad Ship lying at anchor, instead of the overgrown canoes I had half expected. My eyes were not deceiving me. The three ships, I learned, had been built in Yugoslavia (Yugoslavian oak, according to the Bergen shipbuilders, is the best in Europe) under the supervision of Danish and Norwegian Viking experts, following the exact plans of the tenth-century Gokstad Ship I had seen on display in Oslo. After inspecting all three of them carefully and testing their sailing qualities, I selected the one I liked best and rushed back to New York to convince the directors of Columbia Pictures to donate the vessel to me. They agreed (not pure altruism, of course; they would be receiving their share of publicity from the voyage), but only on condition that I sign a statement releasing them from any liability in connection with the voyage. A routine precaution, no doubt, but too bad I did not take it as a warning of things to come.

Just about this time it was announced to the world that the Norwegian archaeologist, Dr. Helge Ingstad, had uncovered the indisputable remains of a large, tenth-century Viking settlement in Newfoundland. After centuries of controversy, even the die-hard skeptics had to admit that other mariners had preceded Columbus to America, and the time was ripe for me to prove the possibility of pre-Columbian voyages across the mid-Atlantic as well.

The season was too far advanced for a crossing that year, and I planned to leave the following spring instead. But this time I was determined to make careful preparations, instead of scurrying around at the last minute and leaving undone half of the essential tasks, as had happened with the *Niña II*. I resigned from my job at *The Saturday Evening Post* in October 1963 and headed for Europe.

The first step was to plan my route. Finding the Portuguese very interested in the voyage, probably because they too have consistently disclaimed Columbus' discovery of America, I decided to make Lisbon my point of departure. I would then sail down to the Cape Verde Islands, across to Yucatan, and then back to Europe via the northern route, all without the aid of an astrolabe or even a compass. The trip from Yugoslavia to Lisbon would be a shakedown cruise with a skeleton crew in which we could test the ship's sailing qualities and seaworthiness. At Lisbon she would be completely overhauled, new sails and rigging would be fitted, the bulk of my crew and provisions would be taken on, and then on to America.

Busy making preparations throughout the winter, I discovered that everyone was extremely interested in the voyage—everyone except the Italians and the Spaniards, who undoubtedly felt that it would steal some of Columbus' thunder—and I received letters from hundreds of volunteers. Out of these I selected a crew of twelve men from ten different European nations; my second-in-command was a Portuguese naval officer, a direct descendant of Ferdinand Magellan, the first circumnavigator of the world. Many countries also offered supplies: the Danes offered mead, a drink made from yeast malt and honey; the Dutch sent a half ton of goat's milk cheese; the Portuguese offered dried fish and fresh provisions; and other sources offered a variety of foodstuffs, all of which had to be items that were common fare in the tenth century.

Finally, in mid-February of 1964, everything seemed ready. After a last-minute check with the Columbia Pictures people, who informed me that all three ships had been taken for safe-keeping to the shipyard where they had been built, I packed my duffel bag and headed for Punat Island, not far from the Yugo-slav border with Trieste, to take possession of my *Long Ship*. I rushed straight from the ferry down to the shipyard, eager for a glimpse of her. Instead all I saw was the high mainmast and the two elaborately carved figureheads on the bow and stern; the rest was submerged in a fathom of water, flanked by the two other vessels, which had suffered the same fate. I scoured the island in search of someone who knew some English and finally located the foreman of the shipyard, who was able to unravel the mystery. Someone along the line had neglected to mention the donation to the Yugoslavs, and all three ships had been brought to Punat, not for safekeeping, but to be stripped of all valuable materials and then destroyed. The ship I had selected was the least damaged, but even so, her sides were stove in in several places, some of the supporting ribs and knees had been removed, her sails were serving as an awning over the village market place, and the location of her carefully constructed, authentic Viking rigging was a complete mystery.

The shipyard foreman thought I was a first-class crackpot, arriving unannounced at this isolated spot to take possession of a vessel he had been ordered to destroy and then coming up with some crazy joke about sailing the ship to America. Unable to convince him that I owned it, much less that I was serious about having it raised and prepared for sailing, I decided to make my way to the nearest telephone, which was at Rijeka, on the main-land, to call the Columbia Pictures representative in London. I dug up every forceful expression I could remember from my days as a Marine Corps sergeant, when I finally got through to him, and added a few juicy ones of my own invention. I must have gotten my point across, for the next day a three-man delegation of VIPs from the Yugoslav state film company arrived from Belgrade with an interpreter and ordered the shipyard foreman to raise and restore the vessel under my supervision.

The wheels left, and my interpreter, named Dragon, and I got to work. The shipyard's method of raising the vessel was for a team of oxen to pull it up on a beach, but I put a stop to that: the ship, her structure weakened by the loss of several ribs and many planks, would have fallen to pieces. The whole shipyard then went on strike, demanding that I be kept off the premises until the vessel was ready, but the strike was very short-lived. Dragon, like most official interpreters, turned out to be a member of the Yugoslav Secret Service, and since the shipyard was state-owned, the boys were back at work within hours. In the meantime I decided that I would have to raise the vessel myself, since it was really a job for a diver. It was bitterly cold, even in the Adriatic, but luckily I had brought along my rubber diving suit, as well as my snorkeling gear. On my first dive I discovered that the ship was much more seriously damaged than I had thought. I should have given up the whole idea of the voyage right then, and let the *Long Ship* stay there as a home for octopi and moray eels, which was about all she was good for. But setbacks and hopeless cases only have the effect of making me more determined than ever. Sometimes I like to call it persistence; in this case it was sheer lunacy.

My first plan for refloating her by pumping air into large oil drums attached to cables slung under her keel had to be ruled out, since I could not find enough drums, or any valves at all. Pumping air into the ship was out of the question; there was nothing to pump it into—she was a giant version of an open row boat with no deck or hold or anything but a tiny cabin in the bow. My efforts were a constant source of merriment to the shipyard workers, who sat around drinking the local plum brandy called "slivovitz" while I scurried around the yard. Then

I thought up a new plan. Dragon and I managed to collect about a dozen ordinary car jacks, which we put to work after I covered over all the holes in the hull and nailed reinforcing planks over the weak spots. At each low tide I was able to raise the vessel a little farther off the bottom and after four days, when her gunwales were above water, we started to pump her out. This rather haphazard engineering feat so amazed the hecklers that they decided I was not such a bad guy after all, and they all offered to cooperate fully in repairing the ship.

The following morning we pulled her carefully up on the ways, and the men went to work, sometimes as many as forty or fifty at a time. We had to replace the forty-five-foot mast, which we found cracked in several places, and more than a third of the hull planking, make a number of new ribs and knees, and completely new rigging. Dragon extricated the sails from the market place; they were badly stretched, but new sails were being made in Lisbon, and I had also decided that for the Punat–Lisbon shakedown cruise I would have the film company's engine reinstalled as an auxiliary. The engine, like almost everything else, had been removed, and it had to be bought back from some fishermen the foreman had sold it to.

As the repair work neared completion, I sent word to the five crew members who were to make this leg of the voyage to join me at Punat. Three weeks to the day after I had arrived to find the ship under water, she was ready to sail (Dragon more than anyone else deserves the credit for this feat), and right on schedule my five crewmen arrived on the evening ferry boat. They were five good men: an Englishman, Bill Holmes, a chemist on land and a real sailor at sea; two Norwegian descendants of the Vikings, Knut Adeler and Per Christiansen; and two Yugoslavs, Jevtic Slobodan, an artist and sculptor, called "Jumbo" because of his size, and Plavsic Slavoljub, who had fortunately been nicknamed "Bell" for short when he worked as a stuntman on the movie for which the ship was built. They ranged in age from twenty-two (Per) to thirty-one (Jumbo), a real change from the venerable crew of the *Niña*, of which I had been the junior member by a wide margin. There was one problem: neither Jumbo nor Bell knew a word of English, which was to be our lingua franca. I was afraid I would have to take a quick course in Serbian from Dragon but discovered that Jumbo knew some Italian, and then they both started to pick up English words very quickly from the rest of us—but not the sort of words they would have learned at a Berlitz school, I'm afraid.

After dropping their bags off at the local inn, they all trooped down with me to see the ship. A bitter snowstorm was blowing at the time, and the ship looked ghostlike, covered with ice and snow, but at least she was afloat and ready to sail. They set to work with a will, sweeping the snowy shroud from the deck and examining every inch of her structure. Neither Jumbo nor Bell had had much sailing experience, and both had heard the local fishermen and even the shipyard workers remark that the vessel was only a movie prop and not fit to paddle around a lake in, much less sail across thousands of miles of open sea. Her lines were graceful—seventy-six feet from stem to stern and eighteen feet across the beam—and with a draft of only three feet, she appeared to be built for speed. But could she withstand heavy seas? The huge Jumbo started to jump all over the gunwales to test their strength (someone had told him they were the ship's weak point), and Knut inspected the planking with a critical eye. I was hurt that the boys should doubt her sturdiness, for at that time I considered her the soundest vessel ever built. Later I was to remember that scene with bitter amusement.

That night, as we sat drinking the potent slivovitz to warm ourselves against the cold, I went over my plans for the voyage again, warning them that this would be no pleasure cruise. They all knew the conditions: to save time on the voyage to Lisbon, we would have the auxiliary motor, charts, and a compass; but from then on our only means of propulsion would be the one large square sail, our only navigational aids the sun and stars, and our only food the kind that would have been carried by

tenth-century mariners. And of course we would have no radio
or life rafts. But I wanted to make sure they understood and to
give them a chance to back out if they wanted to. Not one of
them did. Bill Holmes said, "Chief, we'll get there if we have to
paddle this canoe across." I wondered at the time how much of
their enthusiasm depended on the slivovitz, but I never had
cause to wonder again: although the ship let me down, the men
never did.

The snow melted the next day, and we made the final
preparations—checked out the engine, filled the fuel tanks, and
loaded the decks with gear and supplies. We were ready to cast
off when the second stroke of bad luck occurred. (Looking back,
I can't decide whether the first stroke of bad luck was the
scuttling of the ship or my raising her.) The port authorities and
customs officials suddenly announced that we would not be able
to leave without changing the ship's registration and paying a 20
per cent export duty. When I discovered that the ship had
originally cost $30,000, I was panic stricken. Anxious to be away
before the next snowstorm began, I persuaded them, with
Dragon's help, to let us leave, on the condition that we leave the
ship's papers behind. I was sure that the ancient seamen had not
bothered with such petty matters as owner's papers, registration,
and national flags and was almost happy to be sailing without
them.

Around noon on the ninth of March we were underway at
last. The old seadogs in the port of Rijeka, where we had to go to
receive official clearance, could not dampen our spirits, in spite
of their warnings that March was the worst month for sailing
those waters and their advice to make for the nearest sheltered
cove the moment the barometer started to fall. We planned to
sail around the clock and hit port only when we ran low on food
and water. I set up continuous watches and calculated that
we could make the twenty-four-hundred-mile trip to Lisbon
within fifteen days, twenty at the most: the least we could do
was six knots using the engine; under sail with a good breeze, we

could do ten. But our first day out established a pattern that was to repeat itself with frustrating monotony during the three weeks that followed—an unending struggle to keep our flimsy ship afloat and headed toward Lisbon.

That evening, as we were running south at more than eight knots along the Yugoslav coast, a violent squall struck us without warning. The problem I had feared most, heavy seas breaking over the gunwales (which cleared the water by only three feet) and swamping the ship, was only minor. The Vikings had known what they were doing when they designed their ships: she could ride the big tail seas as easily as a gull lobbing on the waves of a bay. But if the design was good, the construction was not. Whenever we were hit by head seas, which plagued most of our journey, the whole frame shook, and the sides heaved in and out like bellows. Instead of being held together by the heavy spikes, wooden treenails, or walrus-hide thongs the Vikings had used, this ship was joined by short nails with spike heads soldered on to give the appearance of solidity that had deceived us. We could have minimized the damage by never venturing out unless we had a perfect tail wind, but in that case we never would have left port, since we had head winds 95 per cent of the time. Also I wanted to put the ship through the severest tests possible; if she were going to fall apart, better in the Mediterranean than in the middle of the Atlantic.

Lowering the sail, we quickly started the auxiliary engine, and as the crew made frantic efforts to keep up with the small geysers sprouting from bow to stern (made worse, if anything, by the vibrations of the motor), I steered for a small cove. There we sheltered until dawn, plugging leaks most of the night and dining on canned tripe and raw onion and ketchup salad prepared by Jumbo, the ship's cook.

Anyone superstitious, and most sailors are, would say that our bad luck was only natural. In the movie the vessel had been a funeral ship, stolen by a renegade band of Vikings who then suffered a series of disasters ending with the ship's wrecking on the coast of North Africa. Bill had warned me that I was making a big mistake in using the black "death sail" from the movie, but I had no choice. The ordinary Viking sails were being made in Lisbon, and we had to test the ship's sailing ability on this part of the voyage, bad omen or not. Per and Knut, who both knew the old Viking myths, had said jokingly that the only way we could break the curse on the death ship was to sacrifice a maiden to the Norse Gods. We all had a good laugh over that one, but we soon began to think we might have made better use of our time in port by hunting around for a suitable victim.

Fair weather returned with daybreak. The wind was perfect and we raised the sail again, averaging slightly over nine knots that day—over twice the best speed that the *Niña* ever averaged. Bill eyed the billowing black "death sail" suspiciously, suggesting that we should at least paint it another color as soon as we made our next port. "Daddy, you're entirely too superstitious," I answered. "It'll be a breeze reaching Lisbon."

Yet that evening, when again we were hit by a sudden squall, which caused a large tear in the sail before we could haul it down, a fire developed in the propeller shaft when I ordered the engine started, and a fuel line snapped moments after we put out the fire, I began to wonder if we were not really cursed after all.

The next morning produced fair weather again, and I decided to cross the Adriatic to the Italian coast, where we could make repairs and rig a tarpaulin over the forward deck for shelter from the heavy spray that had drenched everything and everyone on board. There was no doubt that our ship had been designed for speed. With a fair wind we covered the 125 miles across to the Italian port of Vieste in eleven hours, an astonishing average speed of over eleven knots. At that rate and without any prolonged calms, we could cross the Atlantic in fifteen days!

From Vieste we made our way down the Italian peninsula, taking refuge in several ports along the way whenever a particularly bad sirocco blew up, bringing blasts of hot wind straight from the North African desert. We were completely unaware that we were the objects of a massive sea and air search mounted by the Yugoslav government. Our failure to put in at the Island of Vis, south toward Dubrovnik, which had mistakenly been reported as our next port of call after Rijeka, had started a rumor that the ship and all hands were lost. The story reached the press as far away as London and New York and sent our families into a needless panic. Ironically, we were the only ones who didn't know we were missing. We learned of the search a week later when we were passing Crotone and a police launch came out loaded with reporters and photographers to congratulate us on our "miraculous survival." Even the Italian navy and air force had joined in the search, and it is still a mystery to me how the rumor continued for so long when we had reported to the harbor master every time bad weather drove us into port. It isn't as if a seventy-six foot, open-decked Viking ship could be mistaken for a fishing trawler, either.

The almost constant siroccos, the innumerable leaks, and the other mishaps did not deter us from our original plan. We thought there would be no problem once we reached Lisbon for a complete overhaul, removed the motor, which was the main cause of the damaging vibrations, and started across the Atlantic with a good tail wind filling our sail. Hugging this rockbound coast was really more dangerous than crossing open water, and we suffered one particular mishap that never could have occurred in the middle of the Atlantic. Around noon on the fourth day out, a dense fog covered us suddenly, reducing our visibility to a bare twenty yards. Bell, who was always interested in how I plotted our course, asked me, "Chief, do you really know where we are in this fog?"

"Bell, I have a built-in radar. There's nothing to worry about."

Then Per, who was stationed at the bow as a lookout, said, "Your radar isn't working so well, Chief. I can see bottom."

At the same moment we heard voices, which I thought

came from a passing fishing boat, but seconds later a large truck appeared out of the fog and hurtled across our bow. We were almost aground, no more than ten yards from a coastal highway. I yelled for Bell to throw the engine into reverse as Bill, who was on helm watch, made a 90 degree turn to port, but as we swung away from the shore we became entangled in a fishing net suspended from several buoys. After freeing ourselves from the net and sacrificing all the cigarettes and a good portion of the slivovitz aboard to placate the angry fishermen, we headed seaward. Losing our position entirely and colliding with other boats in the dense fog were risks we could cope with, but not a head-on collision with a truck.

Luckily we did not lose our position (my radar was working again), and six hours later we put into Bari, the next port down the coast, to take on fuel and make more repairs. But even in port we never had a moment's relaxation. We usually entered without the harbor pilot's help, and always without the proper papers. The port captains were invariably incensed that we flew a large Viking pennant with a dragon insignia instead of the compulsory Italian flag. We had nothing against the Italian flag, but we always arrived after nightfall when all the stores were closed and we could not buy one. Things got so bad in Otranto that the harbor police confiscated our rudder, refusing to let us leave until we flew the Italian flag. Per and Knut offered to pull a Viking raid and steal one from an Italian navy boat in port, but a quick reconnaissance stroll down the pier revealed that security measures were too stiff, and Bill finally had to sew one together out of different items of clothing. It wasn't very pretty, but it had the right colors and it was more or less rectangular.

There were plenty of other annoyances. Throngs of curious locals scrambled all over the ship, staring at the disheveled crew and interfering with our work of calking and patching. That was when we were lucky enough to find a place to tie up that was neither a restricted naval zone nor already jammed with other boats taking shelter from the foul weather. About the only good thing about putting into port was that we were able to get some decent food. I had made the grave mistake before leaving Rijeka of letting Jumbo buy all the provisions, and it was not until we were well underway that I found out what his idea of a well-balanced shipboard diet was: canned tripe (eight cases of it); six cases each of very hot peppers, pickled cauliflower, and ketchup; three sacks of onions (but no cooking oil; he liked them raw); one sack of garlic; and a small acount of crackers and cheese. While Jumbo and Bell gobbled down these Yugoslav delicacies, the rest of us munched on cheese and crackers until we could buy some cans of sardines and other more palatable food in Vieste. "Very good *mangiare*, Chief," Jumbo would say, looking very hurt when I refused a plate of tripe and raw onions. In fact, he liked the stuff so much that most of the time in port he would volunteer to guard the ship while the rest of us trooped off to stuff ourselves with antipasto and lasagna.

We never could get a reliable weather forecast in port. Whether in Monopoli, Otranto, Crotone, Reggio di Calabria, or any of the other places we stopped, the story was always the same: the radio gave storm warnings, the harbor master predicted a flat calm, and each fisherman prophesied anything from a hurricane to a hailstorm. It made little difference; no matter what the weather was when we left port, it always became foul or fouler within a few hours out. Not that foul weather is unusual in the Mediterranean at that time of the year; in fact, March is considered the worst month, so bad that fishing and sailing practically come to a standstill until April or May. However, the gale that hit us in the Gulf of Taranto our seventh day out was unusual even for March.

We left Otranto at daybreak and headed around the heel of Italy's boot, intending to cut across the 120-mile wide Gulf of Taranto and to make Malta, or, if luck held out, some port on the coast of North Africa, our next stop. Everyone was in high spirits as we bowled along before a good tail wind for the first time in days. But the stiff breeze soon became a twenty-, then a thirty-knot wind and while we were lowering the huge spar to put on a small storm sail—Viking sails have no bonnets—it veered around almost 90 degrees and before long a seventy-knot gale was upon us in full force. "The hell with the storm sail," I shouted. "Start the engine."

The seas became enormous. Whipped up by vicious cross currents, they swamped the ship in spray and foam so that she seemed more like a torpedo than a floating vessel. After several hours in which we made absolutely no headway, I decided to run for the port of Gallipoli. About halfway up the east coast of the gulf, the chart showed a large rocky bank near the surface and about a mile offshore. My plan was to get sea room and pass on the outside, but the seas had other plans. They lifted the ship, thrusting her forward like a surfboard no matter which way we tried to steer her. I finally decided that we would have to pass between the bank and the shore, but moments later even this choice was impossible. Suddenly we found ourselves on the bank, so shallow that when the trough of a wave passed over, we could see the jagged rocks all around us.

Only the courage and resourcefulness of the crew pulled us through. Throwing everyone a life jacket, I quickly grabbed the helm and sent Per to the bow to guide me through the labyrinth of murderous rocks. Bill and Knut smashed open several drums of diesel fuel and began throwing bucketsful over the weather side of the ship to prevent the high seas from breaking and smashing us down on a dry bottom. Jumbo and Bell heaved over ballast rock at breakneck speed to reduce our draft. Jumbo was thrown against the mast and sprained his shoulder, but he never let up for a minute. Several times we crossed over rocks with barely a few inches of water to spare, but the death ship curse seemed to desert us at the right moment, and each time a big sea lifted us high and sent the ship dashing across. After three hours of this strain on nerves and muscles, we had zigzagged our way safely out of the rocky bank into deep water. Looking back, all we could see was a solid mass of foam.

I had been afraid that the crew would all desert the moment we reached Gallipoli, and I could not have blamed them if they had. But I had chosen my men well. In spite of what they had just been through, they vowed to stick with the ship and even joked about the danger we had faced. We soon learned how narrow our escape had been: several fishing trawlers, whose distress flares we had seen while we were battling across the bank, had foundered in the same area and had been smashed to pieces on the rocks; fortunately most of their crews had been rescued by larger vessels, but six men had drowned.

We stayed in port the following day, calking, pounding back loose nails, and driving in new ones to replace others that had fallen out altogether, while we waited for the gale to blow itself out. We finally crossed the gulf the next day, even though the weather was still rough and became steadily worse as we made our way south along the Calabrian coast and the eastern shore of Sicily. For four days and nights the ship was battered by heavy seas and drenched by continual rain squalls, while we bailed constantly and even resorted to plugging leaks with honey-soaked rags. Again I had hoped to reach North Africa without another stop, but the men had gone without sleep since we left Gallipoli, and I decided to put into Sciacca to give them a rest before we set out across open water for Tunis. Some rest they had. The little Sicilian port was so jammed with sheltering fishing boats that the only place for us to tie up was against a twenty-foot-high mole enclosing the harbor, and after a few hours of being lifted and pounded against the wall—the seas were so rough that occasionally waves came right over the mole to break over us on the other side—we headed seaward again. About four hours later, as we approached the southwestern tip of Sicily, an Italian naval vessel came alongside and signaled a gale warning suggesting that we put into the nearest port, which was Mazaro del Vallo on the southwestern tip of Sicily. It seemed as if the weather was determined never to give us a break.

The familiar radio forecast of *mare agitato* kept us in Mazaro del Vallo for four full days. We had arrived there on March 21, our thirteenth day out from Rijeka, when according to our original plan, we should have been within landfall of Lisbon. As we waited for the weather to improve we were entertained royally by "Big Shot" Tony, a retired Chicago gangster who had been deported from the United States a few years before and was eager to show off his knowledge of English and his wealth to the people in his home town. Besides wining and dining us while we were in port, he loaded us down with enough food and wine to reach America.

We almost lost Per in Mazaro del Vallo. He fell in love with a local girl and had a hard time deciding between the voyage and his Sicilian beauty. In the end we made up his mind for him by getting him drunk and carrying him aboard just as we were leaving. When he finally woke up with a horrible hangover a few hours later, we were well out to sea, and there was nothing he could do but threaten to murder the lot of us. Actually we probably saved him from being murdered himself, for the few times he had been able to talk to the girl, by waiting outside the local church where she attended daily Mass, about a dozen glowering brothers and cousins had gathered around to protect her from our Norwegian lover boy.

Although we enjoyed "Big Shot" Tony's hospitality, we were anxious to press on to Lisbon and each day we delayed in port was agony, except for Per. We seized the opportunity of the first favorable weather forecast and at midnight on the fifth day in port we waved goodbye to Tony, thanked him for all the cigars and spaghetti dinners, and set out for Tunis. The weather was perfect: calm seas, a light but steady tail wind, and the skies so clear that for the first time we were able to navigate just by the stars and without a compass, in practice for our Atlantic crossing.

I don't think I'm particularly superstitious, but that black death sail definitely had some kind of an attraction for gale-force winds. About five hours out of port, only minutes after Knut had remarked, "Maybe Mediterranean weather isn't as bad as Norway's, after all," another sirocco hit us, this time bringing particles of sand as well as blasts of hot air all the way from the North African desert. This storm was even worse than the one in the Gulf of Taranto, but at least we were in open water, which any sailor will prefer in a storm to a rock-strewn coast. Mazaro del Vallo lay only 25 miles to our stern, and Tunis over 130 miles ahead, but I decided to strain our luck and head for Tunis under power. Per wanted to go back and see his girl, but all the rest of the crew were as sick of lying in port as I was and preferred to keep on, even if it meant battling this granddaddy of a sirocco.

Fighting a storm in the *Long Ship* demanded the utmost in skill, nerve, and back-breaking work. In other types of vessels, deck hatches could be battened down and the ship made fairly safe unless it capsized. Ours was completely open, so that every drop of rain, spray, and breaking wave had to be bailed out, even if she had not leaked like a sieve as well. Just when we had bailed out most of the water and thought we could collapse for a moment of rest, another large sea would break over the gunwales and we would have to start all over again. The long narrow hull made the helmsman's job particularly nerve-wracking. He had to judge the speed and direction of each wave, because a direct hit amidships from a heavy sea would have swamped us and possibly overturned the ship completely. For the next forty hours all we could do was pray and force our aching arms to keep bailing.

The gale diminished in force as we entered the Gulf of Tunis. Exhausted, but thankful that we had made it, we crept slowly along the channel toward the faint lights of La Goleta, Tunis's seaport. After tying up at the first empty berth we saw, we all fell asleep as if drugged.

Although only halfway to Lisbon at this time, it never occurred to any of us to give up. The delays and dangers only made us more determined to reach Lisbon as quickly as possible, to make the major repairs the ship needed, fit a tarpaulin over most of the deck, change our black death sail for the more cheerful red and white striped one, and set off for America. From the newspapers I learned that most of the other seven crew members were already in Lisbon—all the more reason for our impatience to reach there ourselves. When the harbor master gave us permission to leave, after extracting a heavy fine for our having entered, as usual, without a pilot, proper papers, or a flag, we eagerly pored over the charts, checking distances and calculating that with no trouble we could reach Morocco, three quarters of the way to Lisbon, in a few days.

At sunup on March 29, Good Friday and the twentieth day out of Rijeka, we set out for Algiers. The weather was good (rarely did we *start* under bad conditions) except for an unusually heavy swell running from the northwest. I knew this could not be the aftermath of the sirocco we had just battled through, since it was coming from the opposite direction, and we stopped off briefly at Bizerta to get a weather report. Although the forecast was favorable, just to be on the safe side we did not even attempt to use our jinxed sail. It made no difference. About half a day out of Bizerta a strong wind started to blow from the northwest. I just could not believe that another storm could hit that coast so soon after the last one, but it did, the only difference being that this one was an icy cold mistral sweeping down from the mountains of France, instead of a sirocco. Once again our ship was lifted high on the crest of one wave, dashed into its trough, and pounded by the next. We began to hear sharp cracks and snaps: she was breaking into pieces like a handful of twigs.

By then we were nearly halfway between Bizerta and the next port, Tabarka, on the Tunisian-Algerian border. I made up my mind to continue on, but soon regretted my decision. The sky became pitch dark, and the seas enormous. Per, seeing the strain on my face, offered me a cigarette. I rarely smoke, but I snatched that one up. "The way things are going," I said, "I'd better smoke three at a time."

One by one the planks separated from the ribs, and the nails flew out like bullets. Frantically we hammered in more nails, trying to fasten the planks back on the ribs, but in places there were six-inch gaps, which Jumbo stuffed with more honey-soaked rags to keep out the gushing water. As each sea hit us, the entire hull began to twist and squirm like a snake, the mast worked loose from its base on the keel, and the gunwales heaved in and out as much as eighteen inches. My *Long Ship* was now like the branches of a tree shaking in a strong wind: she re-sembled a ship only in outline.

Realizing now that we had no hope of making port before the full fury of the storm was unleashed, I had two choices: either run her ashore on some beach or find a safe anchorage. Ahead lay a rocky headland running north and south, and I made for the small cove on the lee side to shelter from the gale. As soon as we dropped anchor I put on my diving gear to patch the hull underwater, since we could not locate most of the leaks from above. I got a shock when I saw that many of the spikes holding the planks to the ribs below the water line were missing, while others were pulled in as far as half the thickness of the wood. But the crusher was the keel. Instead of being made of one solid piece of oak, like on the Gokstad original and all other Viking ships, it had been laminated. The two inches of special resin covering the bottom, topped by thick tar, had hidden this fault from me when I had dived to inspect her in Budva and again when she was up on the ways at Punat. The keel, the vessel's backbone, was now broken in many places and whole sections were missing altogether.

When I climbed aboard to spring this thunderbolt on the crew, who were all bailing furiously I saw that the wind had increased to gale force. The ship was now beyond repair; without a solid keel, not even a complete overhaul could make her fit for an ocean crossing. I felt like abandoning her right there, but the nearest town was more than thirty miles away, and between it and our cove lay a rugged mountain range and a desert, both of which we would have to cross on foot. I decided that we would have to keep the vessel afloat and try to hail a passing vessel to carry us to some port. We had been relatively protected at this anchorage, but the huge seas began to swing around the point and enter the cove, increasing as the storm continued. Swells of fifteen to twenty feet passed under the ship, straining our anchor cables, then broke on the shore only twenty yards away, throwing spray as high as fifty feet, which the wind blew back over us.

By dawn the next day, the situation was even grimmer: our anchors had dragged, the seas entering the cove had increased in force and size, and although we had been bailing constantly, the water level, if anything, was higher than the night before. Jumbo said to me, "Chief, you have to do something or we'll be lost."

I said nothing. What could I say when there seemed no chance of saving either the ship or ourselves?

"Where's your Viking spirit, Jumbo?" Per asked.

"Spirit? Huh. We'll all be spirits soon. Dead ones," Jumbo retorted.

I had to make the most difficult decision of my life, and quickly, before the ship broke up under us or we were driven onto the shore. I knew that the expedition was finished and that my main responsibility was for the lives of my crew. My worries increased when Knut reported that both anchor cables were frayed and would soon snap. The breakers smashing against the rocky shore of the cove ruled out abandoning the ship and swimming ashore there, but remembering that about two hundred yards to the east we had passed another cove with a sandy beach, I called the men together and explained my plan to drive the ship aground there.

I was surprised to find that Per, Knut, and Bill were dead set against destroying the ship (Jumbo and Bell, neither of whom could swim, accepted the plan as the lesser of two evils), even though they knew it was beyond repair. Bill took the news the hardest, saying bitterly, "Is this why we've been killing ourselves for weeks, to wreck our own ship? Why not just stay here and let the storm do it for us and save ourselves the shame?"

After awhile he too realized that going down with the ship would be little consolation for ourselves and our families, and he joined in the preparations. We lashed empty fuel drums together to make a raft, loaded it with a cask of water and a sack of canned food, and placed map and compass in a plastic bag so that we could find our way to civilization. Even though we all wore life jackets, Per and Knut were assigned to get Bell ashore if we capsized, while Bill and I would handle Jumbo. Per tried to cheer him up by saying, "Jumbo, with all that blubber, you couldn't sink if you tried."

Unable to raise either anchor, we tied the cables to floats, a fortunate precaution, for when we reached the other cove all we could see was a solid mass of white foam and spray for twenty feet from shore, where the immense waves were breaking with a thunderous roar. Sandy beach or not, to run aground there would be suicide. We turned about quickly and re-entered the first cove, where Bill dove overboard, retrieved the anchor cables, and had us tied up again, safe for the moment at least. Things are really bad when you can't even abandon ship or run her aground—the sailor's two last resorts.

The storm continued the rest of the day along with a steady downpour. Cold, wet, and exhausted, we kept on bailing and plugging leaks. By that time all the rags had been used, and we had to stuff the tarpaulin, sleeping bags, and even spare clothes into the gaps. Somehow the anchors held, and by the following dawn the wind had died down considerably. By noon the seas had decreased enough to permit us to weigh anchor and head seaward in hopes of finding a passing ship. But ships seem to appear only at nighttime or in a dense fog, when you fear a collision, and never when you are adrift, out of water, or about to sink. Finding that the ship was still hanging together and that the seas became even calmer, I decided to take her back to Bizerta.

It was a slow and tedious return. For three full days we inched along, hugging the coast in case the ship should suddenly go under and we should have to swim for shore. Once safe inside the harbor, I chose a sandy beach next to the abandoned French yacht club and ran her aground.

Our final task was to dispose of the hulk that had once been a ship. I wanted to sell the valuable motor and other gear, all still in good condition, but the Tunisian authorities demanded an 80 per cent import duty which, added to the compulsory 20 per cent commission for the agent, would have left me with exactly nothing. I was forbidden to give anything away to anybody but the Tunisian merchant marine, and the American consul in Tunis urged me to make such a gift which, he said, would promote good will between our countries. I might have accepted this official twist of my arm if it had not been for the ill treatment the police inflicted on my crew. First they ordered us to pull the ship off the beach and tie her up at a pier, which meant that we had to bail constantly; then, even though I was permitted to go ashore, the men were kept prisoners on board, with an armed guard stationed on the dock who constantly searched the ship to make sure nothing was being sold to the locals.

The customs officials were almost as bad, threatening arrogantly to keep us all in Tunisia until we had disposed of the ship to their satisfaction—that is, donated everything to the merchant marine, since I was also forbidden to abandon the ship there or take her out and scuttle her. News of our difficulties reached the international press, and the well-meaning articles that appeared, blasting the Tunisian government for harassing us, did not make the authorities any more cooperative. In the end these articles were to be our indirect salvation, but we did not know it at the time and cursed the press for making matters worse.

By this time, more than a week had passed, and it looked as if we might spend the rest of our lives imprisoned on board that leaking wreck. Fed up with Tunisia, even more fed up with the ship, I decided to destroy her, valuable motor and all—if the Tunisian merchant marine wanted it, let them dredge it off the bottom of the sea. The crew pledged their support, with the exception of Jumbo, who had signed up for the voyage in order to visit his brother in America and, determined to reach there if he had to hitch a ride with an albatross, chose to go ashore rather than risk a lengthy stay in some Tunisian prison. The scheme was aided by official incompetence and the obligatory Tunisian siesta hour. I went ashore, wandered around town for awhile and returned, announcing to each guard that his superior had given me permission to move the ship to another berth. While they all scurried off to telephone their napping chiefs—harbor master, head of customs, superintendent of police—for confirmation, we were able to cast off and slip out of port. On the way out we hailed a passing fishing boat and persuaded her crew to accompany us and take us back to shore in return for any equipment they could salvage.

The *Long Ship* was dead. All that was left was a skeleton, straining and creaking with the mere effort to reach open water again. She had failed us, but she still deserved a funeral in proper Viking style. We knew we could not reach the twelve-mile limit before the police discovered our trick and caught up with us, and we dropped anchor about two miles out. Avenging all the frustration and disappointment we felt at the failure of our grand plan to cross the Atlantic, we all took axes and sledge hammers and smashed everything in sight—motor, planks, decks, and mast—drenched her in diesel fuel, and then set her afire, while the greedy fishermen scrambled to grab anything of value they could find on board.

Quickly we jumped aboard the fishing boat. We had already heard the siren of the police launch, and as the fire spread, the launch, along with other fishing smacks and three large freighters, sighted the blaze and made for us. The ship was burning too slowly, and fearing that our pursuers would arrive in time to douse the fire, Bill and Knut leaped back on board amid the flaming timbers, defying the risk of an explosion from the fuel tanks, and smashed more holes in her sides. By the time the police launch pulled alongside, only a small part of the bow remained above water, and in minutes there was nothing left of the *Long Ship* but bubbles and thick, tarry smoke.

During the trip back to port, escorted by the police boat and the harbor master's launch, both filled with angry officials, we were sure that our jinxed expedition would end in a Tunisian prison. However, a fairy godmother in the person of the wife of a friend was waiting for us on shore. Her husband, a wealthy French industrialist with business interests scattered all over North Africa, had read the newspaper accounts of our difficulties and, unable to come himself, had sent his wife to help us out. She had obtained a safe conduct pass for all of us from the president of Tunisia, a family friend, which she handed to the chief of police, who read it with a scowl and reluctantly ordered his men to release us. For Per and Bell this meant being let off the ground, where they were pinned down after taking swings at two policemen. As her reward, our rescuer received enthusiastic embraces from five sweaty, none-too-clean sailors and, just as she thought the worst was over, from Jumbo, who arrived just in time with two taxis. While the officials cursed us soundly, we piled into the taxis and sped off to Tunis and the freighter that was to take us to Marseilles.

The Columbus fans felt secure when they read the news that our *Long Ship* had gone down, but they haven't had the last laugh. No matter what the skeptics say, we know the Vikings made it a thousand years ago, and the Phoenicians more than a thousand years before that, and, with a sturdy ship, so can we.

Epilogue

◆

Our Viking voyage had failed but our determination had not. Toward the end of our expedition, especially during those frustrating ten days in Bizerta, I had decided that maybe I was not cut out to be a sailor and that I had better stick to diving for old shipwrecks instead of creating new ones. But that did not last for long. Even before we docked in Marseilles to scatter to our various destinations, we were making plans for another voyage. This time it would be a 1000–500 B.C. Phoenician ship, and it would be built under my personal supervision, with every spike, every plank of the best material—and with a solid keel.

I was still faced with the same problem that had originally obstructed the Phoenician voyage: no one knew exactly what Phoenician ships looked like, much less how they were constructed. But several months after the voyage a new discovery was made that changed the whole picture. My friend Elisha Linder, the Israeli marine archaeologist, wrote to tell me he and a team of divers had located several Phoenician shipwrecks off the Mediterranean coast of Israel, near Caesarea, and he believed that there were still others in the area. They planned to make a thorough search and to excavate the wrecks as soon as the funds and equipment could be assembled, and the evidence they hoped to recover would enable me to build an authentic and, hopefully, seaworthy replica.

In the meantime, I had been out of the water long enough and was eager to start diving again. In July 1964, with my old friend, Jon "Momo" Kalb from Houston, I headed for "El Bajo de Serrana," a coral bank in the western Caribbean, to search for several promising galleon wrecks I had read about in Spanish archives. Robinson Crusoe's island was paradise in comparison with the barren little cay to which we hitched a ride on an obliging lobster boat—no fresh water, and two wind-stripped coconut palms as the sole vegetation. It seemed like the end of the world, the last place to expect visitors. Yet during our three-month stay there, the various uninvited guests—wreckers fighting over a Japanese freighter stranded nearby, a group of well-armed rival treasure hunters, Castroite gun-runners pursued by a Colombian frigate, to mention a few—were an even greater headache than the hurricanes (several near misses and one direct hit). Nevertheless, we managed to accomplish our mission. Searching the surrounding reefs almost daily, we located more than twenty old wrecks and so many modern ones that we lost count. One turned out to be very old: a small ship, sunk in 1528, from which the sole survivor was the Pedro Serrano after whom the bank was named. According to his own account, Serrano managed to live on this inhospitable cay for eight years (fresh turtle blood and rain water collected in turtle shells were his only liquids) until rescued by a passing ship.

We had to postpone excavating this and the other wrecks until the following summer, since the powerful surf that pounds the reefs during the almost constant winter "northers" make it impossible even to approach the bank. After another six-month stint in European archives, I was ready to tackle the Serrana wrecks with the proper excavation equipment. Jon, never one to leave a job half done, had broken *both* his eardrums in the meantime, but my shipmate from the *Niña II*, Manolo Darnaude, had developed a taste for warm-water diving in the Bahamas and agreed to come along. In the spring of 1965 Manolo, my wife of one year (game to try anything after a Ph.D. thesis exam at the University of London), and I arrived with tons of equipment at the island of Providencia, Colombian-owned but lying off the coast of Nicaragua, ninety miles south of Serrana, to set up our main base of operations for salvaging the Serrana wrecks.

We never did get to Serrana, not even for another look. We were caught in the middle of a diplomatic squabble that had been simmering for years between Colombia and the United States over who owned Serrana. Colombia would not permit anyone to fish or dive on the bank—and two navy frigates patrolled the area just in case—without submitting a written request to the Colombian government. But the United States State Department was against such a request from an American, since it would constitute recognition of Colombian sovereignty. We waited for the matter to be settled, not realizing how slowly diplomatic wheels turn. Providencia itself was not a total loss: there was a seventeenth-century pirate fort to be excavated and several wrecks around the island, which yielded a large number of interesting artifacts, all of which in the interests of good will we were persuaded to turn over to the Colombian government.

But when nine months had passed and Serrana was still off limits, I decided to accept an offer from the Jamaican government to direct a program of excavation at Port Royal, the old pirate base that had sunk into the sea during an earthquake in 1692. I had been fascinated by Port Royal for years, ever since I had read a diver's account of wandering through the coral-encrusted nave of Port Royal's sunken cathedral eighty fathoms down. In the meantime, after diving there myself several times and doing a considerable amount of original research, I had learned that Port Royal had no cathedral, that the sunken church had long ago been covered over by land, that the deepest part of the site is only ten fathoms, and that the whole underwater city has been lying under a thick deposit of mud for at least fifty years. But these facts in no way dampened my enthusiasm. Port Royal is probably the most important underwater site in the Western Hemisphere, certainly the richest and most extensive.

With a small team of divers, I have been excavating Port Royal full time since April 1966, and in one year I estimate we have recovered more artifacts than the combined total from all the old wrecks excavated in North and South America for the past twenty years. The items range in size from a two-inch brass sewing needle to a seventeen-foot oak roof beam and include humble earthenware cooking pots as well as a horde of Spanish silver pieces of eight in mint condition, valued at $100,000.

Yet the section we have excavated so far is only a small portion of the total area and there is enough left to keep us busy for some time to come. That should be more than enough time for Elisha Linder to finish excavating those Phoenician shipwrecks off Caesarea. The Columbus fans felt secure when they read the news that our Viking ship had gone down. But they haven't had the last laugh.